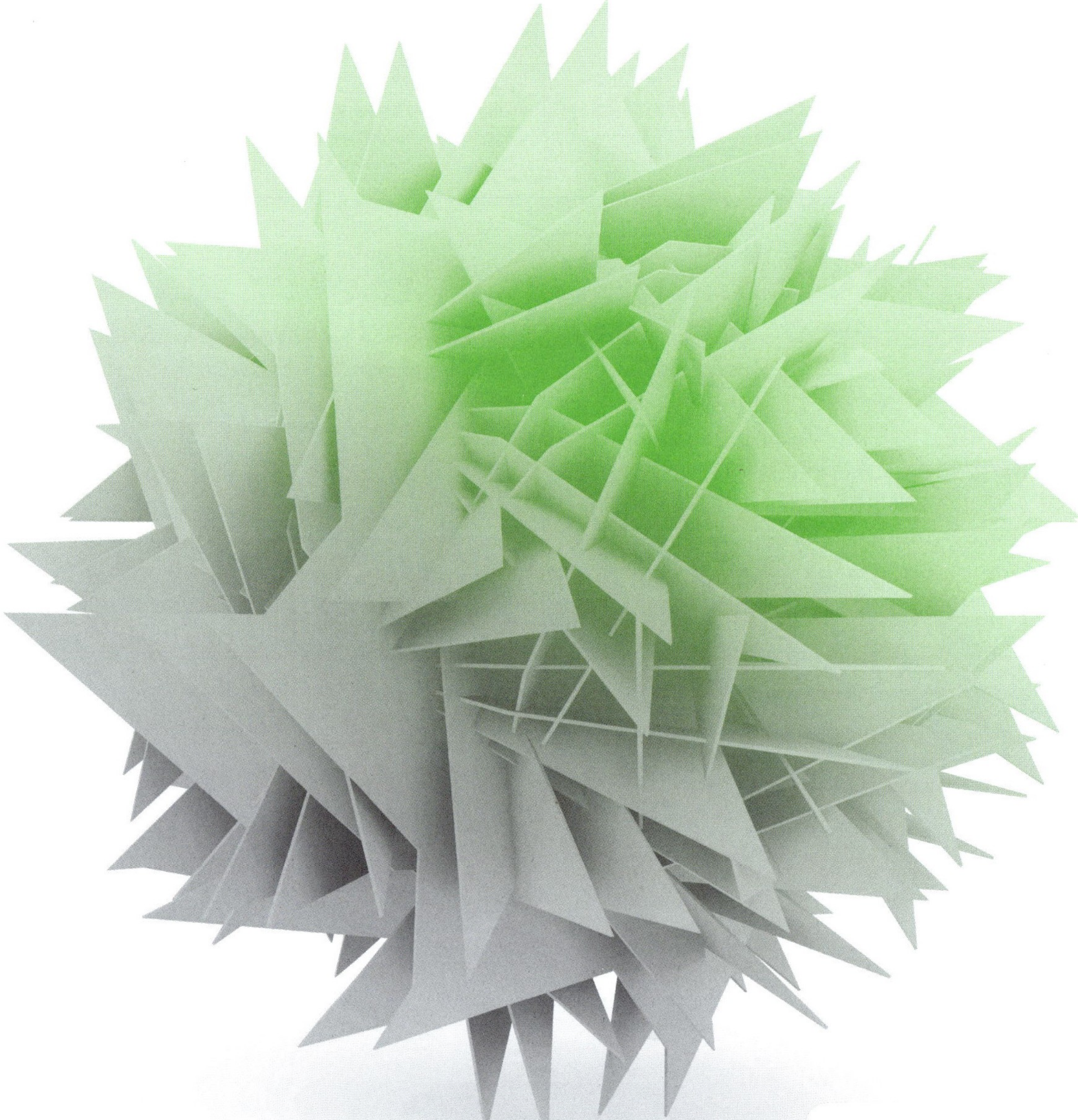

GEOMETRY 5+

Walker Maths Essentials: Geometry 5+
1st Edition
Charlotte Walker
Victoria Walker

Cover design: Cheryl Rowe, Macarn Design
Text designer: Cheryl Rowe, Macarn Design
Production controller: Siew Han Ong

Any URLs contained in this publication were checked for currency during the production process. Note, however, that the publisher cannot vouch for the ongoing currency of URLs.

Acknowledgements
Cover photo courtesy of Shutterstock.

We wish to thank the Boards of Trustees of Darfield and Riccarton High Schools for allowing us to use materials and ideas developed while teaching. Our thanks also go to all past and present colleagues, especially Kath Wilson, who have generously shared their experience and ideas.

For product information and technology assistance,
in Australia call **1300 790 853**;
in New Zealand call **0800 449 725**

For permission to use material from this text or product, please email **aust.permissions@cengage.com**

National Library of New Zealand Cataloguing-in-Publication Data
A catalogue record for this book is available from the National Library of New Zealand

978 0 17 044757 7

Cengage Learning Australia
Level 7, 80 Dorcas Street
South Melbourne, Victoria Australia 3205

Cengage Learning New Zealand
Unit 4B Rosedale Office Park
331 Rosedale Road, Albany, North Shore 0632, NZ

For learning solutions, visit **cengage.co.nz**

Printed in China by 1010 Printing International Limited.
1 2 3 4 5 6 7 26 25 24 23 22

CONTENTS

Glossary

Make your own glossary of key terms:

Term	Definition	Picture/Example
Degrees		
Equilateral triangle		
Isosceles triangle		
Scalene triangle		
Quadrilateral		
Acute angle		
Right angle		
Obtuse angle		
Reflex angle		
Polygon		
Regular		

  ISBN: 9780170447577

Term	Definition	Picture/Example
Irregular		
Symmetrical		
Two-dimensional (2D)		
Three-dimensional (3D)		
Complementary angles		
Supplementary angles		
Translation		
Reflection		
Rotation		
Enlargement		
Locus (plural: loci)		
Phi (ϕ)		
Perpendicular bisector		

ISBN: 9780170447577

Angles

Angle revision

- You may be asked to give reasons for your answers. Acceptable abbreviations are given here.

Angles on a line
- Angles on a line **add to 180°**.
- These are also known as **supplementary** angles.

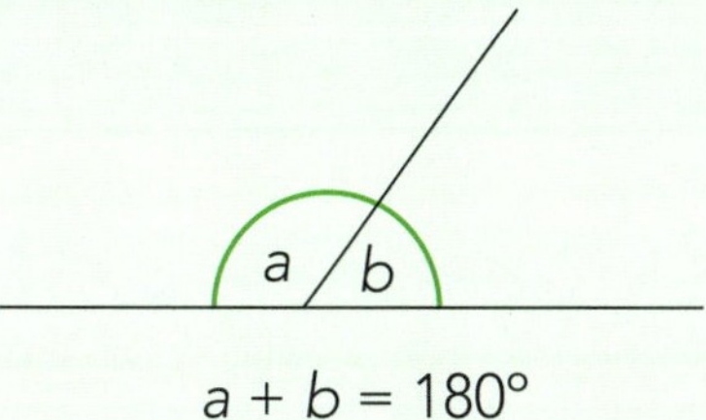

$a + b = 180°$

Reason: ∠s on a line = 180°.

Angles at a point
- Angles at a point, or angles in a full rotation, **add to 360°**.

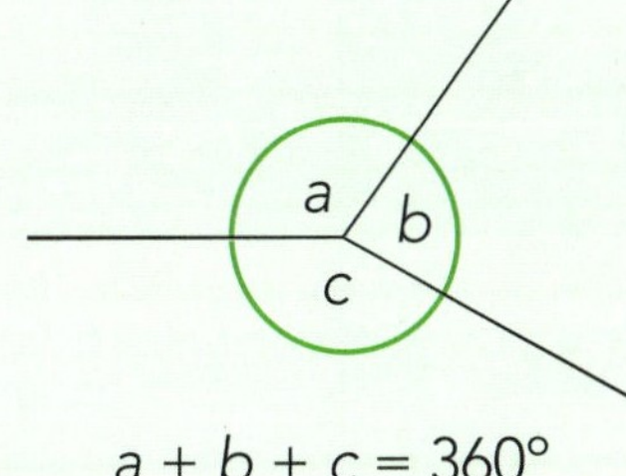

$a + b + c = 360°$

Reason: ∠s at a point = 360°.

Vertically opposite angles
- Vertically opposite angles **are equal**.

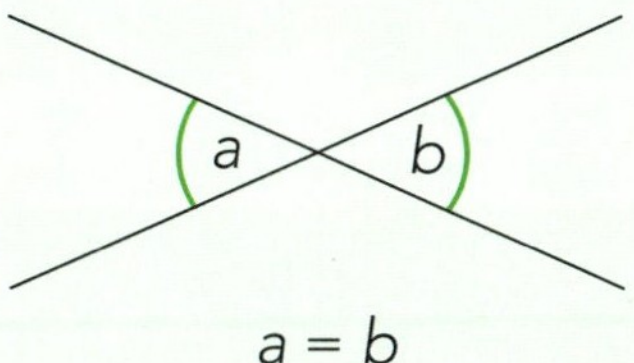

$a = b$

Reason: Vert opp ∠s =.

Interior angles of a triangle
- The angles in a triangle **add to 180°**.

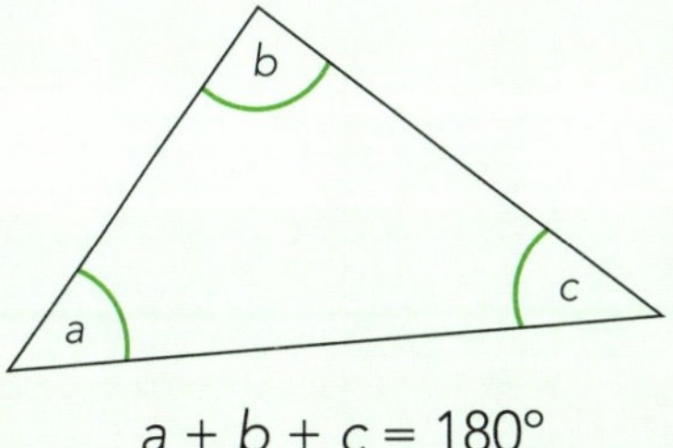

$a + b + c = 180°$

Reason: ∠s in a Δ = 180°.

Exterior angle of a triangle
- The exterior angle of a triangle = sum of the interior opposite angles.

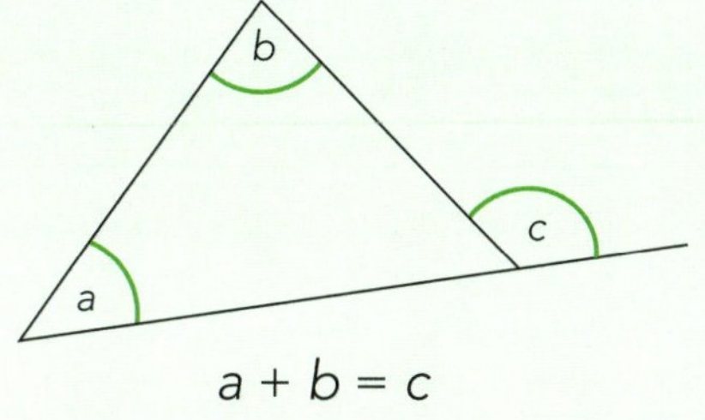

$a + b = c$

Reason: ext ∠ in a Δ = sum of int opp ∠s.

Interior angles of a quadrilateral
- The four angles in a quadrilateral **add to 360°**.

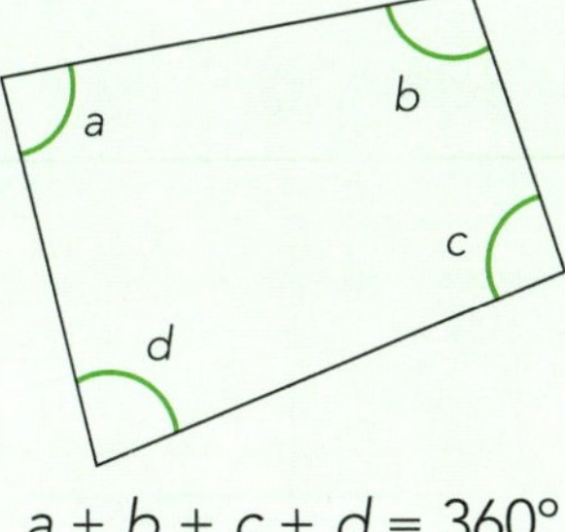

$a + b + c + d = 360°$

Reason: ∠s in a quad = 360°.

ISBN: 9780170447577

Calculate the missing angles and write the reasons. If your reasons are different from those in the answers, check them with your teacher.

1

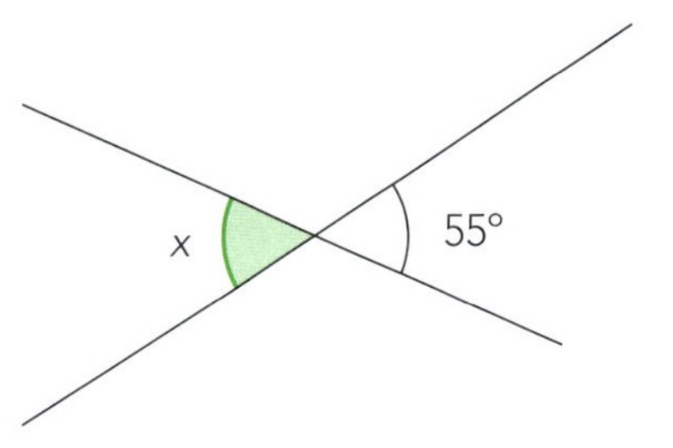

____

Reason: ______________________________

2

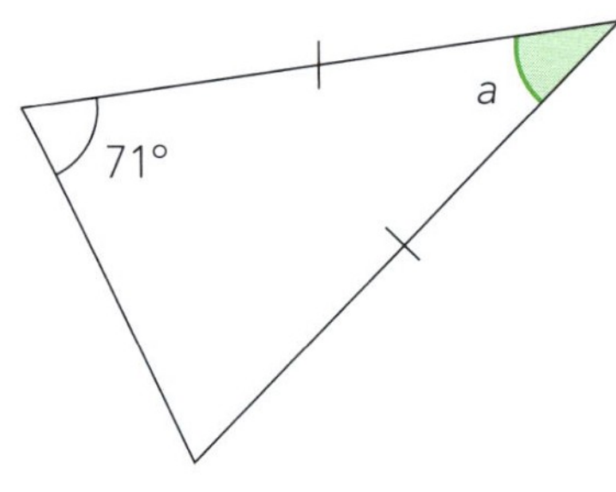

____

Reason: ______________________________

3

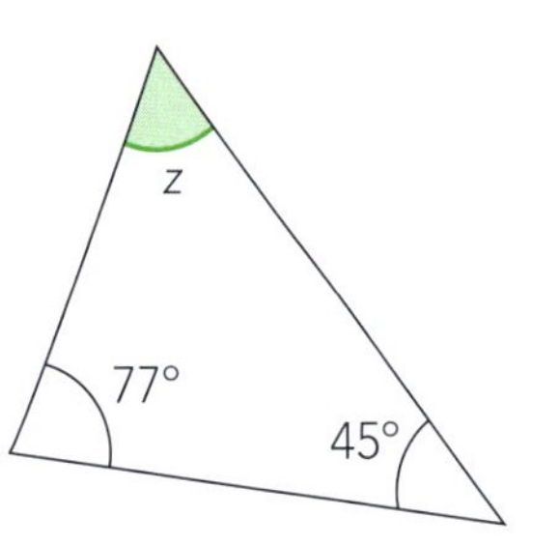

____

113°

Reason: ______________________________

4

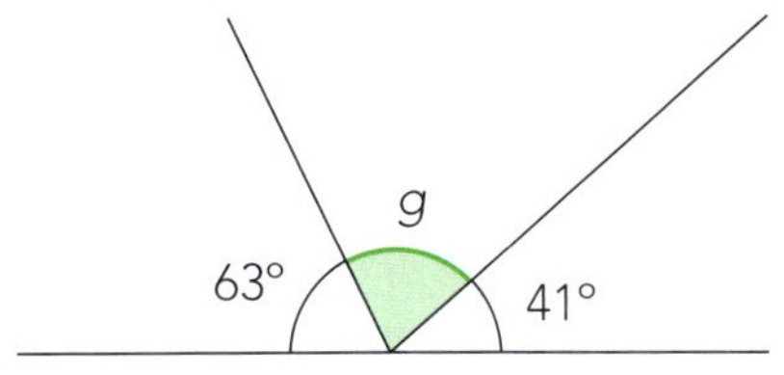

____

Reason: ______________________________

5

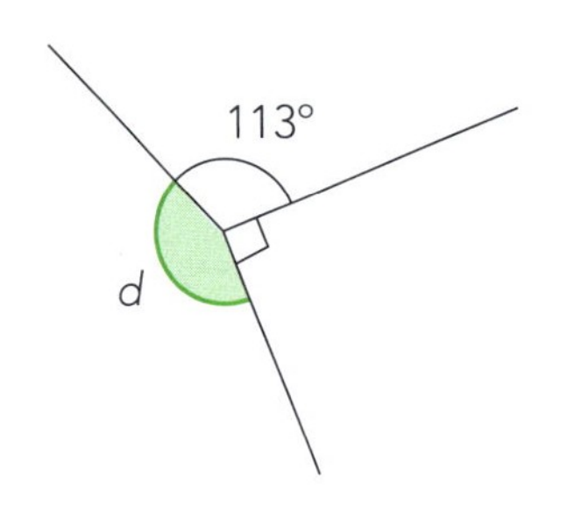

____

Reason: ______________________________

6

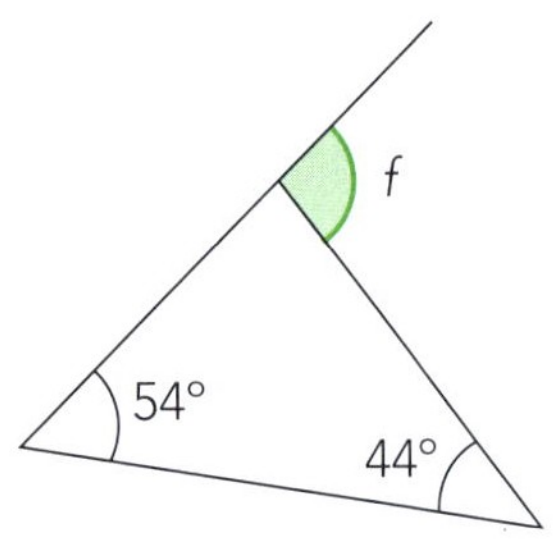

____

Reason: ______________________________

7

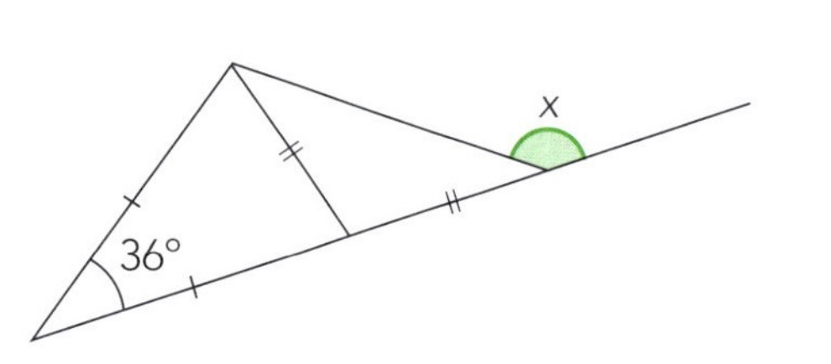

____

Reason: ______________________________

8

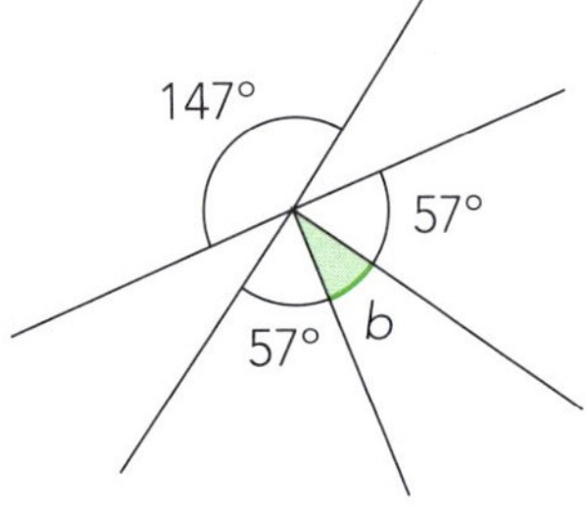

____

Reason: ______________________________

ISBN: 9780170447577

Polygons

- There are different rules for exterior and interior angles in polygons.

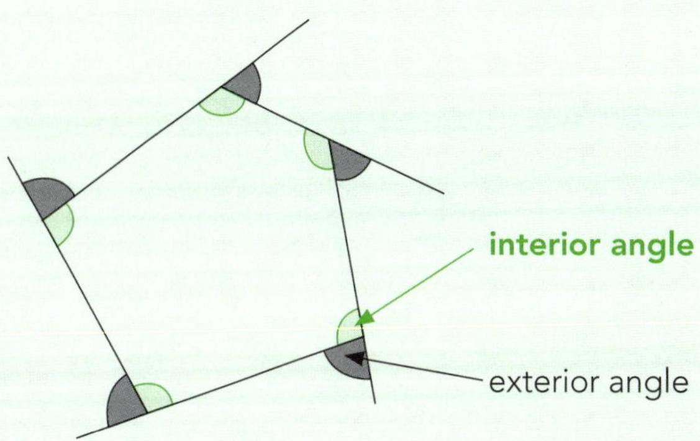

Exterior angles

- Exterior angles of a polygon **always add to 360°**.

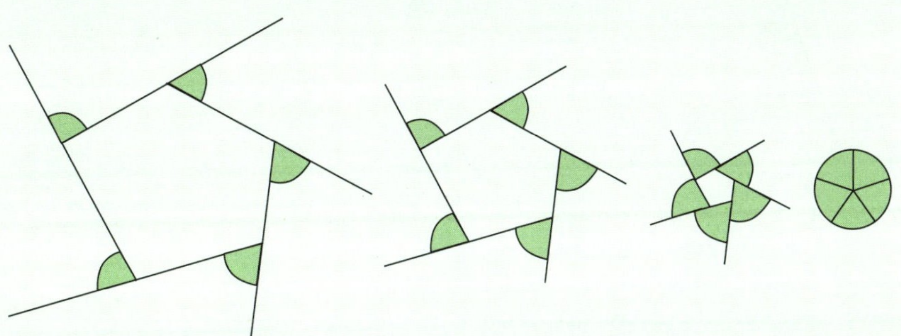

Reason: ext ∠s in a polygon = 360°.

Example:

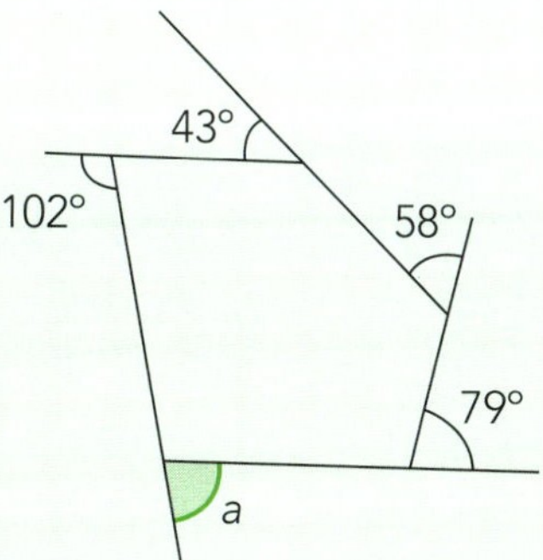

$102° + 43° + 58° + 79° + a = 360°$
$a = 360° - 102° - 43° - 58° - 79°$
$a = 78°$

Reason: ext ∠s in a polygon = 360°.

Calculate the missing angles. The polygons in questions **4**, **9** and **10** are regular.

1

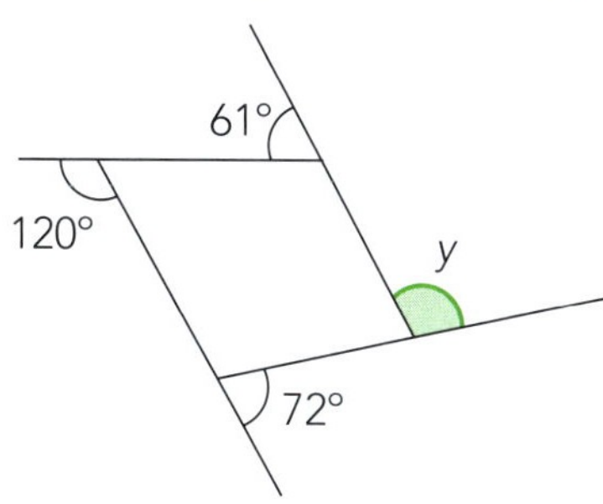

2

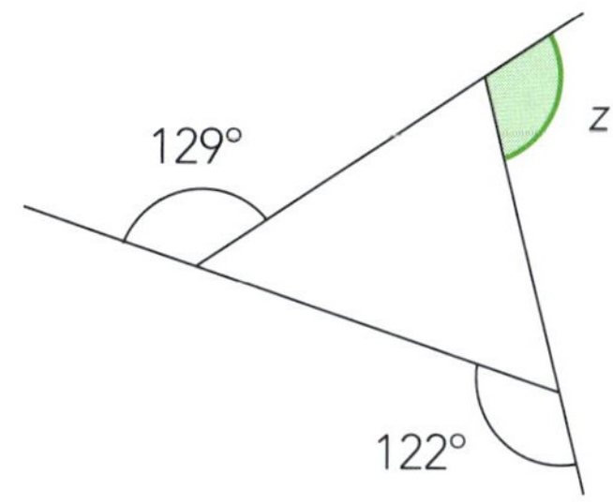

ISBN: 9780170447577

3

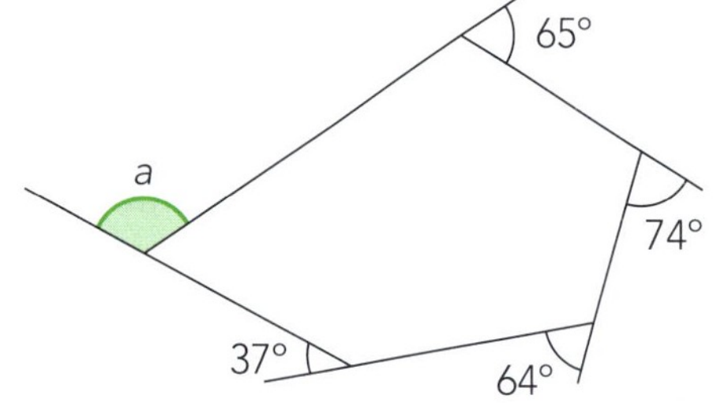

4

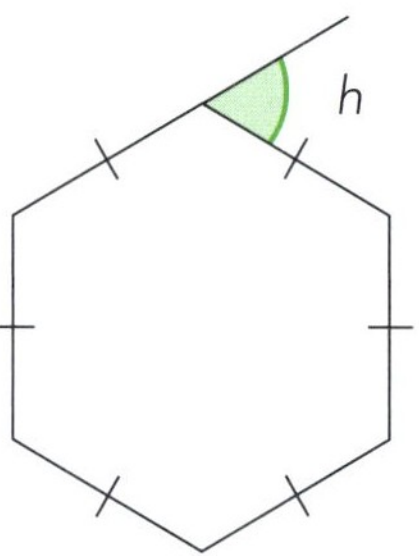

5

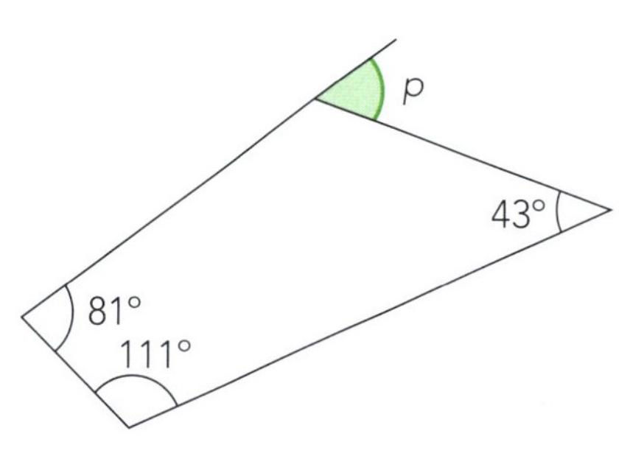

6

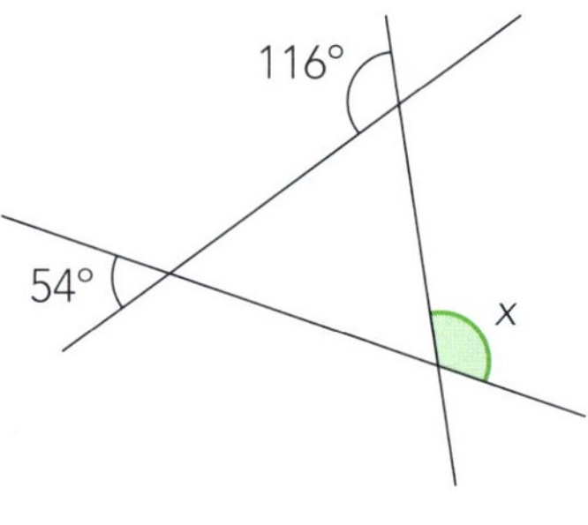

7

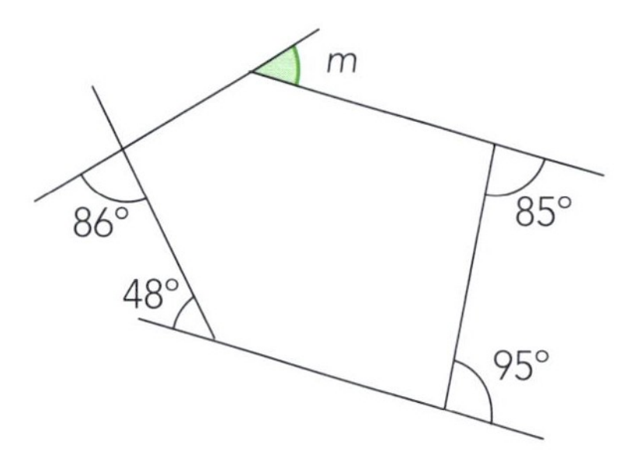

8

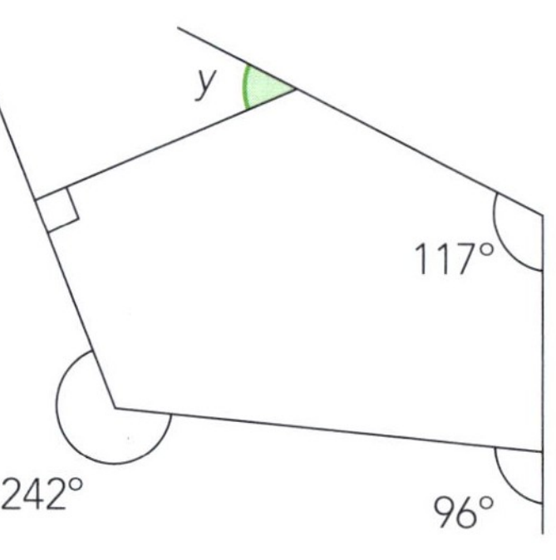

9

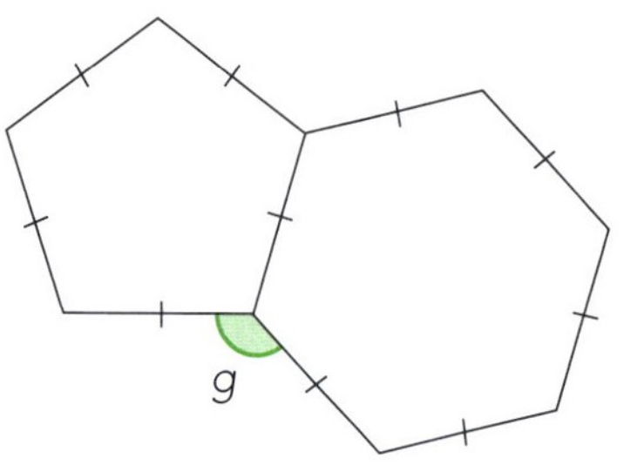

10

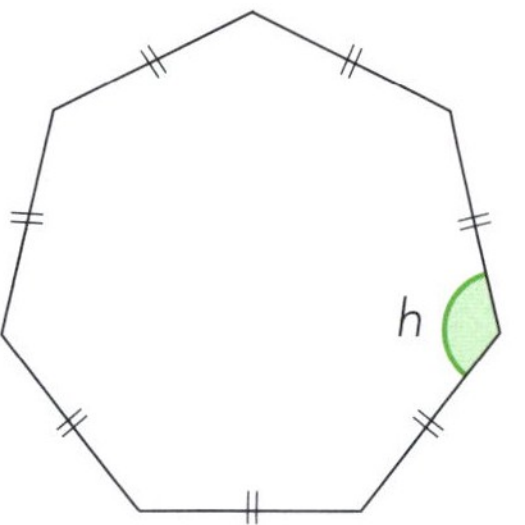

Interior angles

- The sum of interior polygon angles depends on the number of sides.
- Calculate the sum of the interior angles by dividing the polygon into triangles.
- You know the interior angles of a triangle add to 180°.

Name	Number of sides	Diagram	Sum of interior angles	Size of each interior angle of a *regular* polygon
Quadrilateral	**4**		2 x 180° = 360°	$\frac{360°}{4} = 90°$
Pentagon	**5**		3 x 180° = 540°	$\frac{540°}{5} = 108°$
Hexagon	**6**		4 x 180° = 720°	$\frac{720°}{6} = 120°$
Heptagon	**7**		5 x 180° = 900°	$\frac{900°}{7} = 128.6°$
Octagon	**8**		6 x 180° = 1080°	$\frac{1080°}{8} = 135°$
Any polygon	***n***	The number of triangles is always 2 fewer than the number of sides.	**$(n - 2) \times 180°$**	**$\frac{(n-2) \times 180°}{n}$**

Example:

Find the value of *y*.

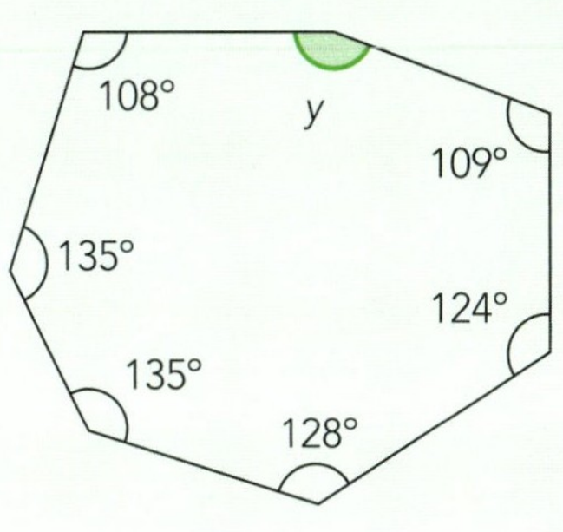

$$\begin{aligned}\text{Sum of interior angles} &= (n-2) \times 180 \\ &= (7-2) \times 180 \\ &= 900°\end{aligned}$$

$y = 900° - 109° - 124° - 128° - 135° - 135° - 108°$

$y = 161°$

 ISBN: 9780170447577

Calculate the missing angles. Polygons in questions **5**, **7** and **8** are regular.

1

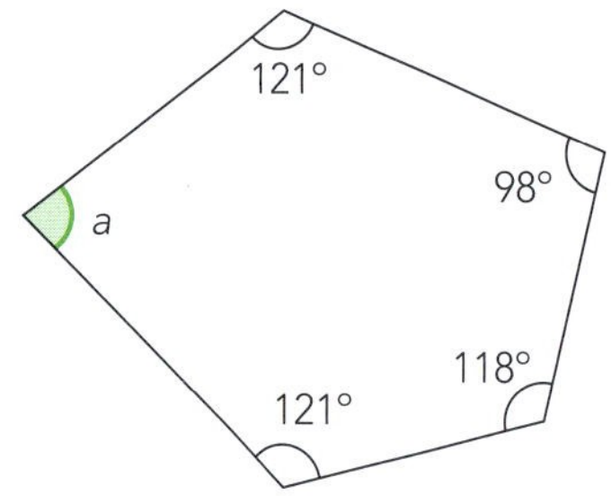

2

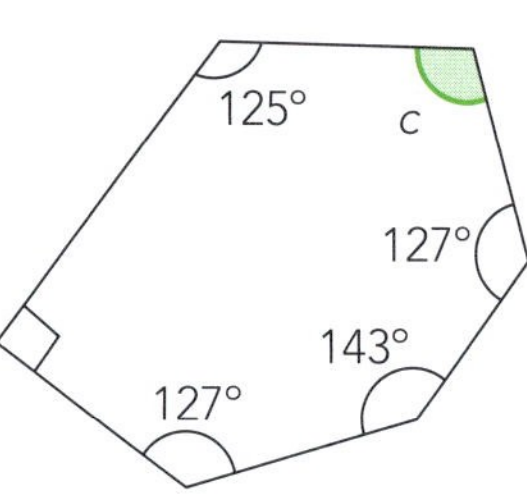

3

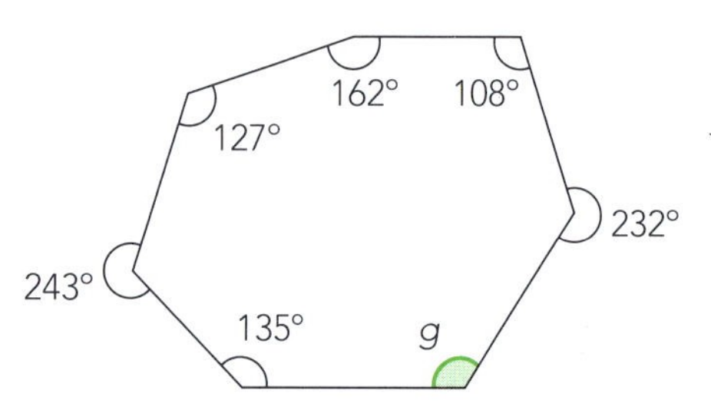

4

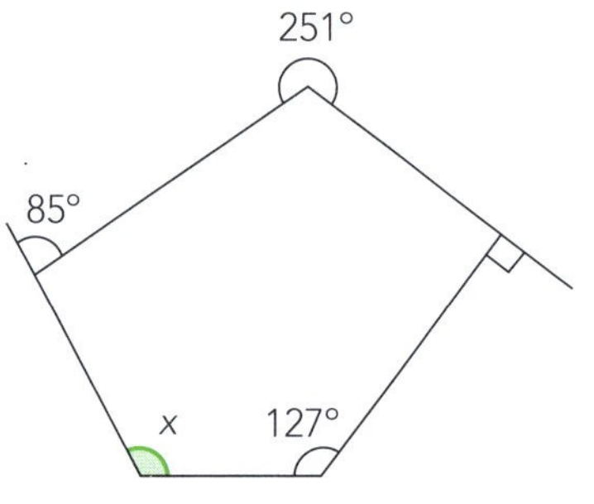

5

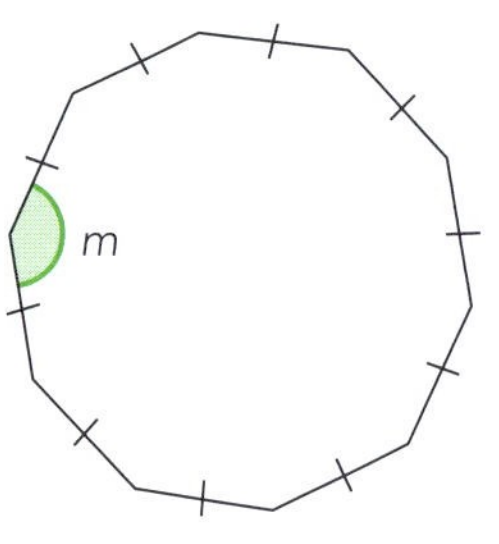

6

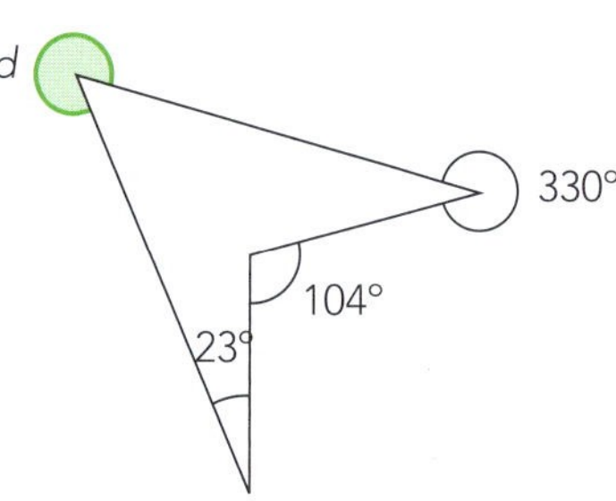

7

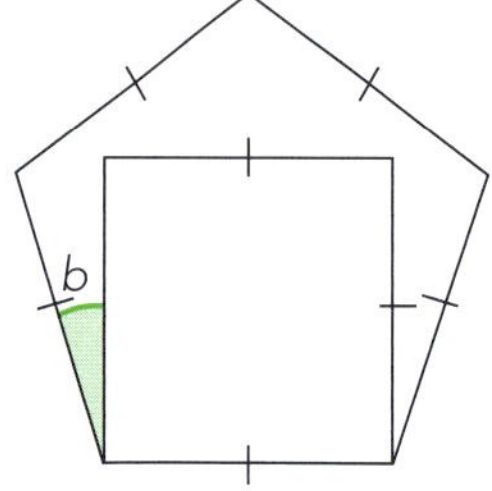

8

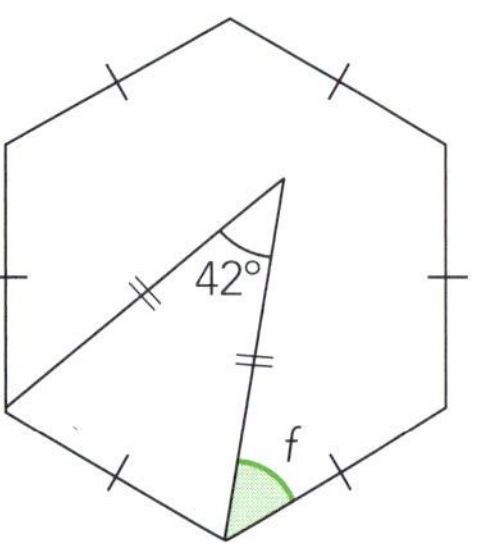

Parallel lines

- You will often need to give reasons for your answers.

Alternate angles

- Alternate angles on parallel lines are **equal**.
- These form a '**Z**'.

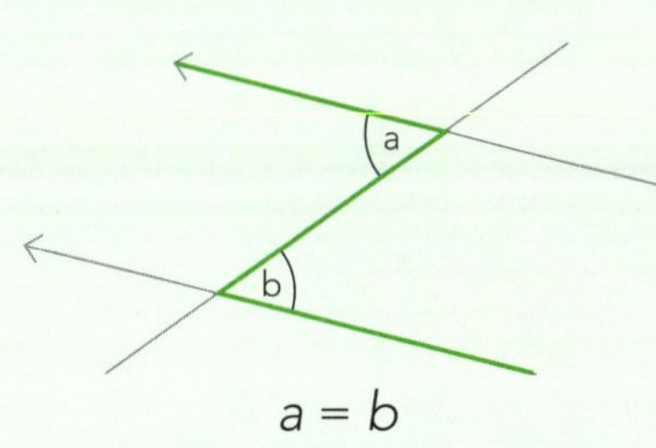

$a = b$

Example:
Find the value of y.

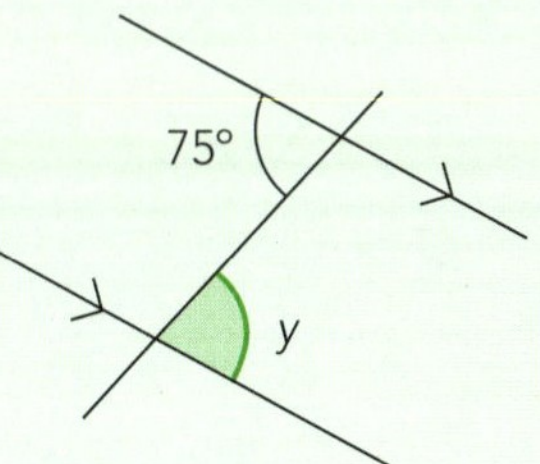

You are allowed to shorten 'Alternate angles are equal, parallel lines' to this:

$y = 75°$

Reason: Alt ∠s =, // lines.

Corresponding angles

- Corresponding angles on parallel lines are **equal**.
- These form an '**F**'.

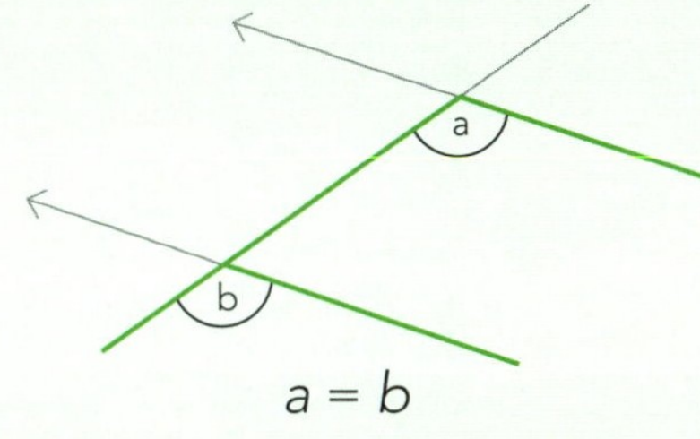

$a = b$

Example:
Find the value of z.

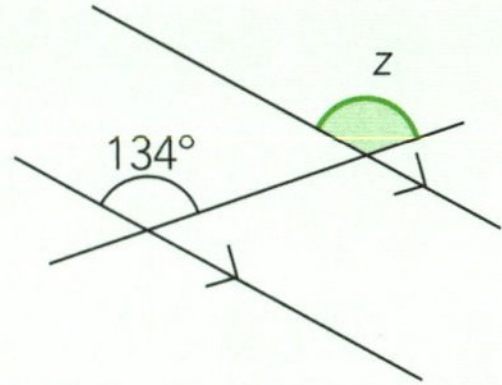

'Corresponding angles are equal, parallel lines':

$z = 134°$

Reason: Corr ∠s =, // lines.

Co-interior angles

- Co-interior angles on parallel lines **add to 180°**.
- These form a '**C**'.

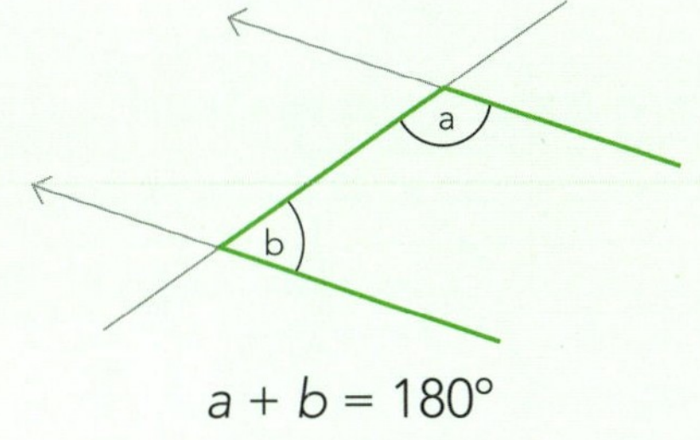

$a + b = 180°$

Example:
Find the value of x.

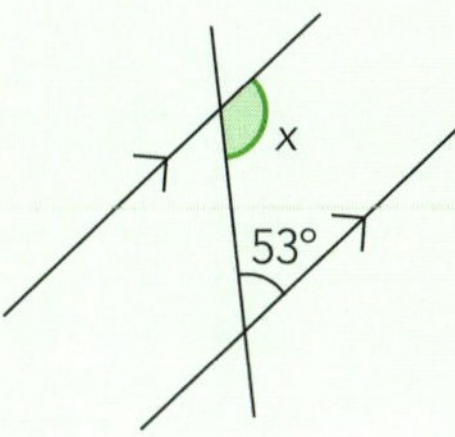

'Co-interior angles add to 180°, parallel lines':

$x = 180° - 53°$
$= 127°$

Reason: Co-int ∠s add to 180°, // lines.

ISBN: 9780170447577

Calculate the missing angles and write the rule(s) used. If your rules are different from those in the answers, check them with your teacher.

1

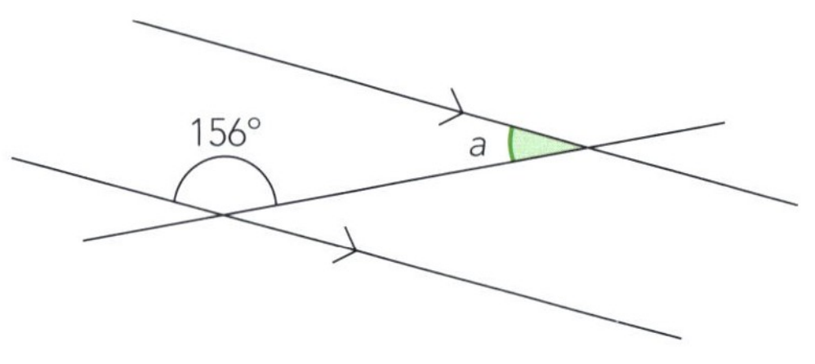

Reason:

2

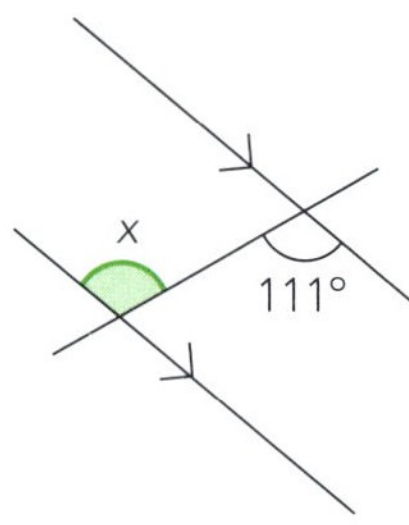

Reason:

3

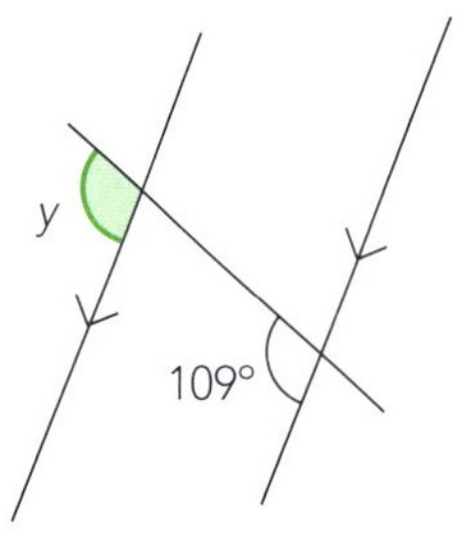

Reason:

4

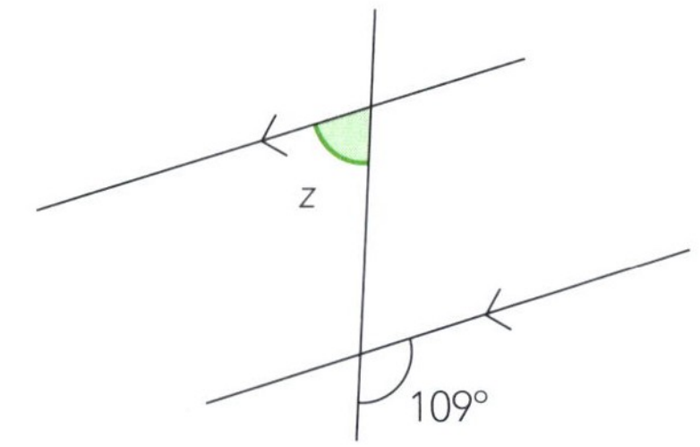

Reason:

5

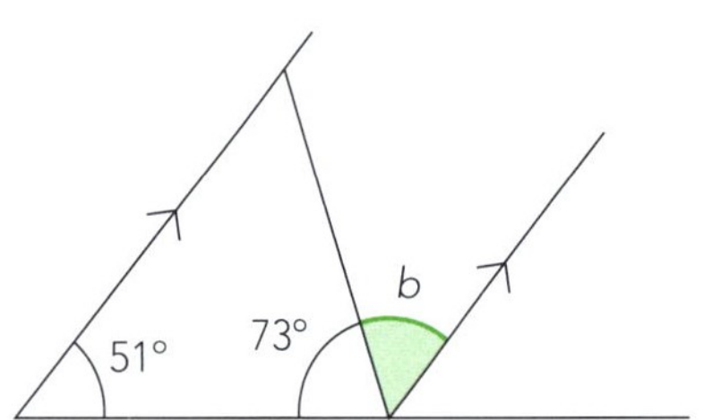

Reason:

6

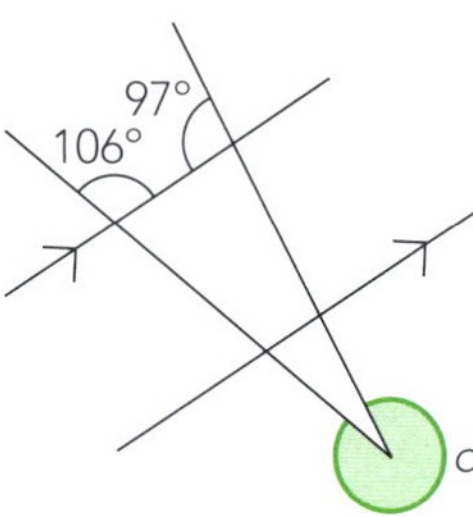

Reason:

7

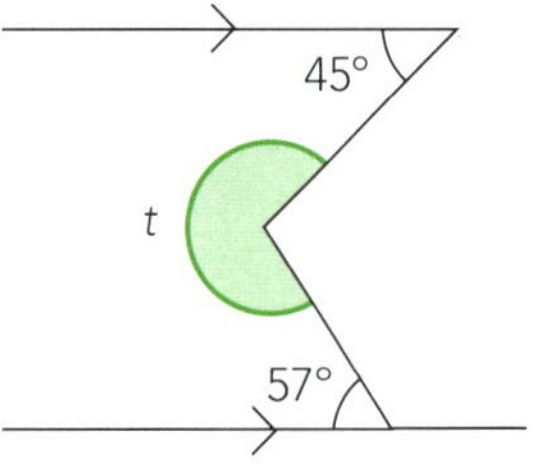

Reason:

8

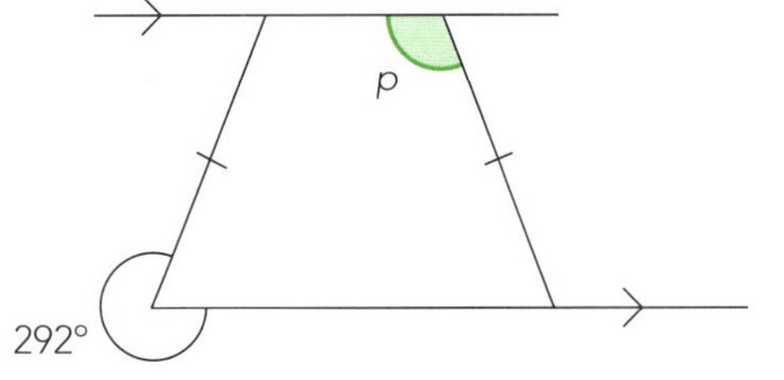

Reason:

ISBN: 9780170447577

Algebra and angles

- Sometimes you will need to use your algebra skills to find the size of an angle.

Examples:

1

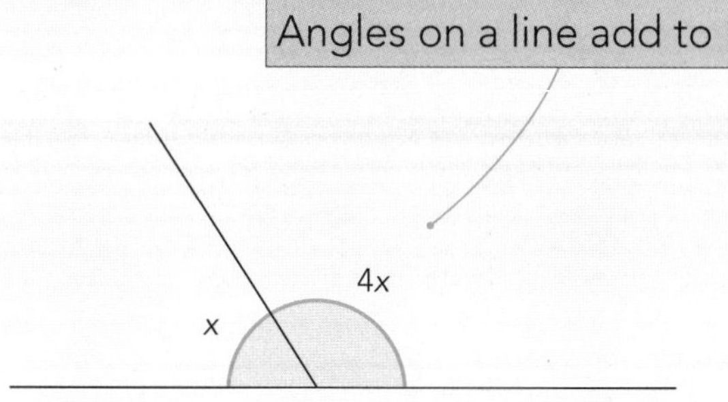

$$4x + x = 180$$

$$5x = 180$$

$$x = \frac{180}{5}$$

$$x = 36°$$

$x = 36°$
$4x = 144°$

2

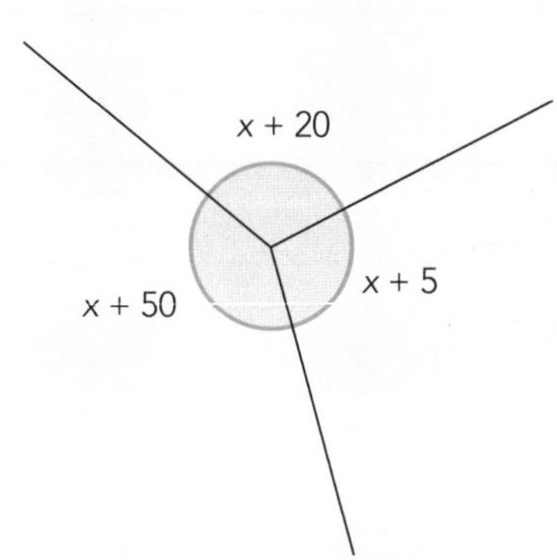

$$x + 20 + x + 5 + x + 50 = 360$$

$$3x + 75 = 360$$

$$3x = 285$$

$$x = \frac{285}{3}$$

$$x = 95°$$

$x + 20 = 115°$
$x + 5 = 100°$
$x + 50 = 145°$

3

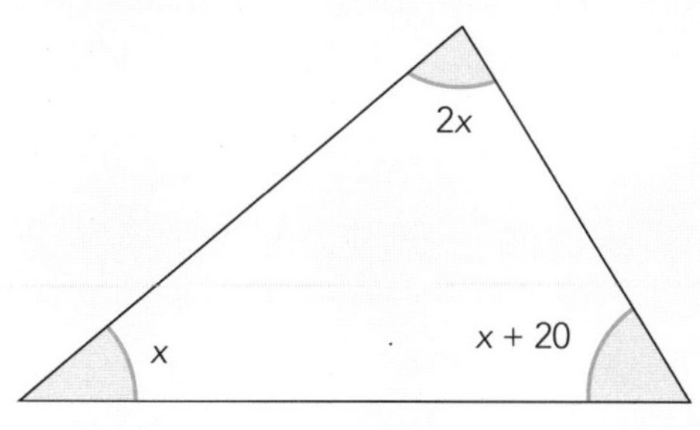

$$x + 2x + x + 20 = 180$$

$$4x + 20 = 180$$

$$4x = 160$$

$$x = \frac{160}{4}$$

$$x = 40°$$

$x = 40°$
$2x = 80°$
$x + 20 = 60°$

  ISBN: 9780170447577

Calculate the values of x and then y.

1

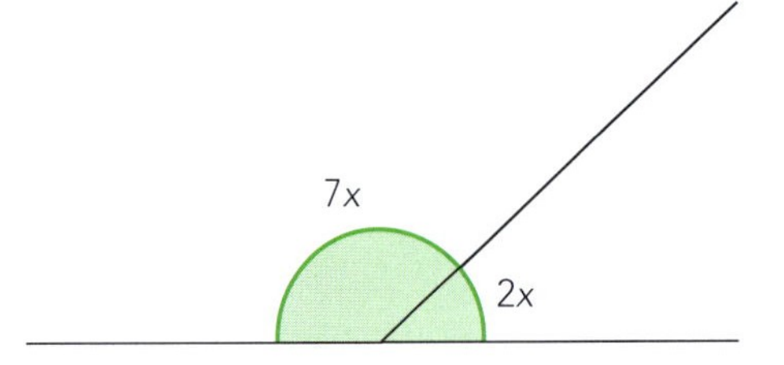

2

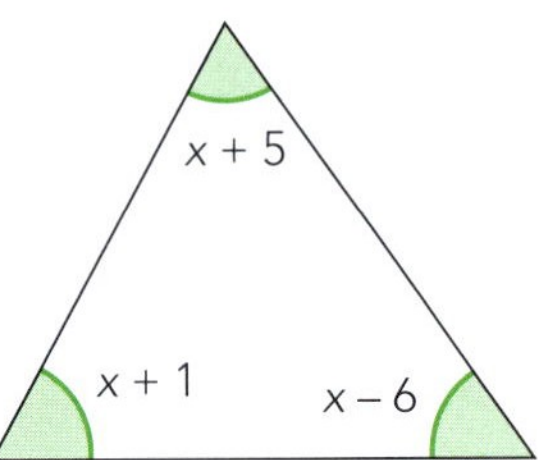

3

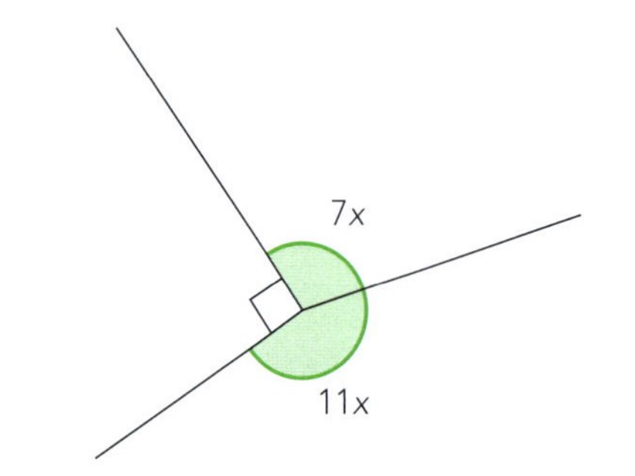

4

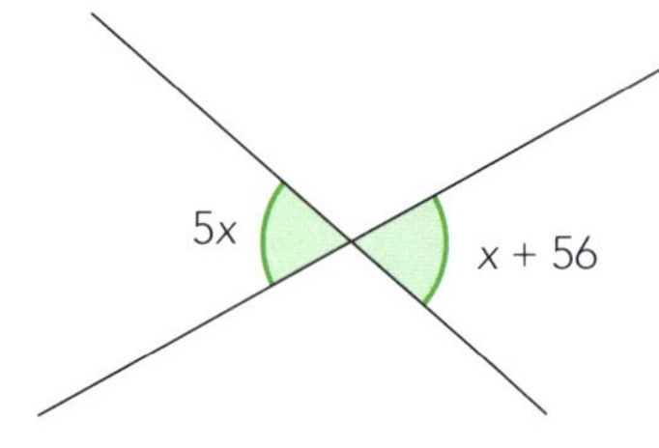

5

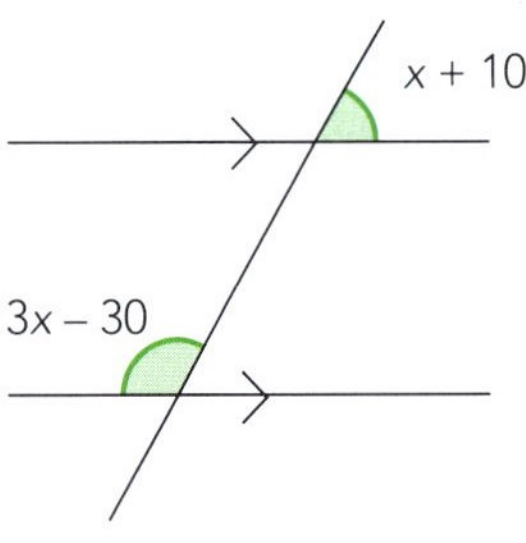

6

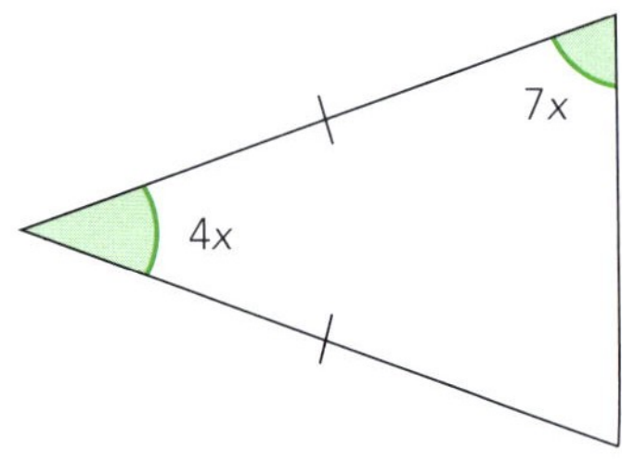

7

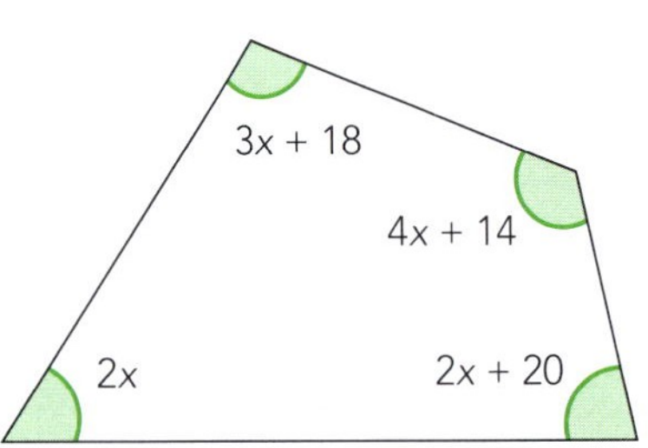

8

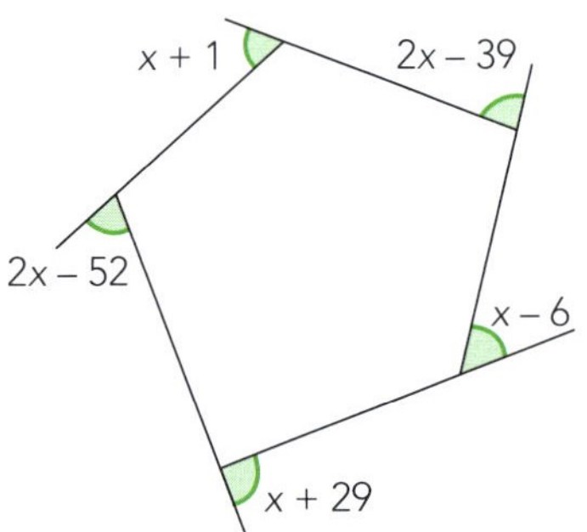

9

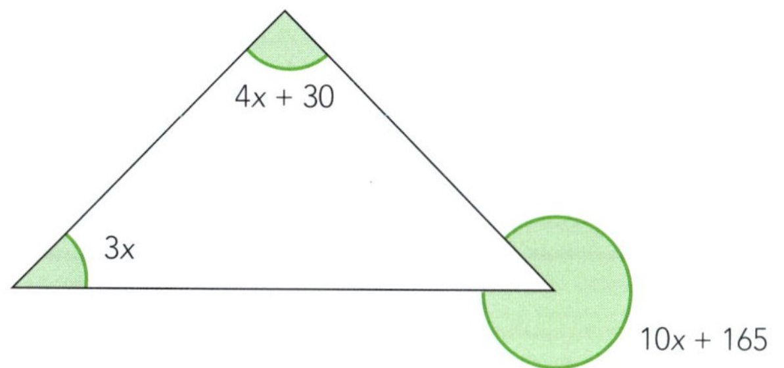

10

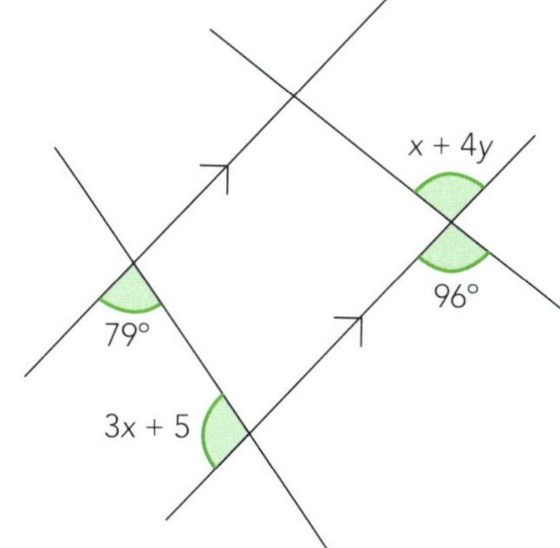

11

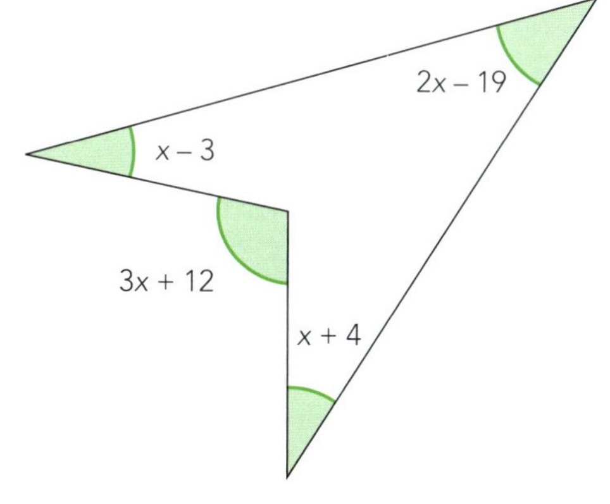

12

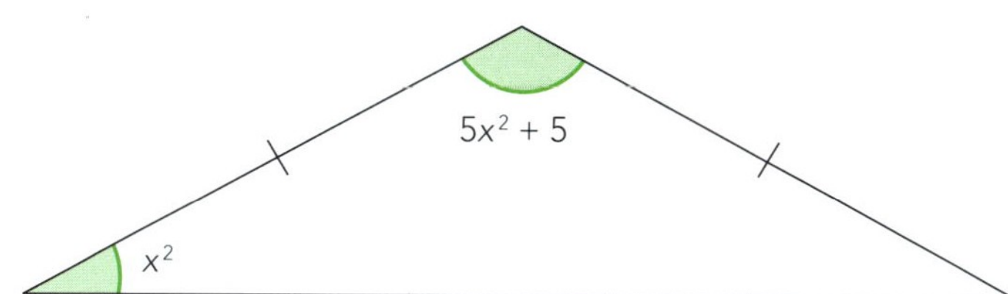

 ISBN: 9780170447577

Position and orientation

Direction: bearings

- Bearings are used in navigation to define **direction** in a **horizontal** plane.
- Direction can be given in terms of north, south, east and west.
- North is always given as the starting point.

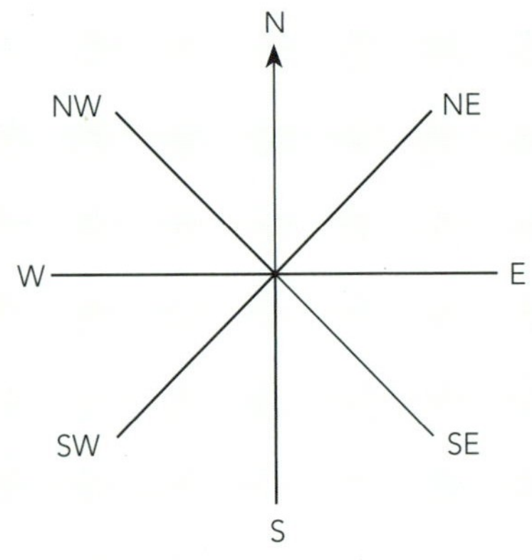

- Bearings are measured in **degrees** in a **clockwise direction from north (000° or 360°)**.
- All bearings must have **three digits**.

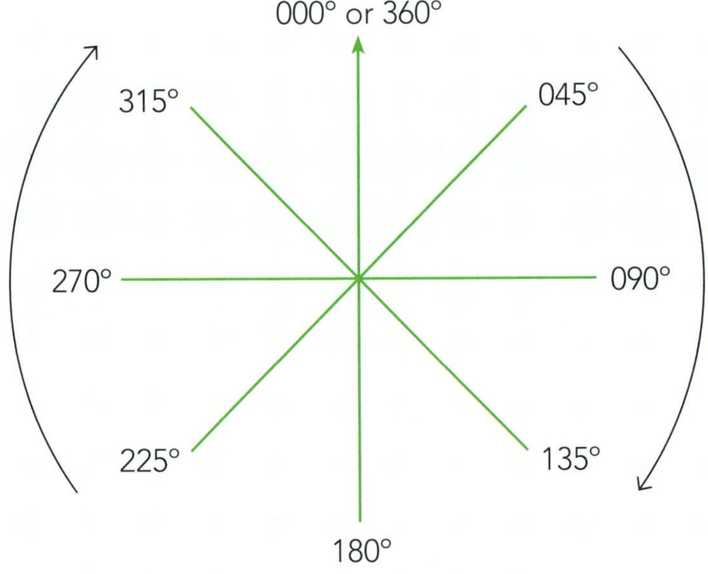

Examples:

1

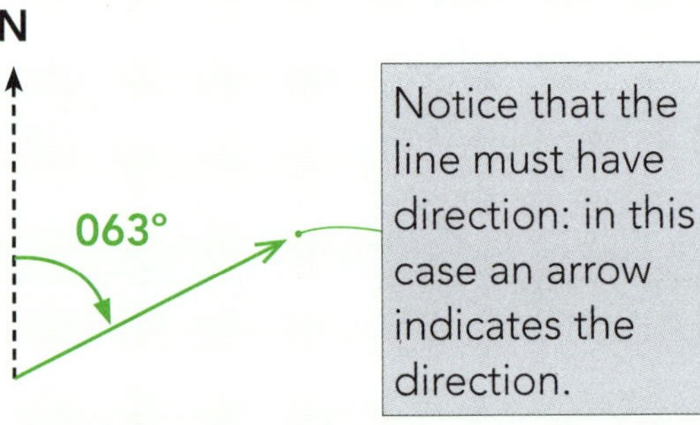

2

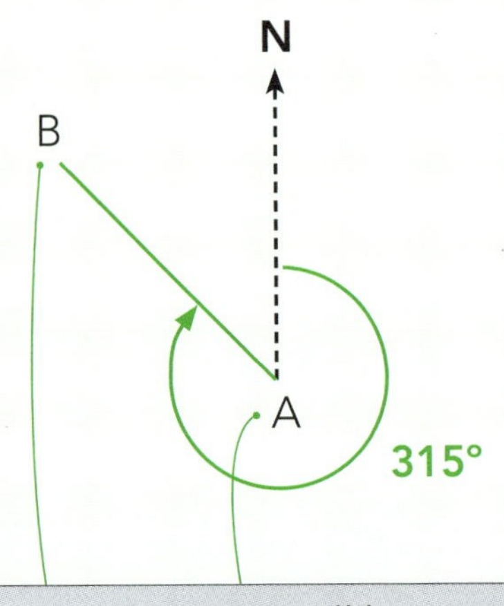

Sometimes the direction will be indicated by words, e.g. 'from A to B'.

ISBN: 9780170447577

Without using a protractor, match the bearings in the lists to each of the diagrams. They are either in the direction of the arrow or from A to B. The dashed line points to north.

321°	031°	257°	238°	293°	153°	061°	103°

N

A B

N

N

B A

1 ________ 2 ________ 3 ________ 4 ________

N

N

A B

B N

A

N

5 ________ 6 ________ 7 ________ 8 ________

9 Ngaire walks anticlockwise around this path, starting at point A. Write the bearings she will need to walk for each stretch of path. Select your answers from the list below.

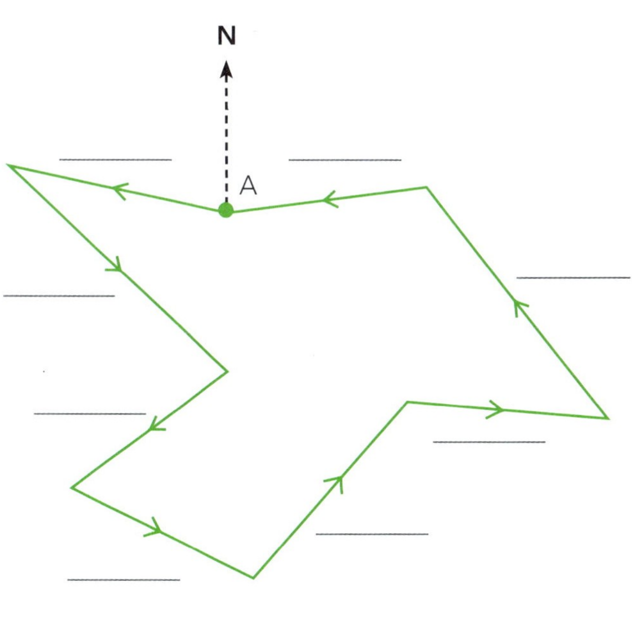

234°	132°
041°	321°
264°	115°
096°	281°

 ISBN: 9780170447577

Using a protractor to find bearings

- You will need a ruler and, ideally, a 360° protractor.

Example: Find the location that is at a bearing of 215° from point A and 137° from point B.

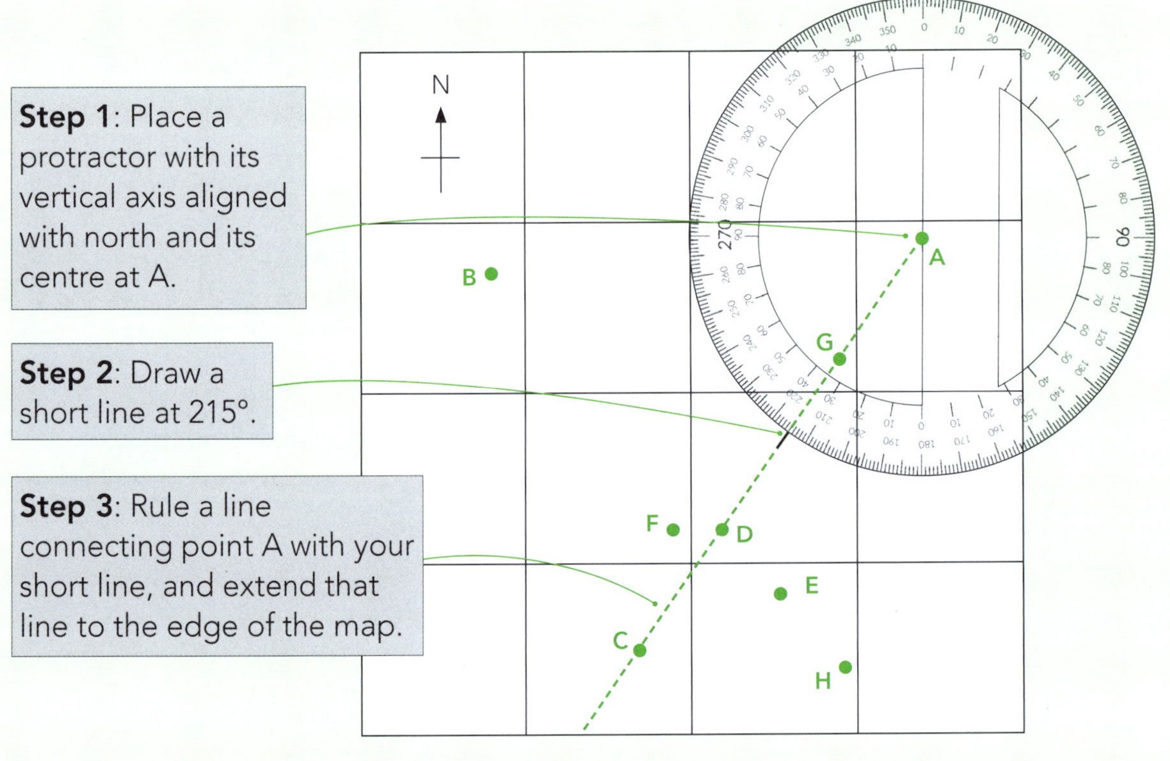

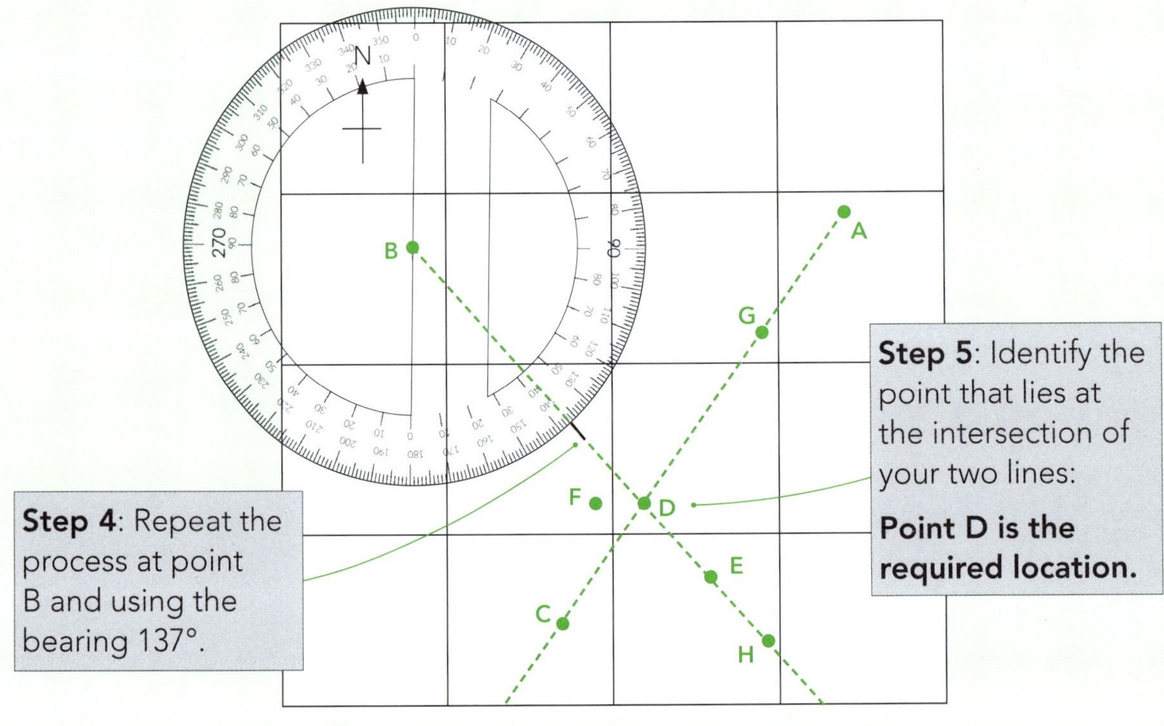

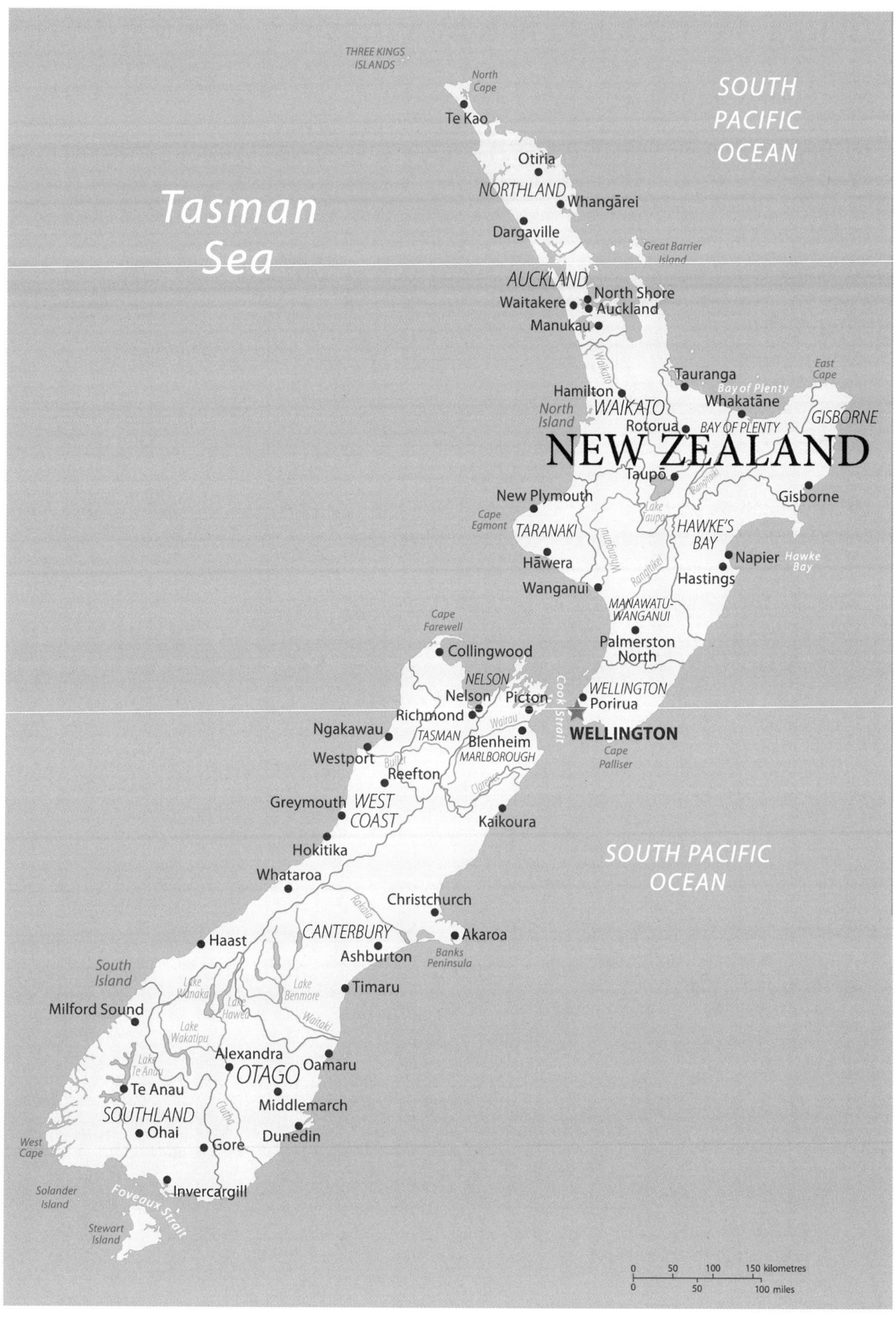

 ISBN: 9780170447577

Rule lines between these locations, and use a protractor to measure the bearings between them. Then use a ruler along with the scale to estimate the distances. Select your answers from the lists below. Some values may be used more than once, and some will not be needed.

Bearings:

085°	220°	315°	150°	110°	030°	350°	225°
330°	065°	150°	295°	010°	185°	210°	035°

Distances (km):

60	110	140	180	220	240	260	270
300	310	340	350	510	560	680	1020

1 Milford Sound to Gore

Bearing: ______

Distance: ______

2 Rotorua to Westport

Bearing: ______

Distance: ______

3 Taupō to Rotorua

Bearing: ______

Distance: ______

4 Christchurch to Dunedin

Bearing: ______

Distance: ______

5 Greymouth to Tauranga

Bearing: ______

Distance: ______

6 Collingwood to Gisborne

Bearing: ______

Distance: ______

7 Whakatāne to Alexandra

Bearing: ______

Distance: ______

8 Gisborne to Hamilton

Bearing: ______

Distance: ______

9 Whataroa to Timaru

Bearing: ______

Distance: ______

10 Whanganui to Rotorua

Bearing: ______

Distance: ______

11 Hamilton to Dargaville

Bearing: ______

Distance: ______

12 New Plymouth to Gisborne

Bearing: ______

Distance: ______

ISBN: 9780170447577

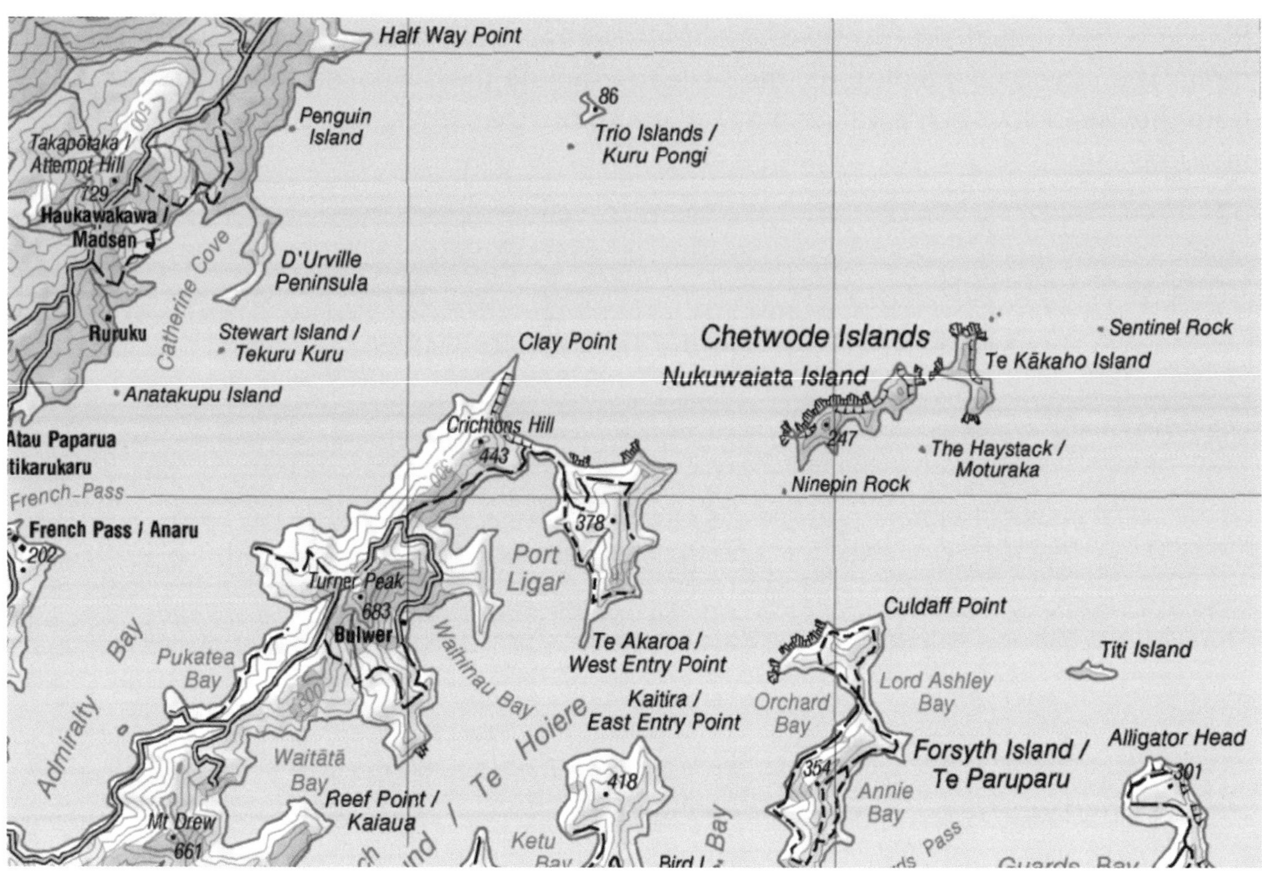

This map shows a part of the outer Marlborough Sounds and D'Urville Island.

Identify the following locations.

13 A bearing of 292° from Sentinel Rock and 018° from Clay Point. ________________

14 A bearing of 170° from Penguin Island and 129° from Anatakupu Island. ________________

15 A bearing of 061° from Te Akaroa (West Entry Point) and 324° from the northern most tip of Alligator Head. ________________

16 A bearing of 320° from Culdaff Point and 244° from Sentinel Rock. ________________

17 A bearing of 078° from Mt Drew and 212° from Ninepin Rock. ________________

18 A bearing of 240° from Half Way Point and 328° from Stewart Island (Tekuru Kuru). ________________

19 A bearing of 241° from the Trio Islands (Kuru Pongi) and 353° from Mt Drew. ________________

ISBN: 9780170447577

Location: loci

- A **locus** is a **set of points**.
- The plural of locus (when we have more than one locus) is **loci**.
- A locus describes **the set of all the points that satisfy certain conditions**.

There are four main types of locus:

1 The set of all points that are the same distance from **one fixed point**.

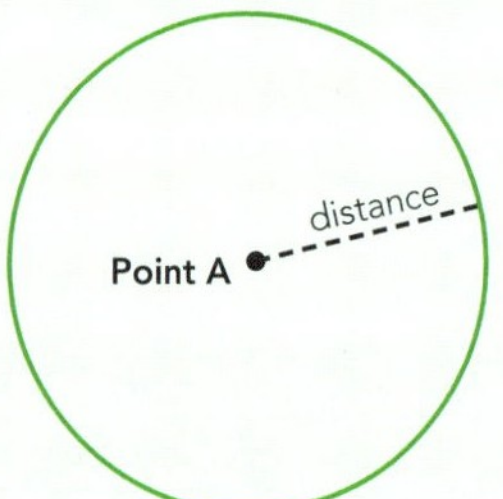

The locus is a circle.
The fixed point (A) = centre.
The same distance = radius.

2 The set of all points that are the same distance from **a line**.

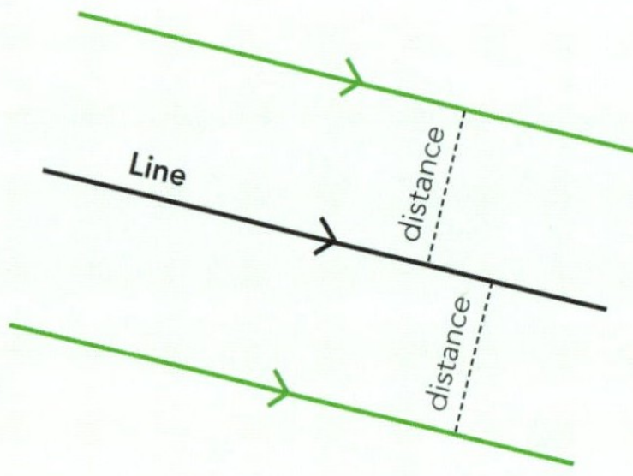

The locus is a pair of parallel lines.

3 The set of all points that are the same distance from **two fixed points**.

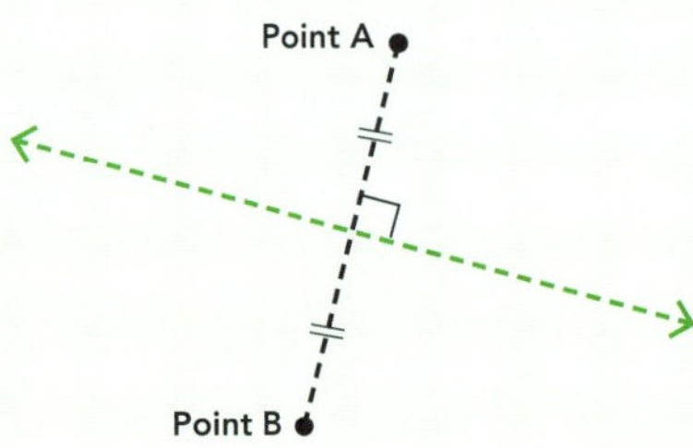

The locus is the perpendicular bisector of the line (AB) joining the points.

4 The set of all points that are the same distance from **two fixed lines**.

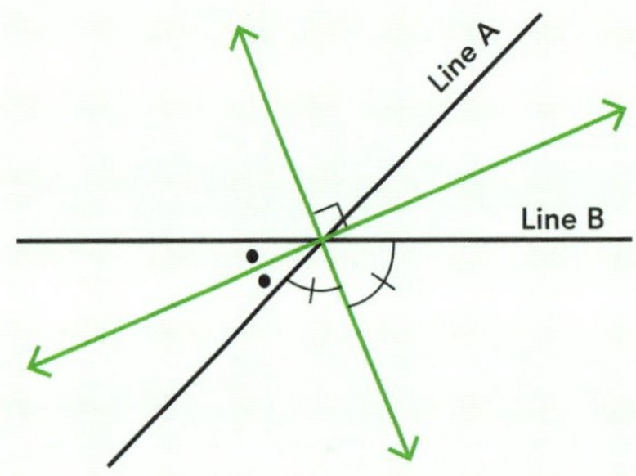

The locus is a pair of angle bisectors that are perpendicular to each other.

ISBN: 9780170447577

Examples:

1 A fireplace (F) has been installed in the corner of a room that is 5 m long and 3 m wide. There is a guard to keep the children at least 1 m away from the fire. Their mum has also said that they must not play in the area where the door swings open. The diagram shows the locus of points for the area where the children can play.

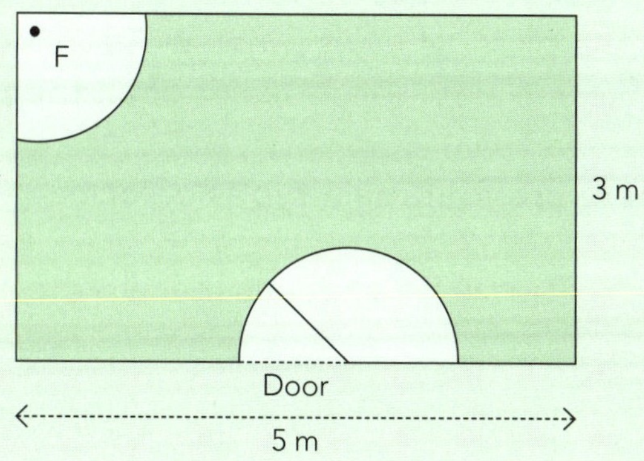

2 A rectangular section is 30 m wide on the side that borders the road and the other side is 20 m long. The building regulations say that the owners are not allowed to build within 4.5 m of the road. Nor are they allowed to build within 3 m of the remaining boundaries. The diagram shows the locus of points for the area that can be built on.

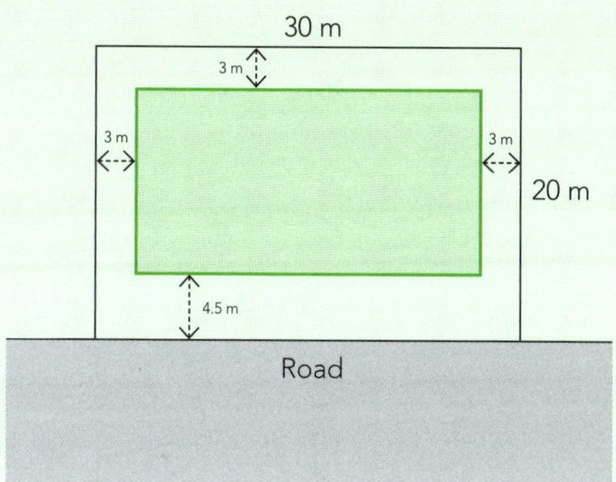

3 Five pairs of buoys mark the approach to a port entrance. The deepest part of the approach is halfway between each pair. The diagram shows the locus for the deepest line of approach to the port.

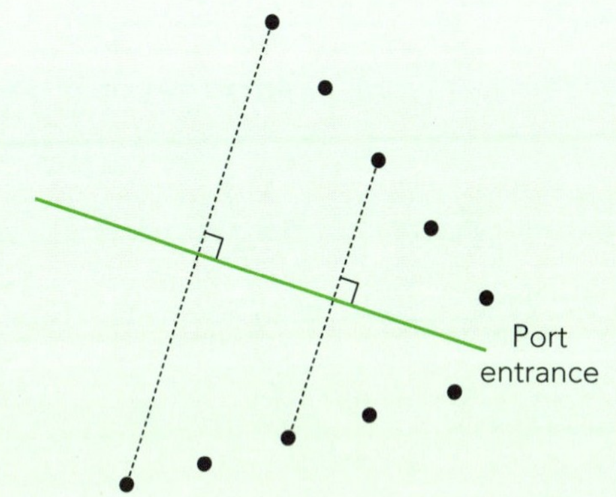

4 Two strings of decorations are fastened between the corners of a rectangular room. The diagram shows the locus for two more strings that are to be located at equal distances from the original two strings.

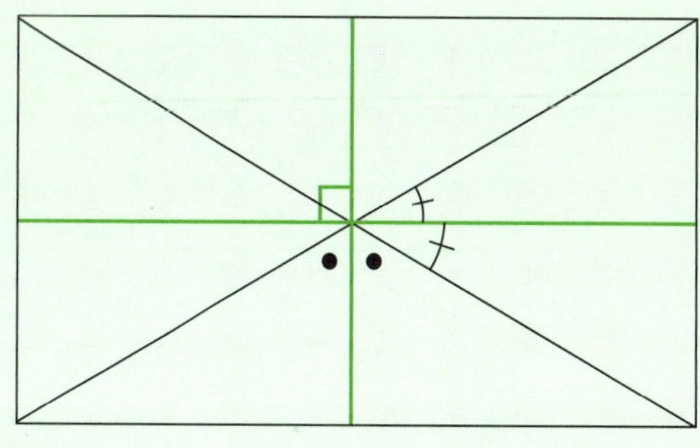

ISBN: 9780170447577

Answer the following.

1 Gurtee the goat has a tether that is 4 m long. She needs to be moved around the farm to different places. Sketch and shade the locus of all the points she can reach for each of these positions.

a She is tethered to a point (A) at the corner of a shed (which she cannot climb onto). The shed is 3 m wide and 5 m long.

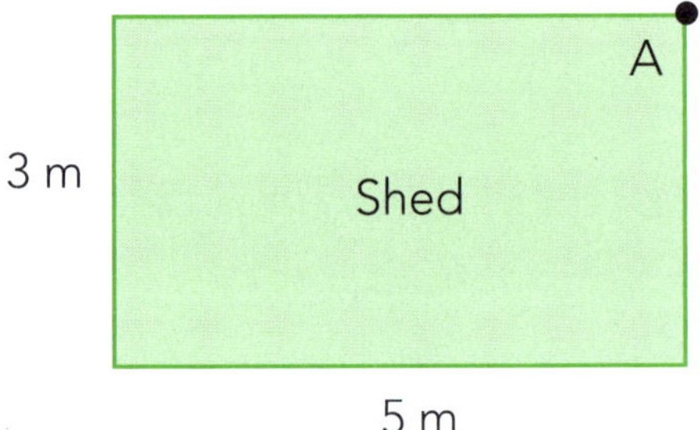

b She is tethered to a post near the corner of a paddock. The post is 4 m away from one fence and 2 m away from the other. She cannot jump the fences.

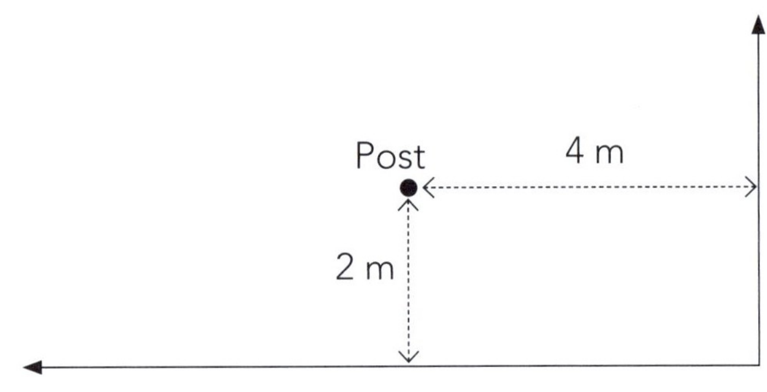

c She is tethered to a wire that runs between two posts (A and B). The posts are 16 m apart. Post A is in the middle of the paddock, but post B is 3 m from the corner of a shed.

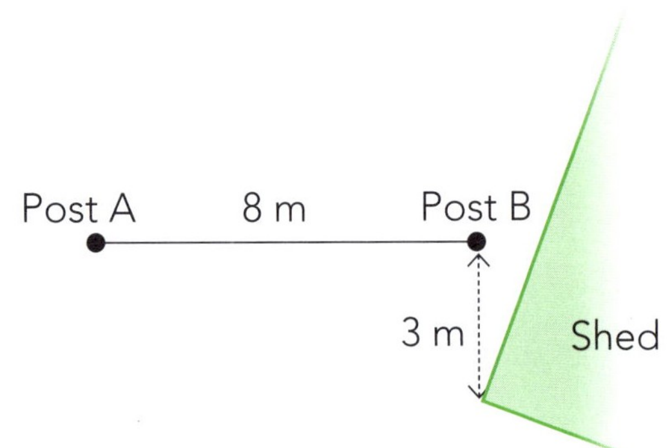

2 Match the diagrams to the descriptions.

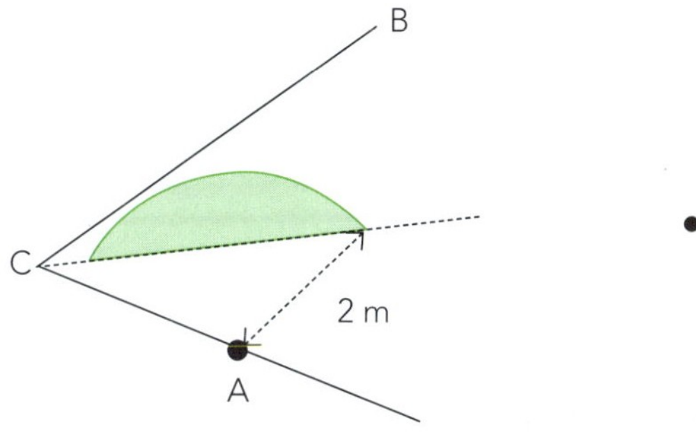

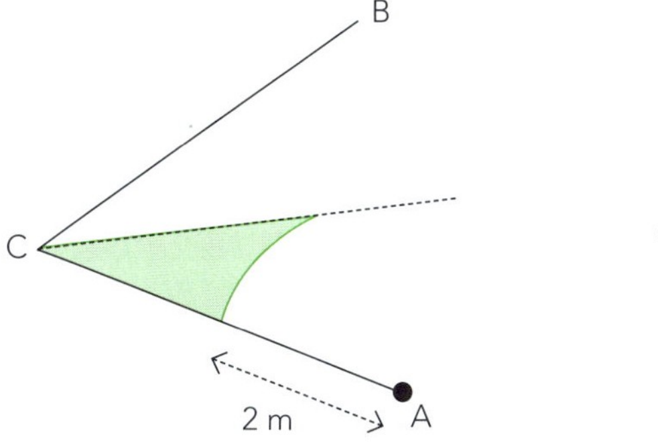

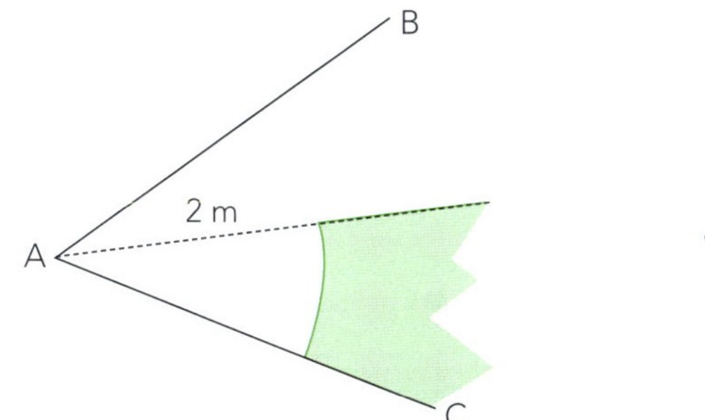

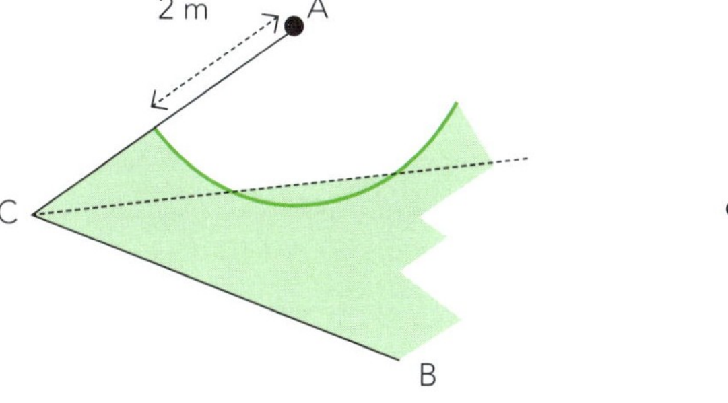

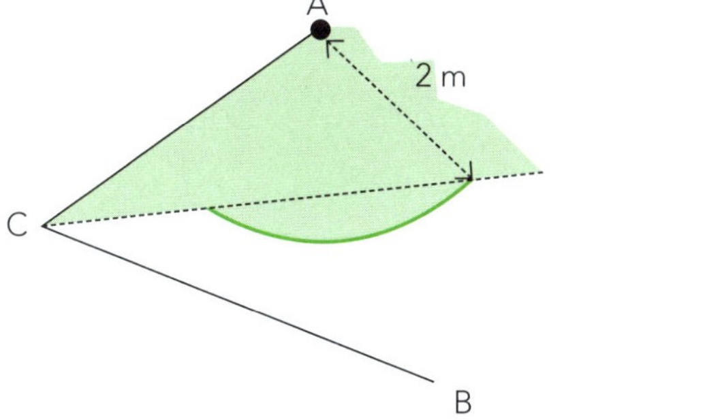

- At least 2 m from A or closer to BC than AC.
- Less than 2 m from A or closer to AC than BC.
- Less than 2 m from A and closer to BC than AC.
- At least 2 m from A and closer to AC than AB.
- At least 2 m from A and closer to AC than BC.

ISBN: 9780170447577

3 Match the following sketches of loci to each of the situations listed below.

A
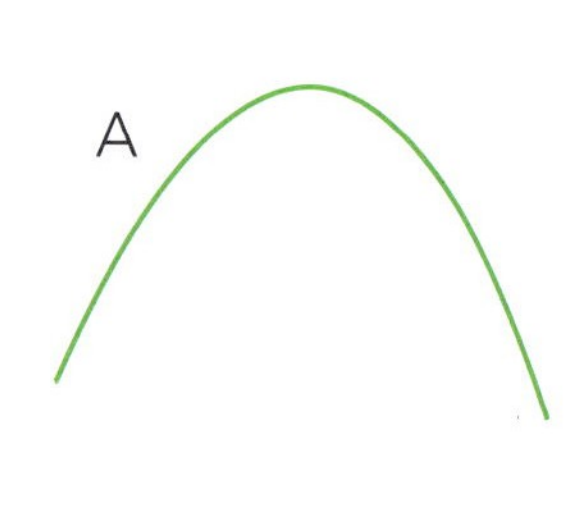

B

C
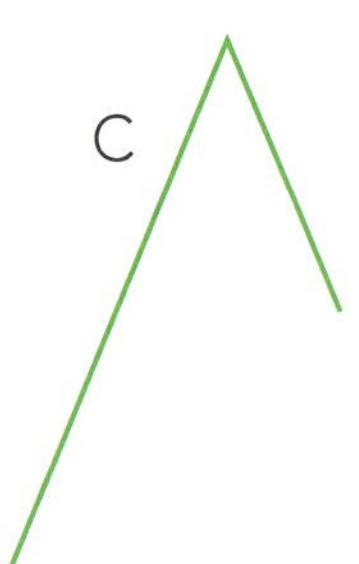

D

E

F
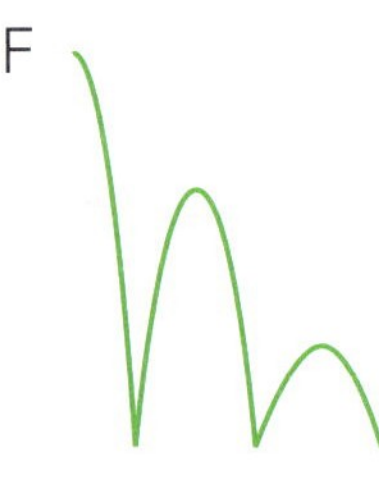

G

H

I
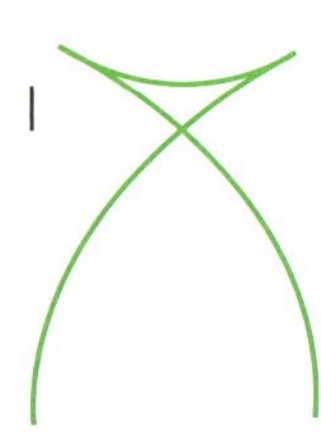

When seen from the side:

a The seats on a seesaw. ____________

b A bouncing ball. ____________

c The valve on a bike tyre while the bike is being ridden. ____________

d A rugby ball when a goal is kicked. ____________

e The ball during a tennis rally. ____________

f A surfer as she paddles out to catch waves. ____________

When seen from above:

g A billiard ball during a shot. ____________

h A car as it does a three-point turn. ____________

i A hockey ball which rebounds off the backboard when a goal is scored. ____________

ISBN: 9780170447577

Distances: scales on maps and diagrams

- Using the terminology of transformation geometry, maps are **enlargements** with scale factors of **less than 1**.
- Diagrams of small things are **enlargements** with scale factors of **more than 1**.
- Scales are generally expressed using **whole numbers**, one of which is **1**.
- Scales on maps and diagrams can come in several forms:

1 Ratios

For maps or large objects:

1:50 000

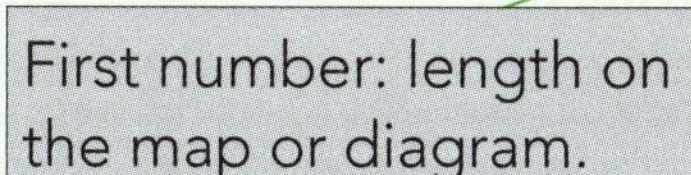

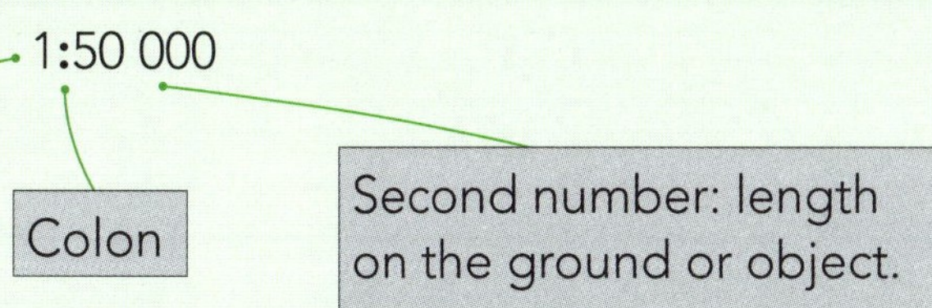

So, 1 cm on the map ≡ 50 000 cm on the ground or object.

≡ 500 m

≡ 0.5 km

≡ means **'is equivalent to'**

For small objects:

100:1

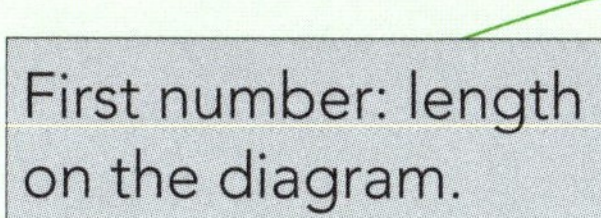

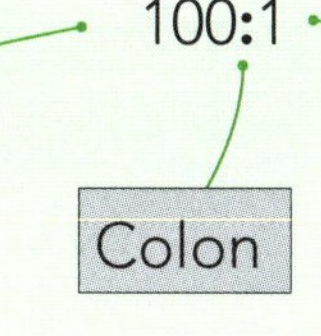

Second number: length on the object.

So, 100 cm on the diagram ≡ 1 cm on the object.

1 cm ≡ 0.01 cm

1 cm ≡ 0.1 mm

2 Diagrams

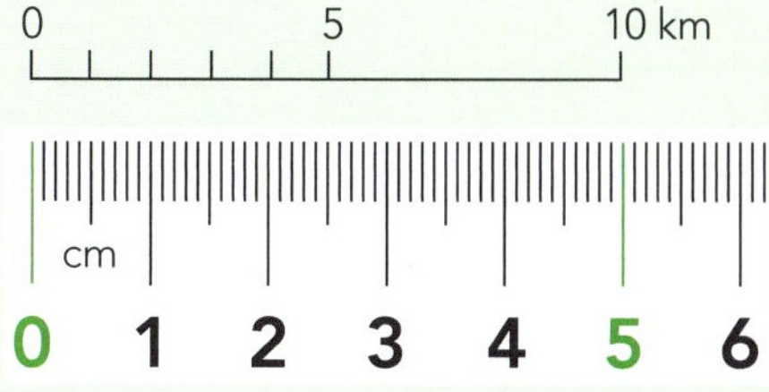

5 cm on the map ≡ 10 km on the ground
1 cm on the map ≡ 2 km on the ground

5 cm on the map ≡ 50 km on the ground
1 cm on the map ≡ 10 km on the ground

3 Sometimes you will be told the scale

Example: 1 cm = 1.5 km

So, 1 cm on the diagram ≡ 1.5 km on the object.

 ISBN: 9780170447577

Examples: Calculate the distance between points A and B.

1

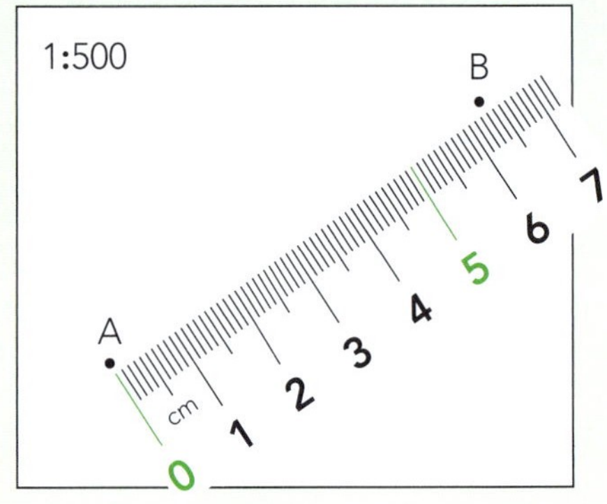

1:500 means 1 cm ≡ 500 cm

∴ 6.3 cm ≡ 6.3 x 500 cm

≡ 3150 cm

≡ 31.50 m

∴ is a short way of writing 'therefore'.

2

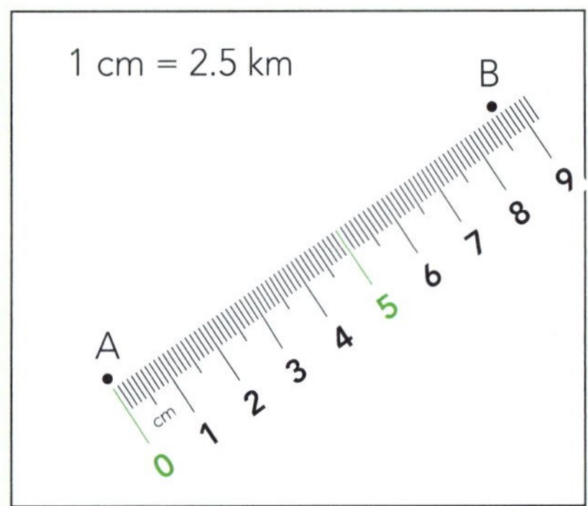

1 cm ≡ 2.5 km

∴ 8.6 cm ≡ 8.6 x 2.5 km

≡ 21.5 km

3

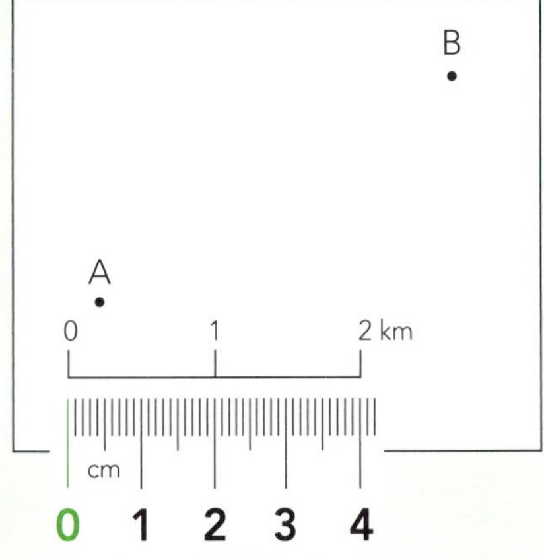

Step 1: Calculate scale

4 cm ≡ 2 km

∴ 1 cm ≡ 0.5 km

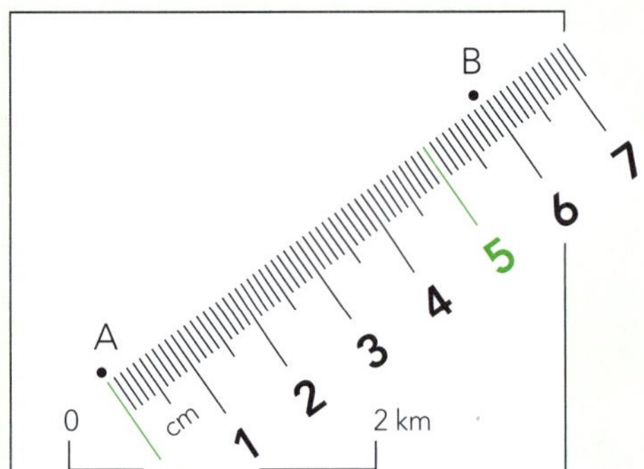

Step 2: Calculate distance

1 cm ≡ 0.5 km

∴ 5.9 cm ≡ 5.9 x 0.5 km

≡ 2.95 km

ISBN: 9780170447577

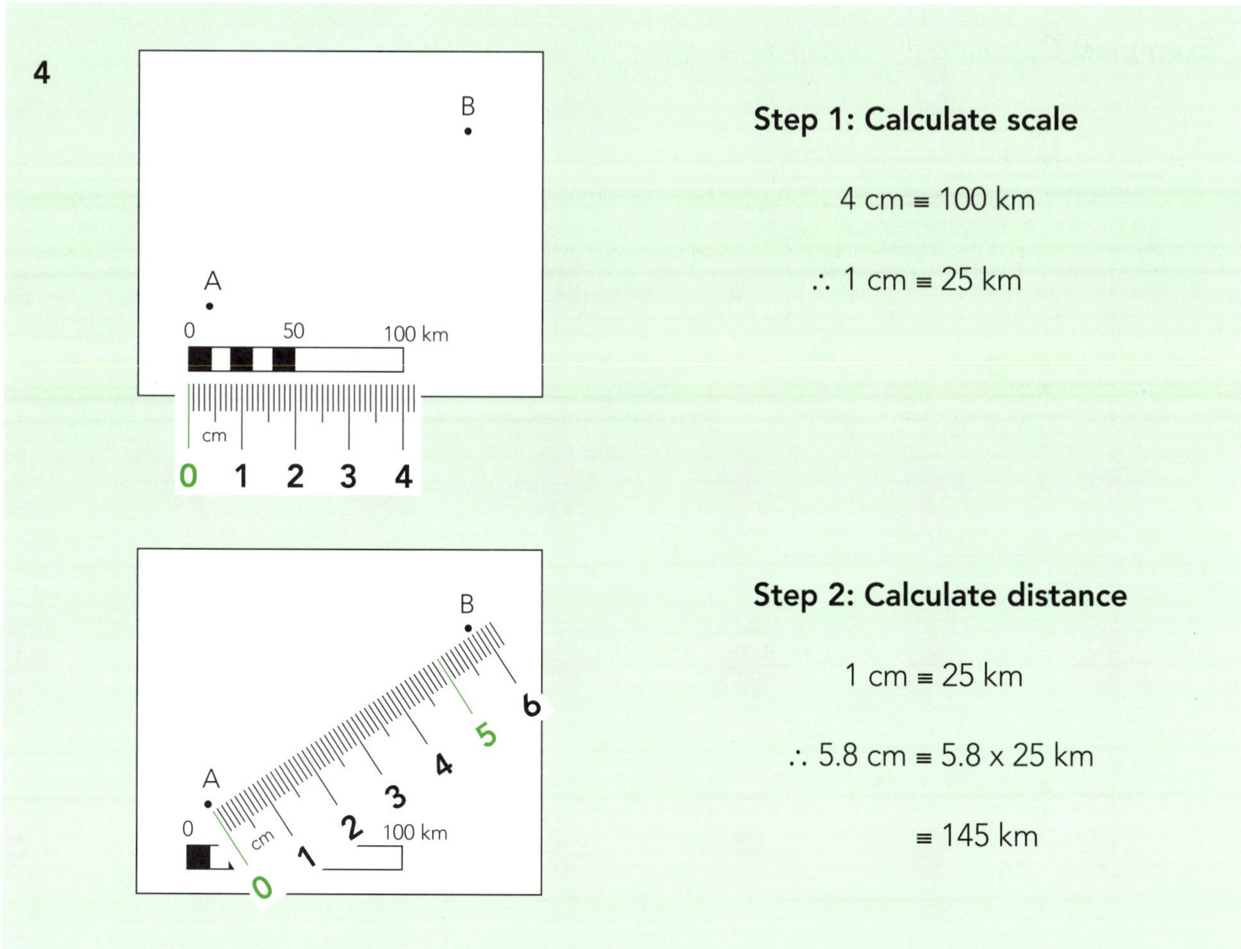

For each of the following ratios, calculate what length 1 cm would represent on a diagram or map.

1 1:10 000

1 cm ≡ 10 000 cm

≡ 100 m

1 cm ≡ 100 m

2 1:1 000 000

______________ 1 cm ≡ ______

____

3 1:200

______________ 1 cm ≡ ______

____

4 1:25 000

______________ 1 cm ≡ ______

____

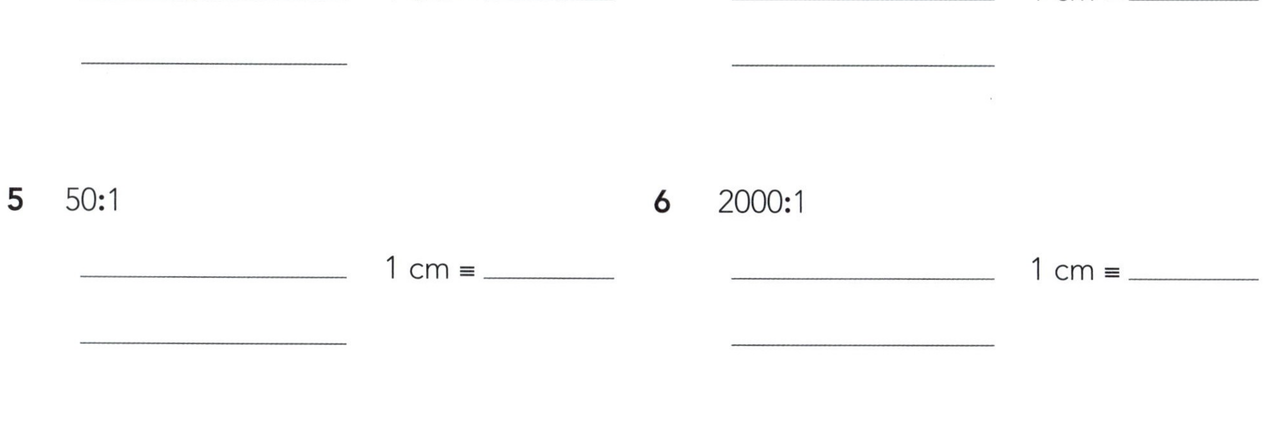

5 50:1

______________ 1 cm ≡ ______

____

6 2000:1

______________ 1 cm ≡ ______

____

 ISBN: 9780170447577

Using a ruler, measure the distances between A and B on this page. Then calculate the distance between the points. Round your answers to the nearest metre.

7

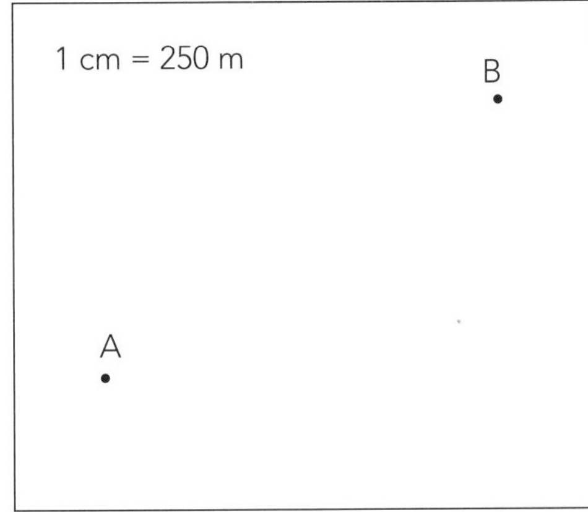

8

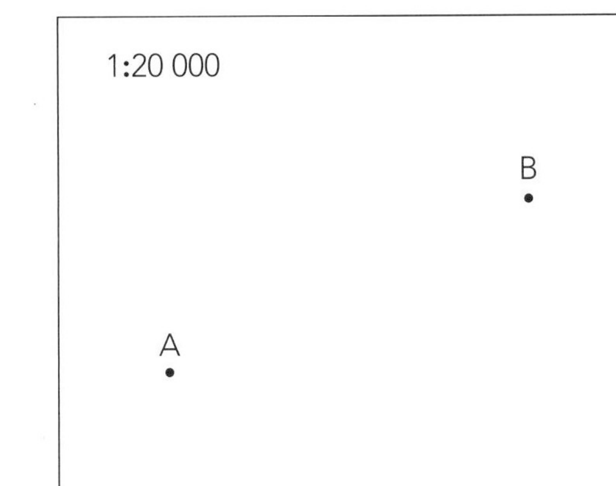

9

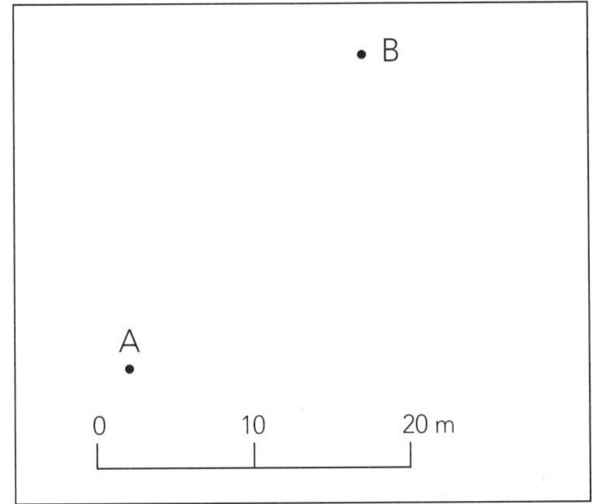

10

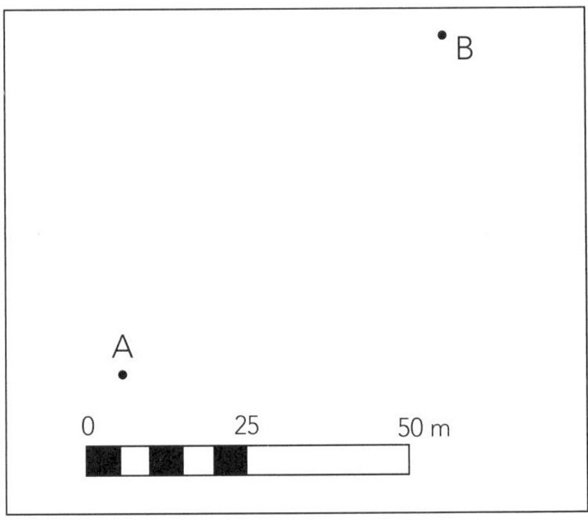

ISBN: 9780170447577

Find the direct distances between the centres of the green crosses on the map below. The scale is 1:500 000.

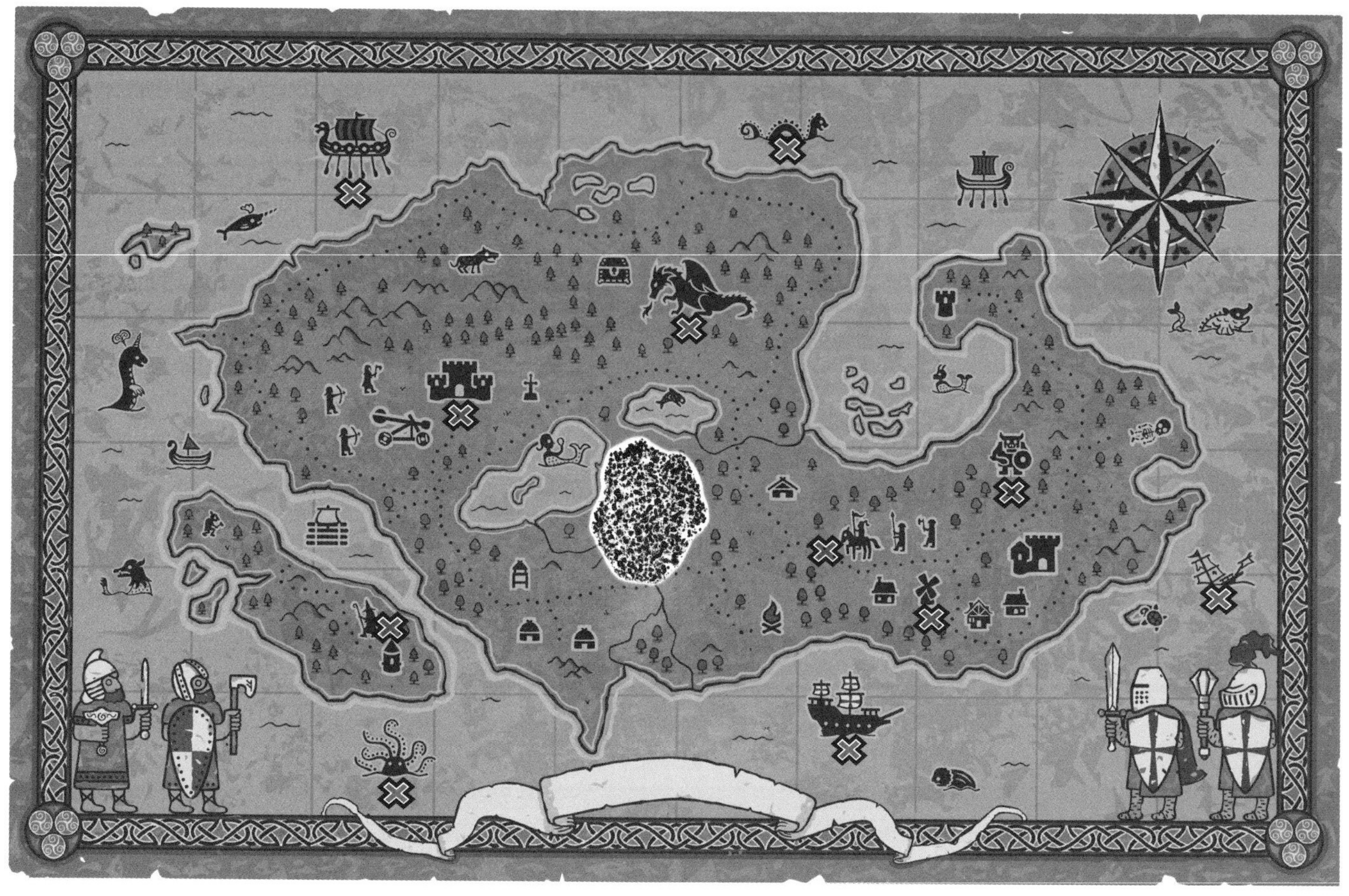

11 **a** Between the Viking ship at the top of the map and the sea serpent.

b Between the sailing ship at the bottom of the map and western castle.

c Between the knight on his horse and the dragon.

d Between the octopus and the sinking ship.

e Between the knight on his horse and the Viking.

f Between the witch and the windmill.

 ISBN: 9780170447577

12 The scale for this house plan is 1:100. Find the following.

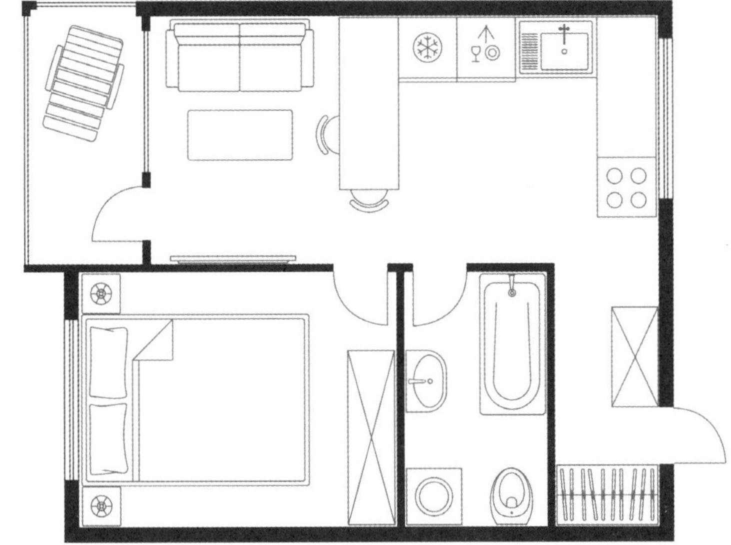

a The internal dimensions of the bathroom.

____

____

____

b The internal length of the kitchen/living room.

____

____

____

c The width of the bedroom window.

____

____

____

13 The scale for this diagram of an ant is 20:1.

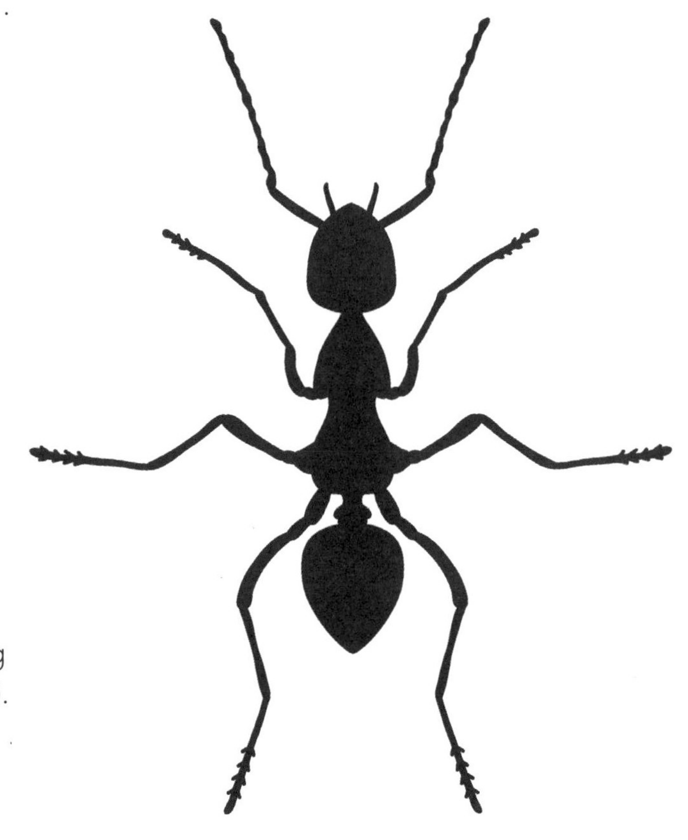

a How long is the body (including the head) of the ant?

____

____

____

b What is the width of the abdomen?

____

____

____

c Estimate the total length of a hind leg (assume it has been straightened out).

____

____

____

ISBN: 9780170447577

Navigation

- For the purposes of navigation, the globe is divided by imaginary **north–south** and **east–west** lines.

East–west lines

- These are lines of **latitude**, also known as **parallels**.

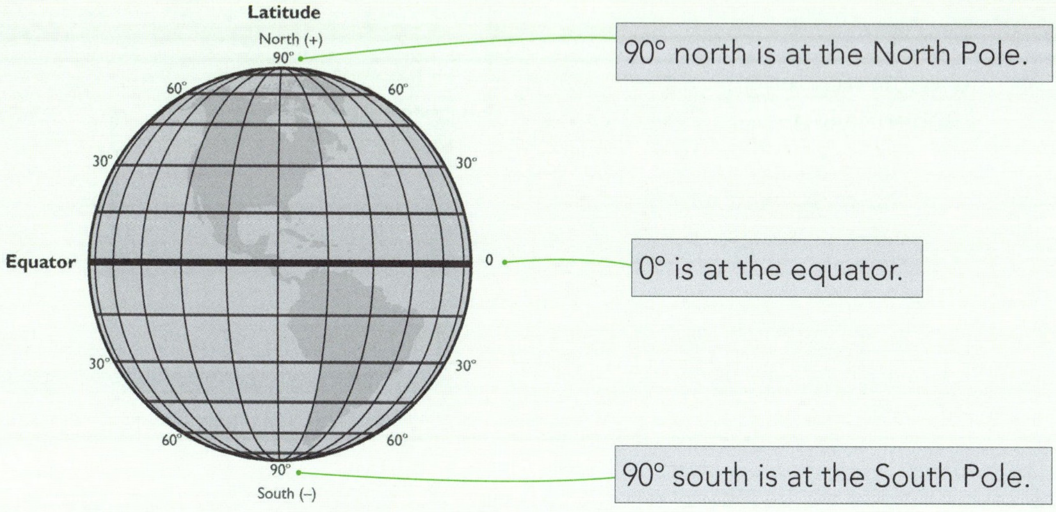

- Latitudes were easily established by navigators because the day lengths are the same at a given latitude. They vary throughout the year, but the relationship was known.

North–south lines

- These are lines of **longitude**, also known as **meridians**.
- Meridians loop through the poles in circles that are all the same size.

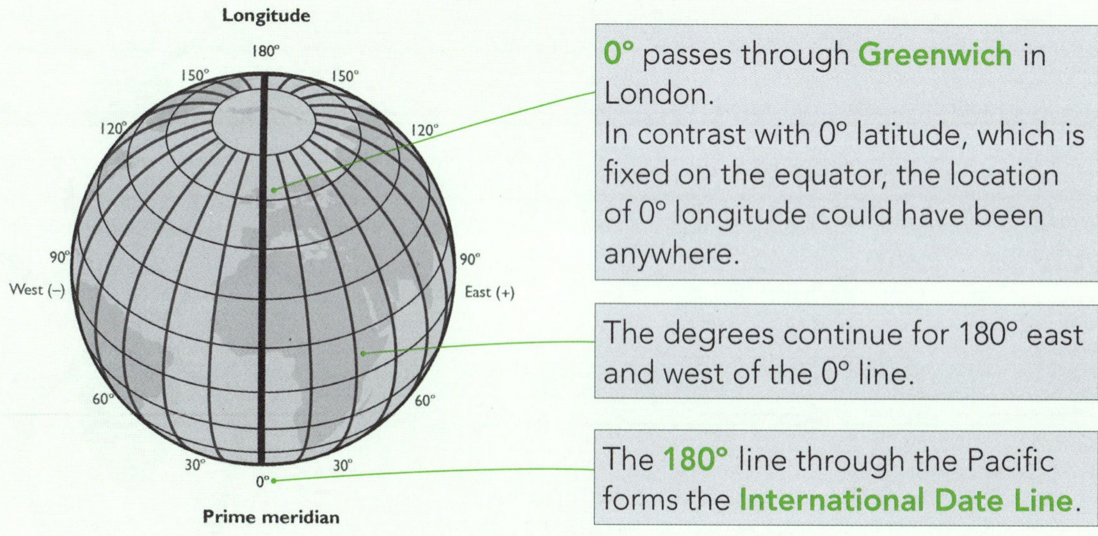

- Notice that the **distance between meridians varies**: 1° is about 1000 km at the equator, but almost nothing at the poles.
- Consequently, establishing longitudes was a massive problem for navigators before the invention of robust and reliable clocks.

 ISBN: 9780170447577

Select the best estimate for the latitudes and longitudes of the following places.

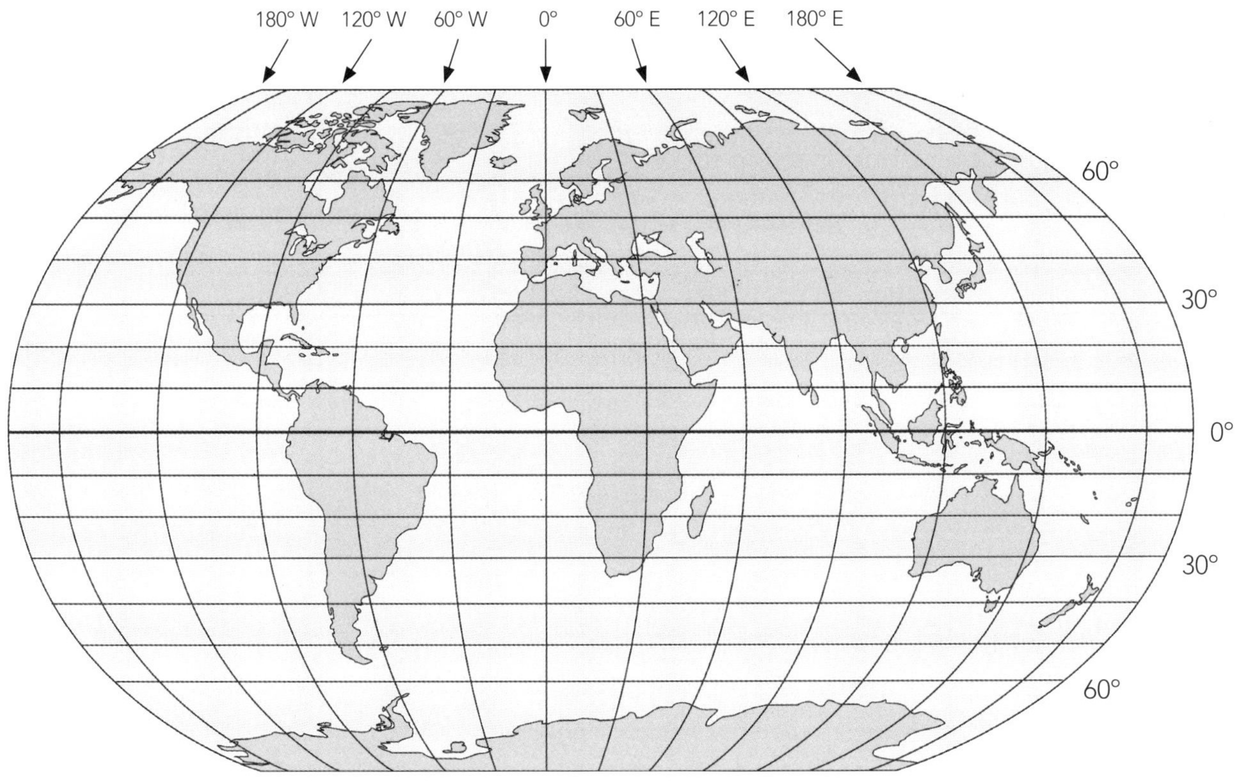

0° E or W	18° E	9° N	170° E	55° S	33° S	78° E	147° E
80° S	70° W	43° S	45° W	74° W	50° N	40° S	41° N

1 The southernmost tip of South America ________ ________

2 Cook Strait ________ ________

3 London ________ ________

4 The southernmost tip of Tasmania ________ ________

5 The only visible island in Antarctica ________ ________

6 The southernmost tip of India ________ ________

7 The southernmost tip of Africa ________ ________

8 There are two values left. Use them to locate New York on the map.

ISBN: 9780170447577

Describing locations more precisely using latitudes and longitudes

- Positions of locations are described using coordinates.

For **longitude**:
1 °E increase from west to east.
2 1° of longitude is longer at the top of the map than it is at the bottom.

Notice that the lines of longitude are **not parallel**.

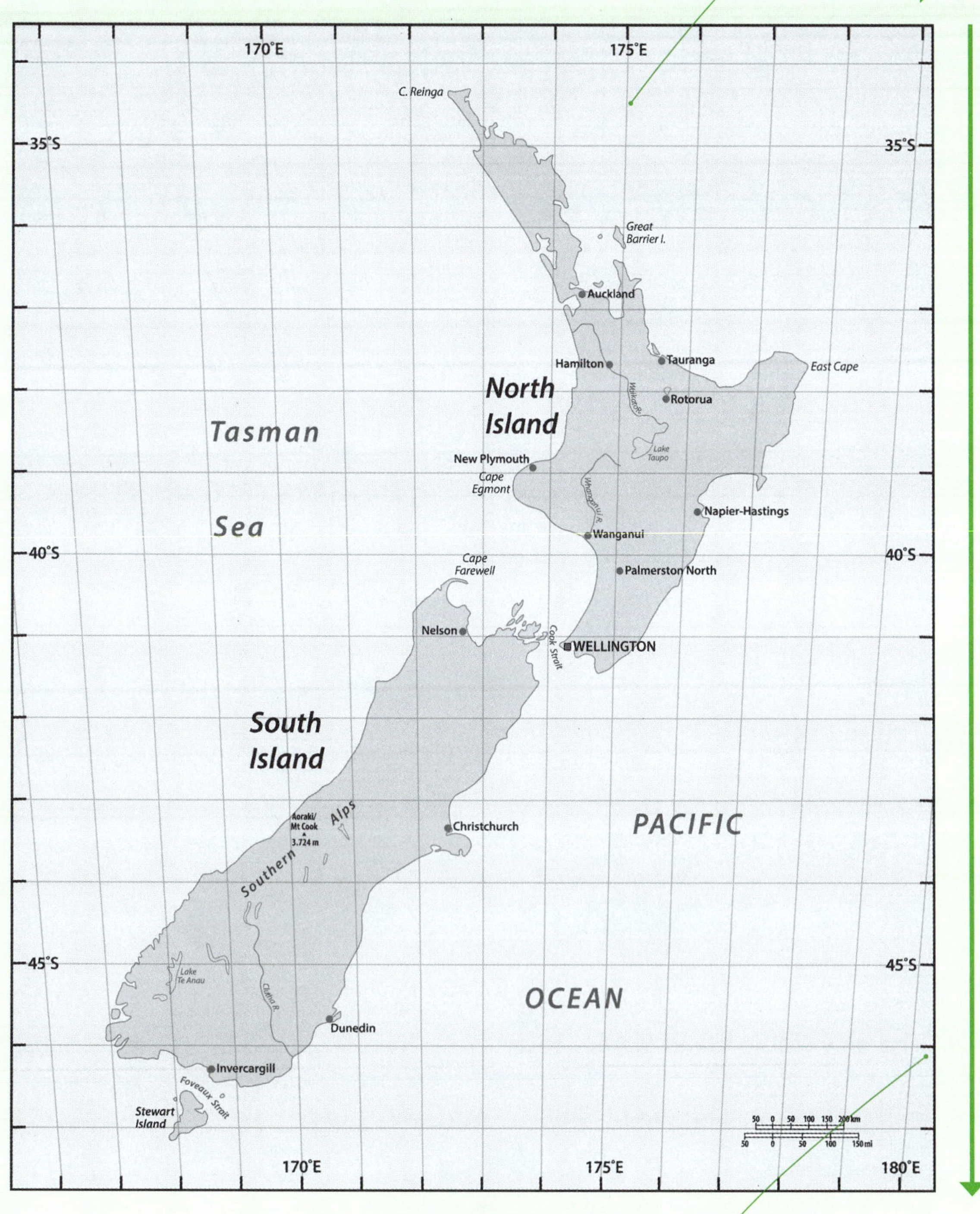

For **latitude**:
1 °S increase from north to south.
2 Every degree is the **same** length.

ISBN: 9780170447577

- There are several different methods for describing a position.
- It is possible to use degrees and up to three decimal places of a degree.

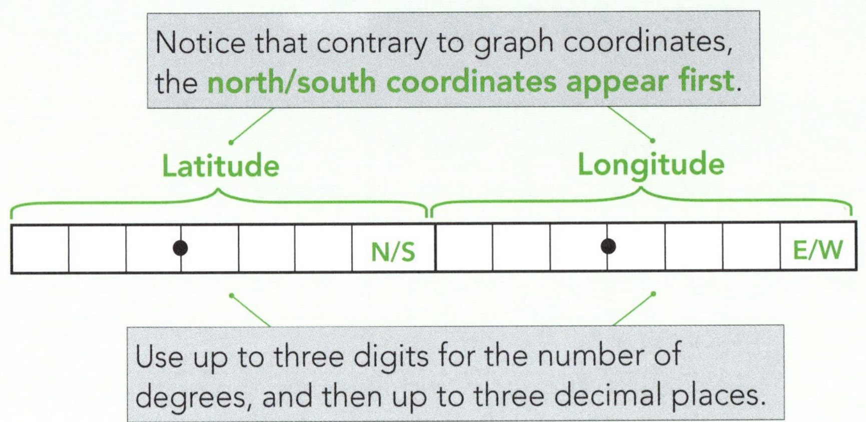

Example: Christchurch to one decimal place is at **43.4°S 172.5°E**.

Which places would you find at the following locations?

9 45.7°S 170.6°E ____________ **10** 37.7°S 177.7°E ____________

11 38.9°S 173.7°E ____________ **12** 34.4°S 172.6°E ____________

Write the locations of the following places to 1 dp.

13 Auckland ____________ **14** Nelson ____________

15 Invercargill ____________ **16** Tauranga ____________

Describing distance and velocity

- In air and sea navigation, **nautical miles (NM)** are used instead of kilometres as a measure of **distance**.

  1 nautical mile = $\frac{1}{60}$ of 1° of **latitude** = 1.852 km (3 dp) ∴ **1° of latitude = 60 NM**

- **Knots** are used as a measure of **velocity**.

  1 knot = 1 nautical mile per hour = 1.852 km/hour (3 dp)

17 Explain why 1 nautical mile must be $\frac{1}{60}$ of 1° of latitude, not longitude.

____

Use a ruler to estimate the distance in nautical miles between the following locations to the nearest 10 NM. Hint: 1° on the vertical scale = 60 NM.

18 Auckland and Hamilton ____________ **19** Cape Reinga and Tauranga ____________

20 Dunedin and Christchurch ____________ **21** Wellington and Dunedin ____________

ISBN: 9780170447577

Transformation geometry

- Transformation geometry is changing figures by following certain rules.
- The transformed figure is called the **image**.
- A transformation may change the size, shape or orientation of the image.
- Properties that **remain the same** when a figure is transformed are said to be **invariant**.

Properties of transformations

Size Is the image **bigger or smaller** than the original figure?

Shape Are the **angles** within the image **different** from those of the original figure?

Orientation Does the image **face a different direction** from that of the original figure?

The property tables for Translation and Reflection have been filled in for you.

Translation

- The figure is **shifted**.

Properties

	Invariant
Size	✓
Shape	✓
Orientation	✓

Reflection

- The figure is **reflected in a mirror** line.

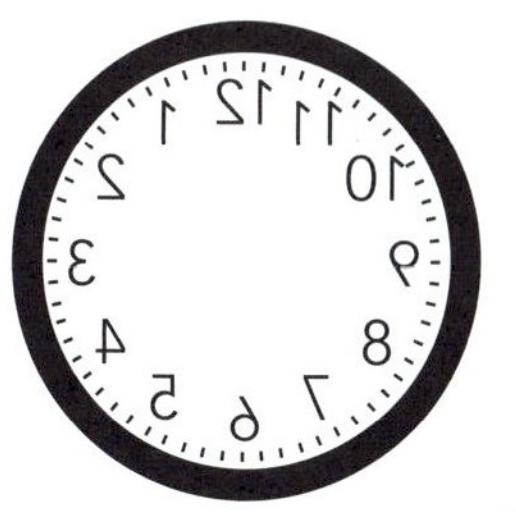

The hands on these clocks would move in opposite direction, so the orientation has changed.

Properties

	Invariant
Size	✓
Shape	✓
Orientation	×

 ISBN: 9780170447577

Fill in the property tables for Rotation and Enlargement.

Rotation

- The figure **rotates around a point**.

Properties

	Invariant
Size	
Shape	
Orientation	

Hint: Do the hands on these clocks move in the same direction or not?

Enlargement

- The figure **gets bigger or smaller**.

Properties

	Invariant
Size	
Shape	
Orientation	

Answer the following questions.

1 Which transformation(s) result in a change of size? ____________________

2 Which transformation(s) result in a change of shape? ____________________

3 Which transformation(s) result in a change of orientation? ____________________

ISBN: 9780170447577

Revision of translation, reflection and rotation

Answer the following.

1 Write vectors for the following word descriptions. (Remember: Translation)

a Left seven and up three.

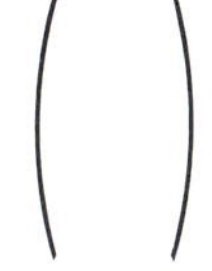

b Down two and right four.

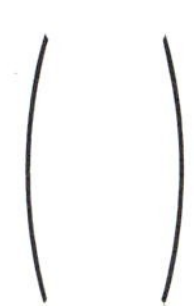

2 Write the vector for the translation of this figure. The green shape is the original.

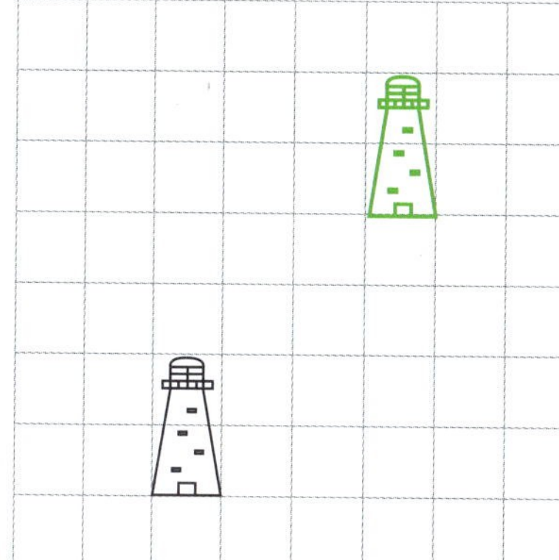

3 Draw the image of the figure after it has been translated by the given vector.

$\begin{pmatrix} -3 \\ -2 \end{pmatrix}$

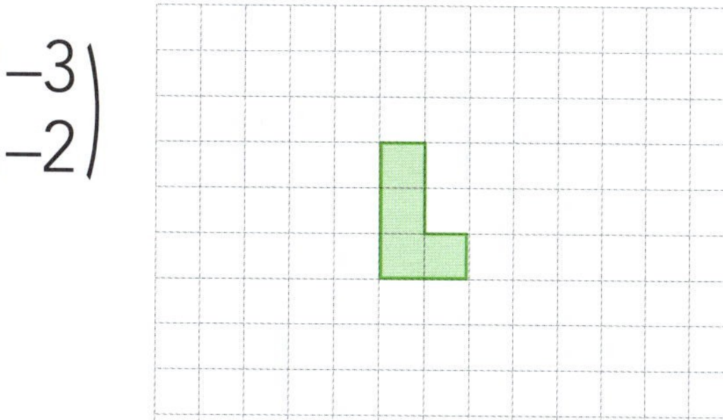

4 Draw the mirror lines for these reflections.

a

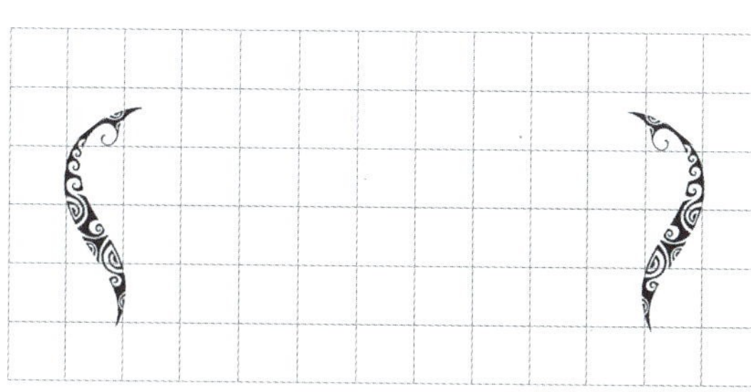

b

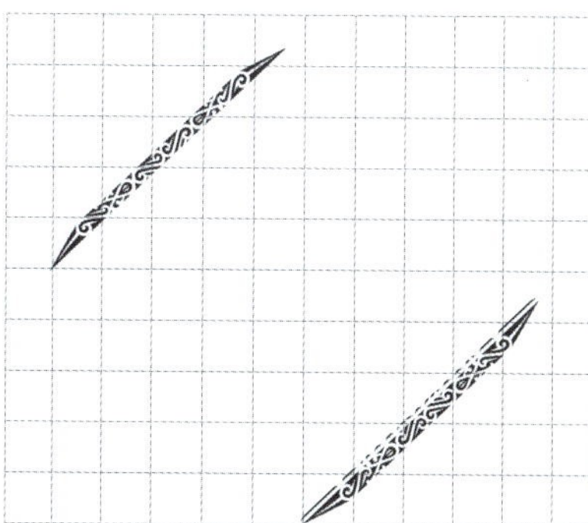

5 Reflect the figure in the mirror line. Label any invariant points.

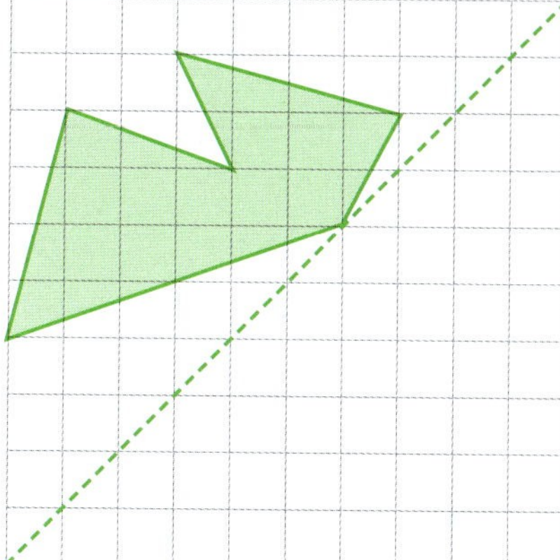

6 Reflect each of the shaded squares in both mirror lines, and shade them appropriately.

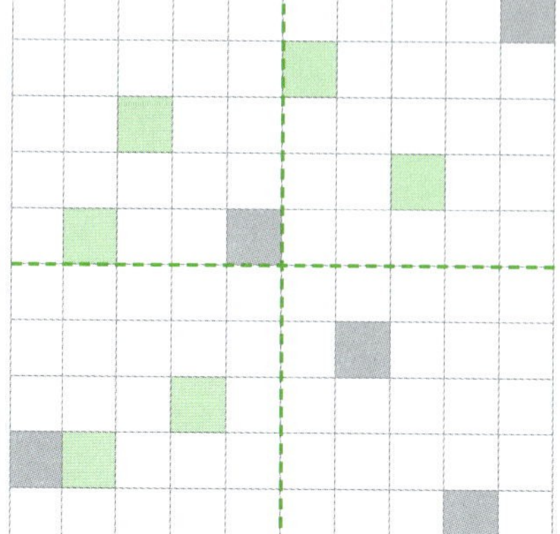

 ISBN: 9780170447577

7 Write the order of line symmetry for these images.

a

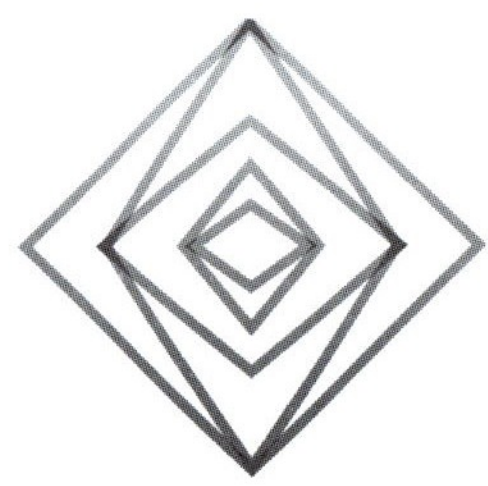

Order of line symmetry = ________

b

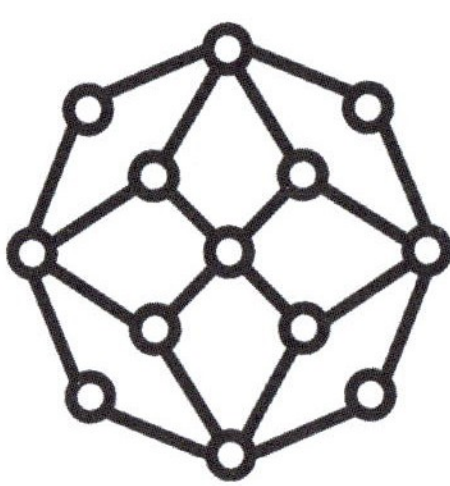

Order of line symmetry = ________

8 Write the angle of rotation for each of these figures. Remember: rotations are clockwise unless otherwise stated; the green shape is the original.

a

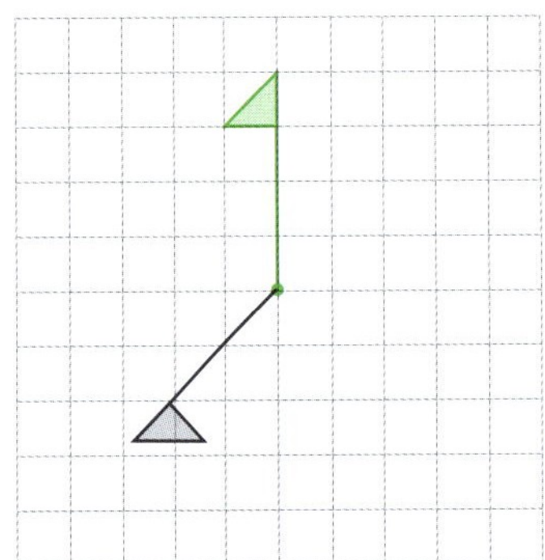

Angle of rotation = ________°

b

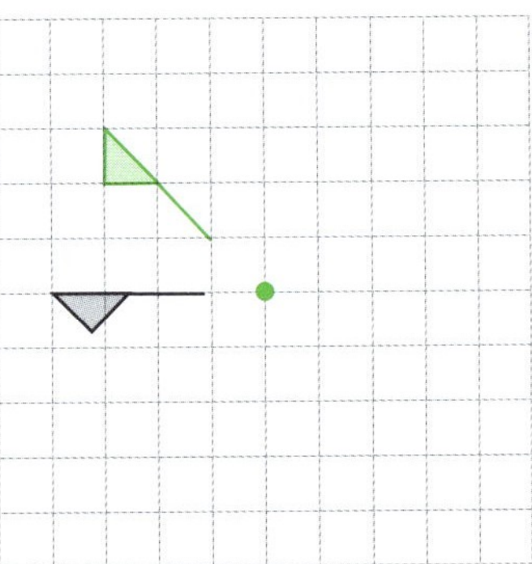

Angle of rotation = ________°

9 **a** Rotate this figure 270° around the point.

b Rotate this figure 90° around the point.

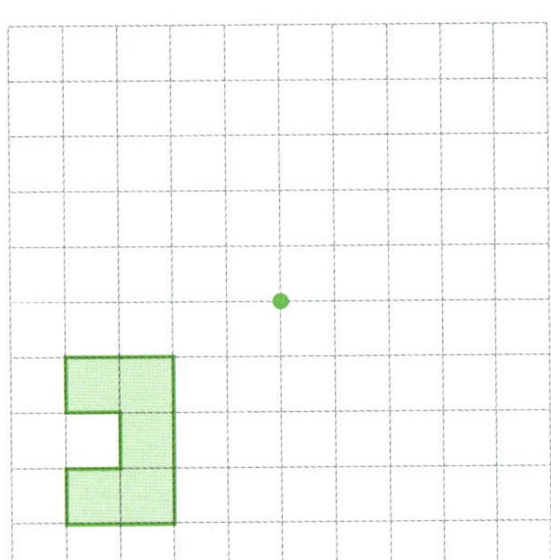

10 Write the order of rotational symmetry for these images.

a

Order of rotational symmetry = ________

b

Order of rotational symmetry = ________

ISBN: 9780170447577

Challenge

Write down the letter/s that you think are represented by these logos. Check with your teacher if you have different answers. Describe the transformations and symmetries in each, if any.

1 Letter(s): ________

Transformation:

____

____

2 Letter(s): ________

Transformation:

____

____

3 Letter(s): ________

Transformation:

____

____

4 Letter(s): ________

Transformation:

____

____

5 Letter(s): ________

Transformation:

____

____

6 Letter(s): ________

Transformation:

____

____

7 Letter(s): ________

Transformation:

____

____

8 Letter(s): ________

Transformation:

____

____

9 Letter(s): ________

Transformation:

____

____

10 Letter(s): ________

Transformation:

____

____

ISBN: 9780170447577

Enlargement

- The figure **gets bigger or smaller**.
- The **scale factor** tells us how much larger or smaller the lines in the figure become.
- The **centre** tells us the position of the image.

Scale factor

$$\text{scale factor} = \frac{\text{length of image}}{\text{length of original figure}}$$

- Notice that the scale factor applies to the **lines**. The increase in **area** = (scale factor)^2.

Examples:

1

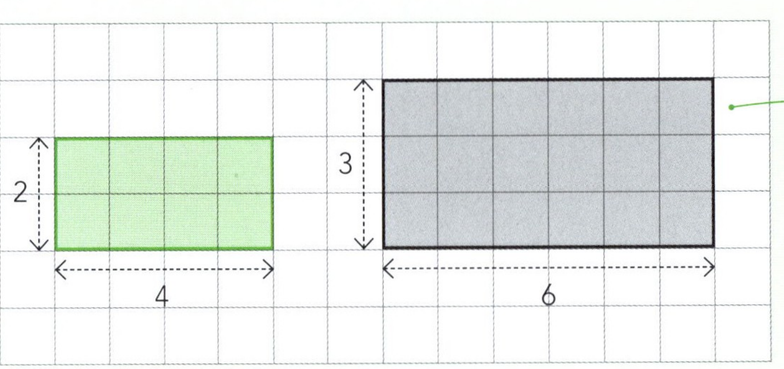

The increase to area $= \frac{18}{8} = 2.25 = \left(\frac{3}{2}\right)^2$. So the scale factor of $\frac{3}{2}$ means the area of the image is 2.25 times that of the original.

$$\text{scale factor} = \frac{\text{length of image}}{\text{length of original figure}} = \frac{6}{4} = \frac{3}{2}$$

You could write the answer as 1.5 or $1\frac{1}{2}$, but it is often more useful to leave it as a simplified improper fraction.

2

$$\text{scale factor} = \frac{\text{length of image}}{\text{length of original figure}} = \frac{4}{6} = \frac{2}{3}$$

ISBN: 9780170447577

Write the scale factor for these enlargements.

1

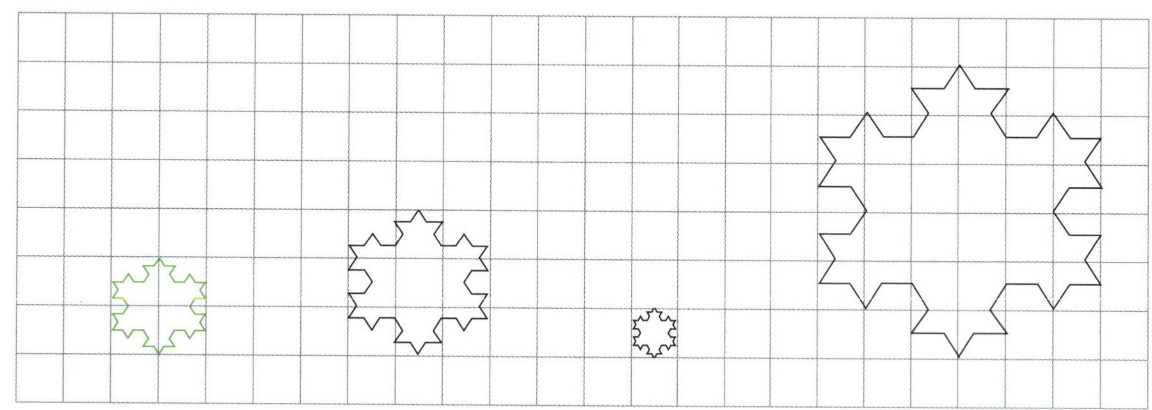

scale factor = ________ scale factor = ________ scale factor = ________

2

scale factor = ________ scale factor = ________ scale factor = ________

3

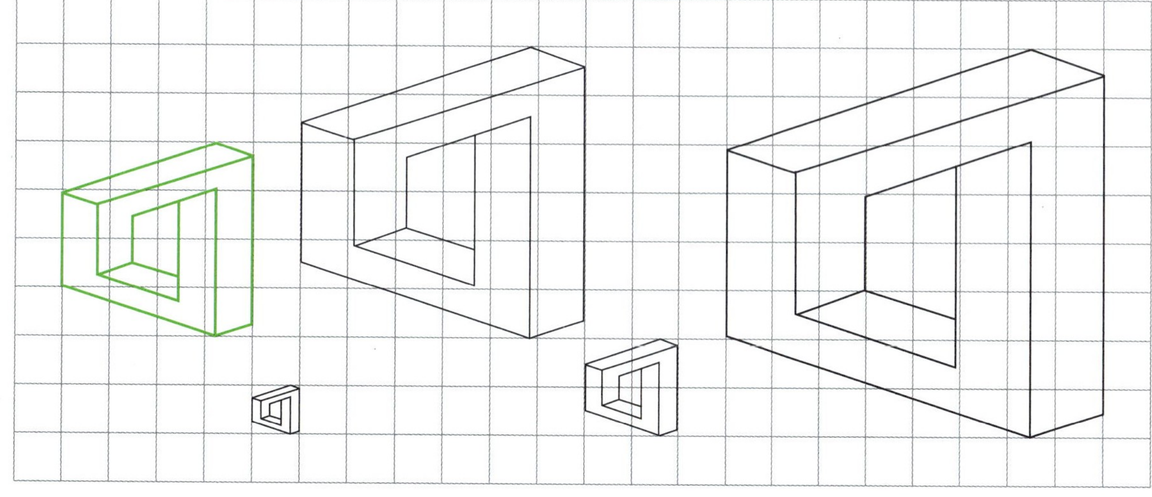

scale factor = ________ scale factor = ________ scale factor = ________ scale factor = ________

 ISBN: 9780170447577

Finding the centre of enlargement

- The centre of enlargement is the point where lines drawn through equivalent points on the figure and the image meet.

Examples:

1

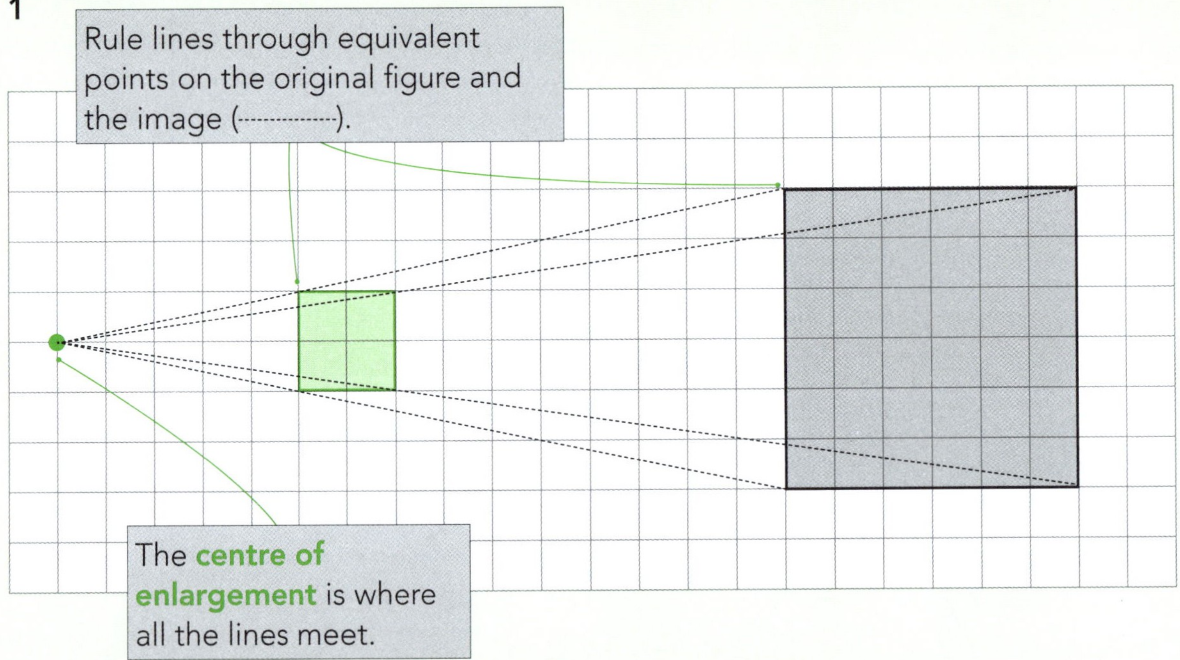

Notice that in this case, the image is **bigger** than the original figure, so the image is **beyond** both the centre of enlargement and the original figure.

2

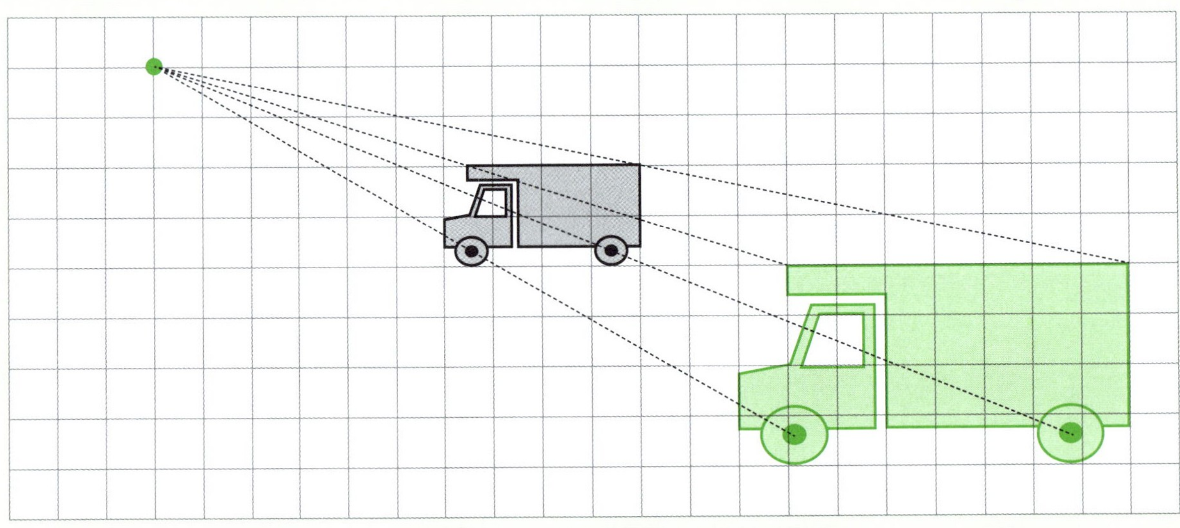

Notice that in this case, the image is **smaller** than the original figure, so the image is **between** the centre of enlargement and the original figure.

ISBN: 9780170447577

Find the centres of enlargement for these images.

1

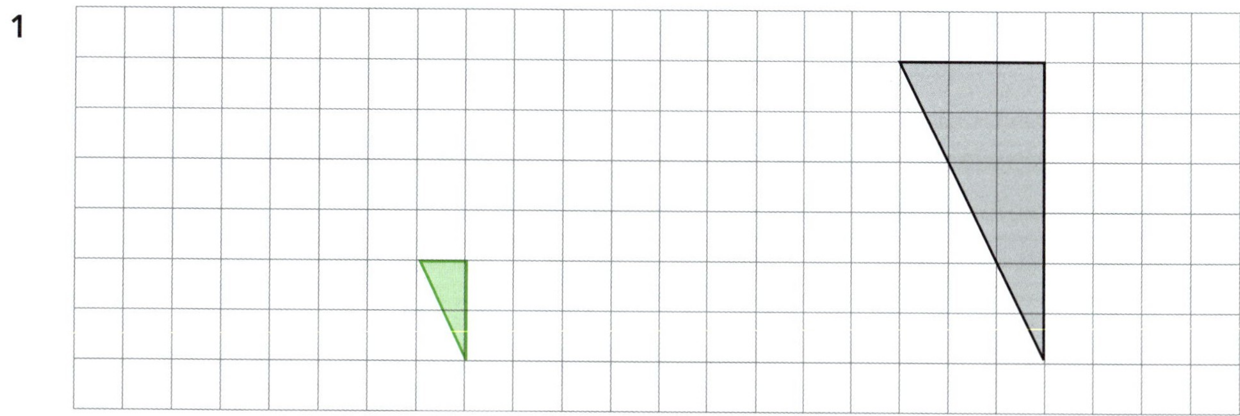

scale factor = __________

2

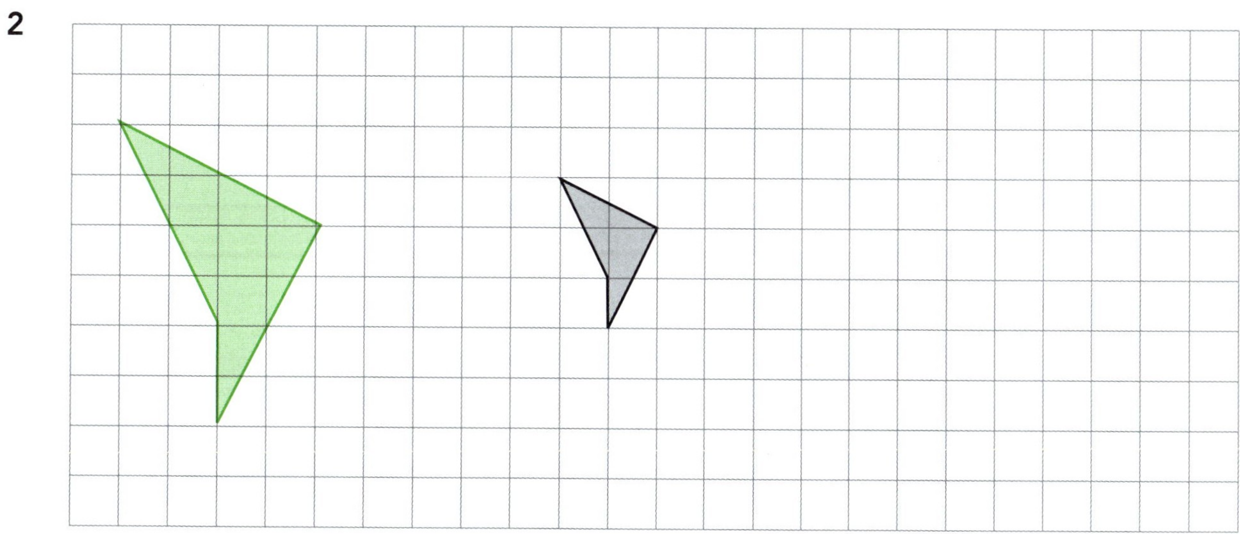

scale factor = __________

3

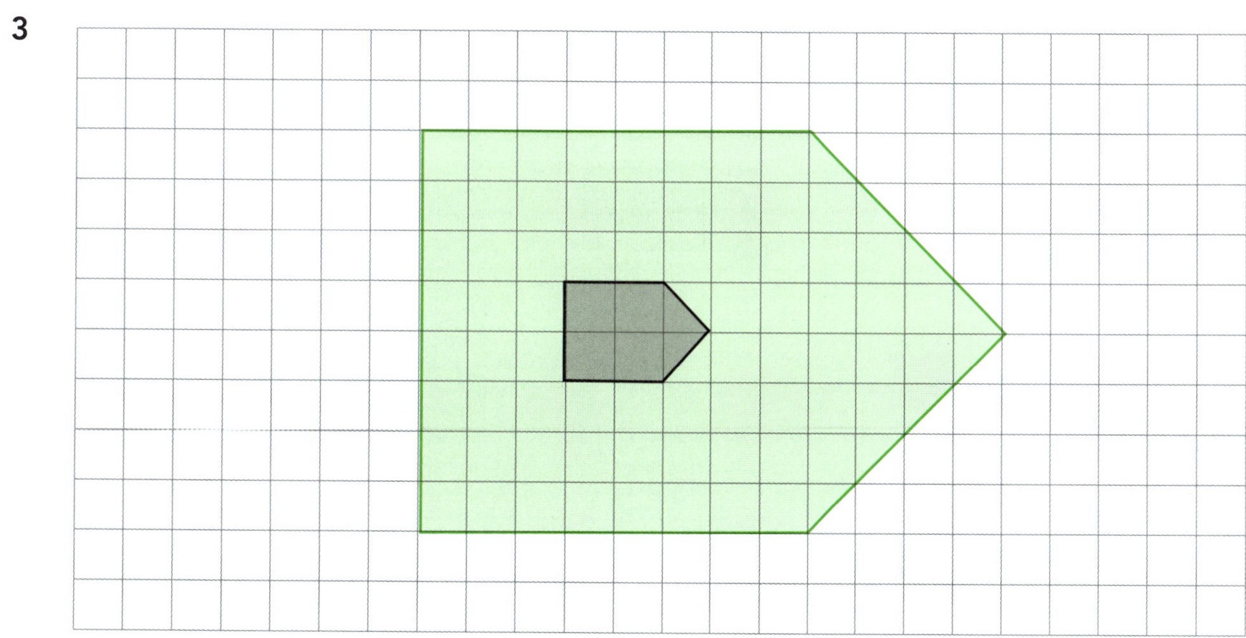

scale factor = __________

 ISBN: 9780170447577

Drawing enlargements

Examples:

1 Enlarge the green triangle by a scale factor of **4**, using the green dot as the centre of enlargement.

Step 1: Write the distance and direction from the centre to points on the original figure.

Point **A**: $\begin{pmatrix} 4 \\ 1 \end{pmatrix}$ Point **B**: $\begin{pmatrix} 5 \\ -1 \end{pmatrix}$ Point **C**: $\begin{pmatrix} 3 \\ 0 \end{pmatrix}$

Step 2: Multiply each vector by the scale factor — in this case **4**.

× **4**

Point A: $\begin{pmatrix} 16 \\ 4 \end{pmatrix}$ Point B: $\begin{pmatrix} 20 \\ -4 \end{pmatrix}$ Point C: $\begin{pmatrix} 12 \\ 0 \end{pmatrix}$

Step 3: Draw the enlarged vectors, starting at the centre of enlargement. The points at the ends of these vectors are at the vertices of the enlarged figure.

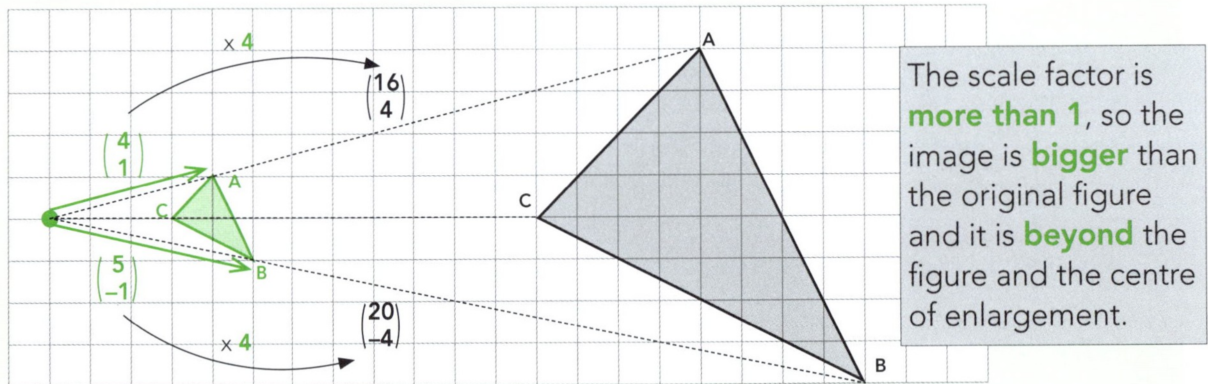

2 Enlarge the green triangle by a scale factor of $\frac{1}{3}$.

Point **A**: $\begin{pmatrix} 9 \\ 3 \end{pmatrix}$ Point **B**: $\begin{pmatrix} 6 \\ -3 \end{pmatrix}$ Point **C**: $\begin{pmatrix} 12 \\ -3 \end{pmatrix}$ Point **D**: $\begin{pmatrix} 15 \\ 0 \end{pmatrix}$

× $\frac{1}{3}$

Point A: $\begin{pmatrix} 3 \\ 1 \end{pmatrix}$ Point B: $\begin{pmatrix} 2 \\ -1 \end{pmatrix}$ Point C: $\begin{pmatrix} 4 \\ -1 \end{pmatrix}$ Point C: $\begin{pmatrix} 5 \\ 0 \end{pmatrix}$

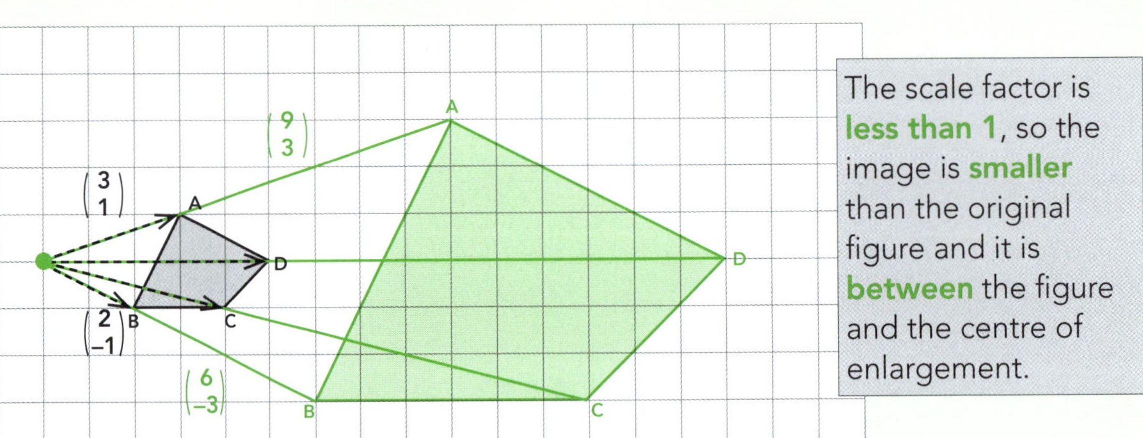

Note: You do not need to plot every point like this. Once you have one or two points, the shape will tell you where the rest are.

ISBN: 9780170447577

Some of these enlargements have been started for you. Complete them.

1 scale factor = 3

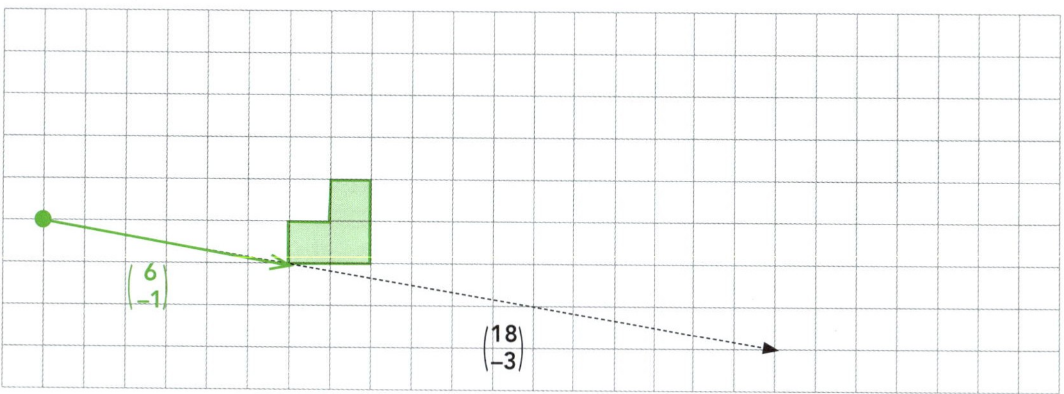

2 scale factor = 2

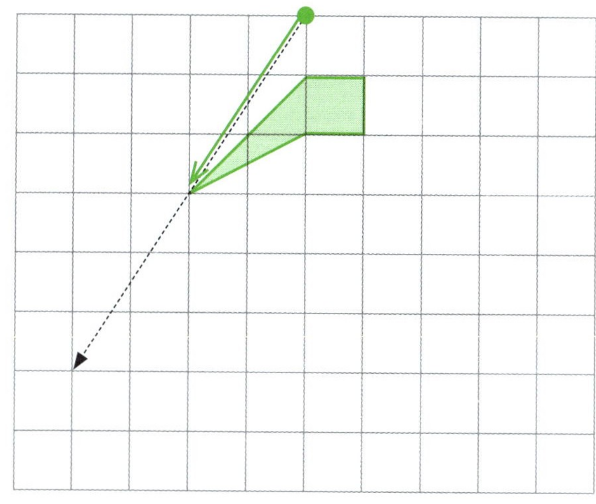

3 scale factor = $\frac{1}{2}$

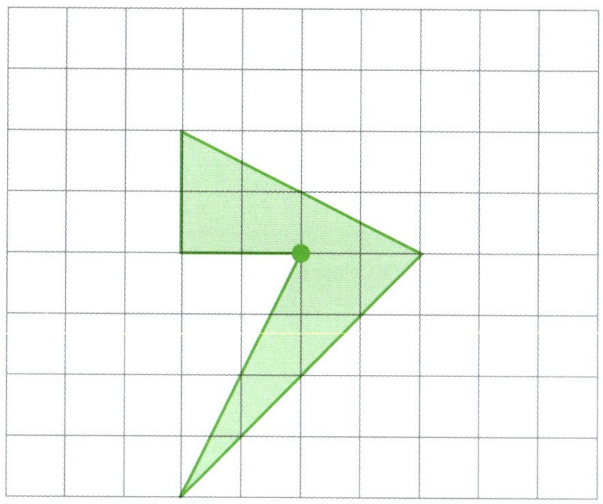

4 scale factor = 3

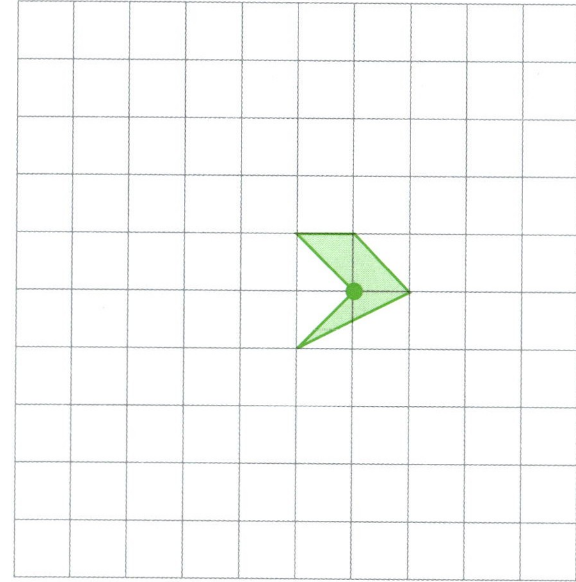

5 scale factor = $\frac{3}{2}$

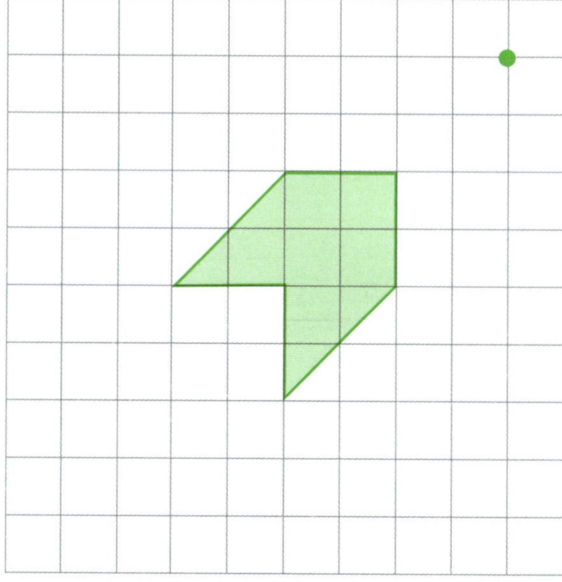

 ISBN: 9780170447577

The theorem of Pythagoras

Activity

1 Trace the two grey squares containing the numbers 1–5 onto a piece of paper.

2 Cut out your copies of these squares.

3 Cut along the dotted lines on the bigger grey square.

4 Like a jigsaw, fit pieces 1–5 onto the large (green) square, and stick them down.

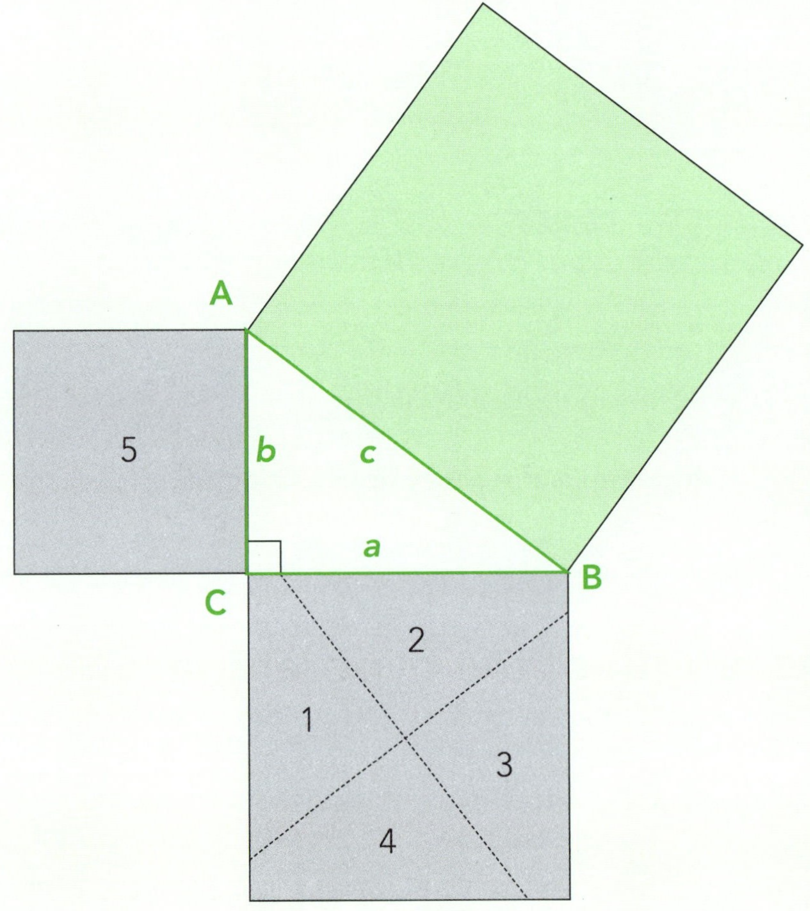

Complete:

- The area of the (green) square = c^2
- The area of the bottom square (containing 1, 2, 3 and 4) = ________
- The area of the smallest square (5) = ________

So c^2 = ________ + ________

You have just illustrated the theorem of Pythagoras.

ISBN: 9780170447577

- The theorem of Pythagoras applies to **right-angled** triangles only.
- The longest side of the triangle is called the **hypotenuse**.
- The hypotenuse is always **opposite the right angle**.
- The theorem of Pythagoras is used for finding **lengths** of sides.

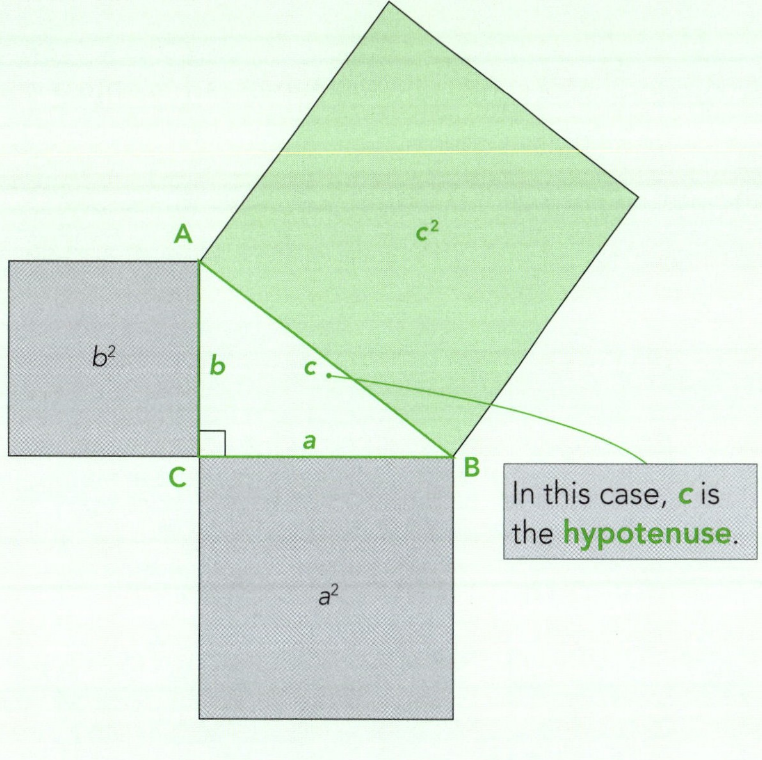

hypotenuse² = short side² + short side²

$$c^2 = a^2 + b^2$$

Finding the length of the hypotenuse

Examples:

1 Calculate the length of c.

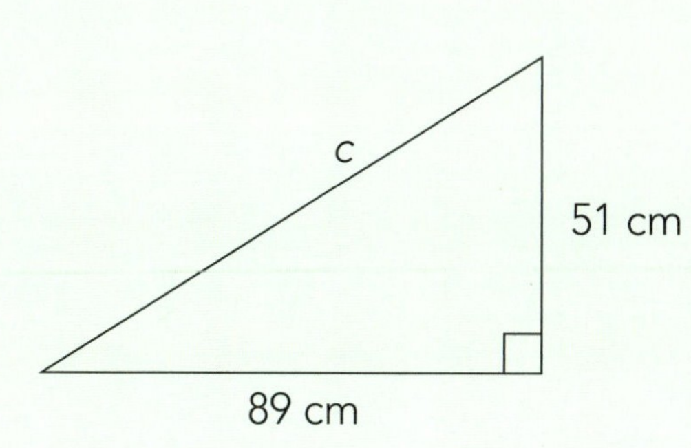

$c^2 = a^2 + b^2$

$= 89^2 + 51^2$

$c = \sqrt{89^2 + 51^2}$

$c = 102.6$ cm (4 sf)

On some calculators you will need to use **brackets**: $\sqrt{(89^2 + 51^2)}$

Don't forget to:
1 include **units** in your answer
2 **round** your answer appropriately.

 ISBN: 9780170447577

2 Sometimes,

- the letters may **not** be a, b and c
- the triangle might be at a **different orientation**.

y is opposite the right angle, so **y is the hypotenuse**. This means that **y^2** must be **on its own** on one side of the = sign.

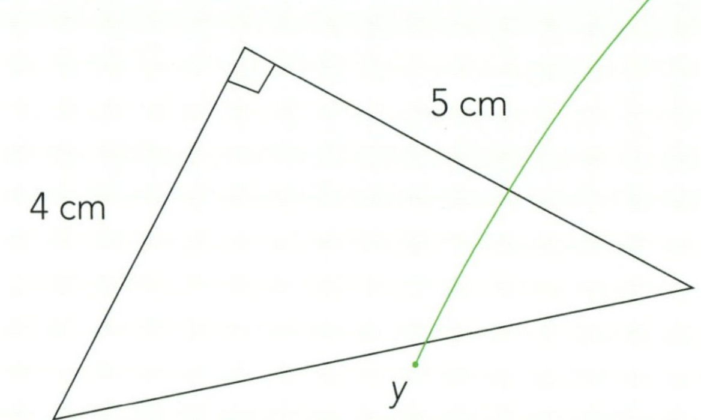

$$y^2 = 4^2 + 5^2$$
$$y = \sqrt{4^2 + 5^2}$$
$$y = 6.403 \text{ cm (4 sf)}$$

Think about your answer. Does it seem about right?

Calculate the length of the hypotenuse in each triangle. Round your answers to **4 sf**.

1

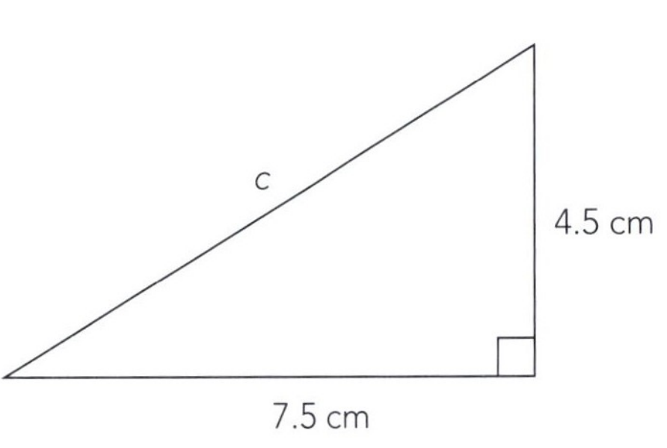

2

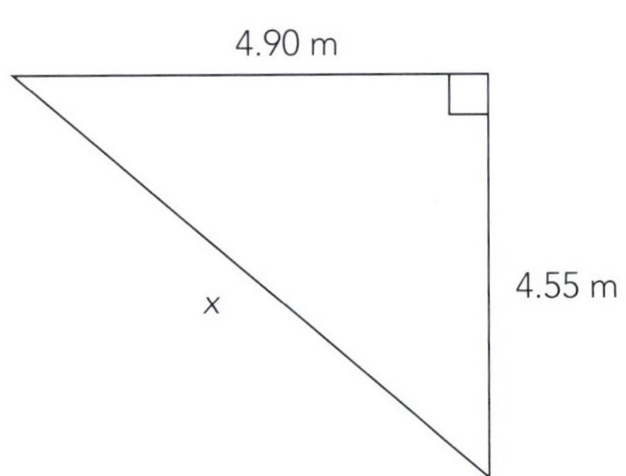

3

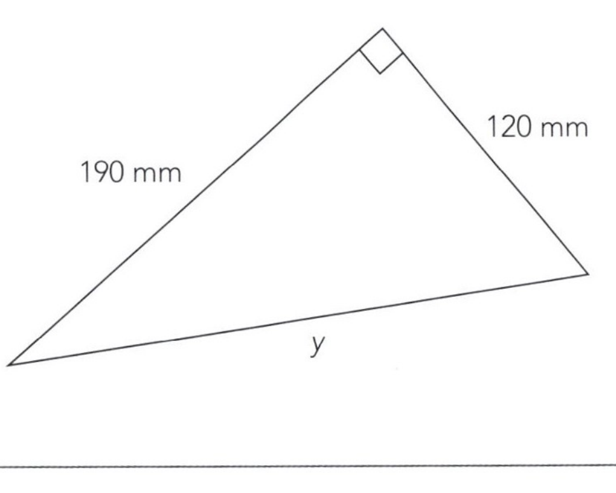

4

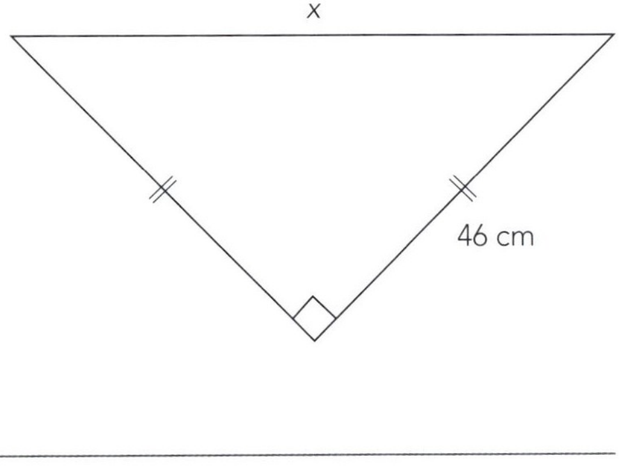

ISBN: 9780170447577

5

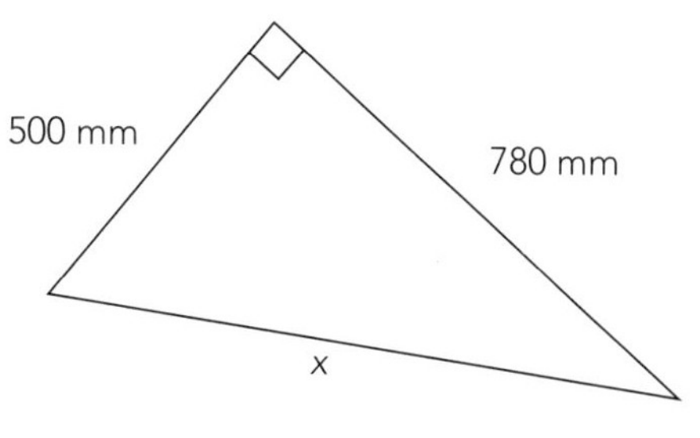

6

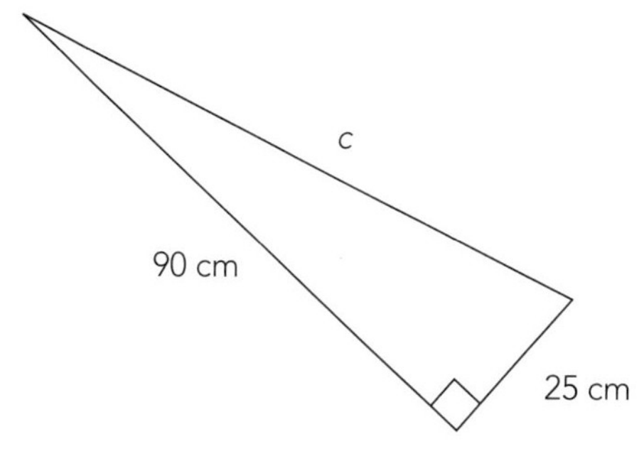

7 ACDE are the corners of a trapezium. The parallel sides are 90 mm and 55 mm, and AE is 50 mm. Calculate the length of the fourth side (CD).

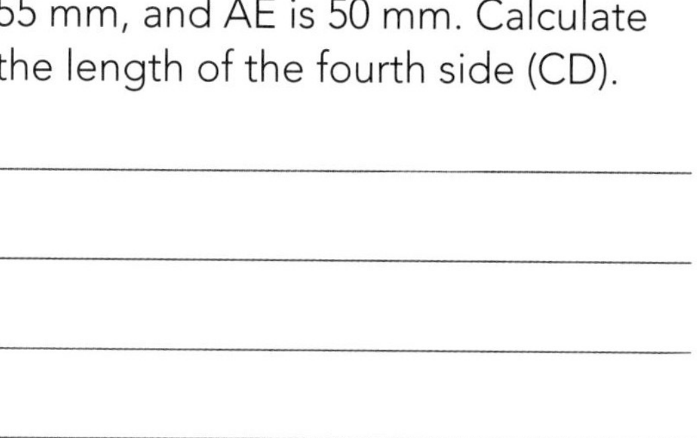

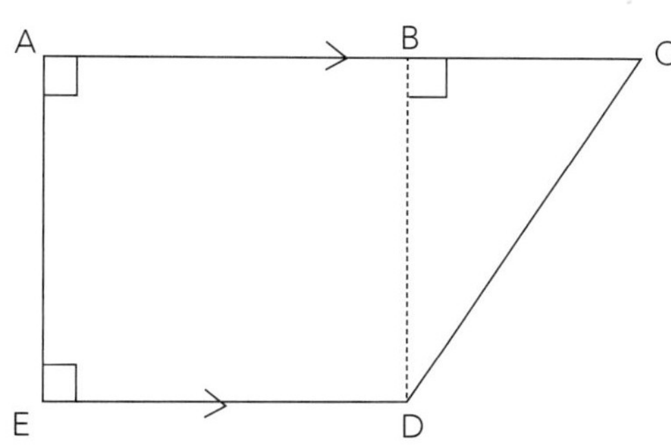

8 Calculate the lengths of the diagonals of a square which has sides that are 10 cm.

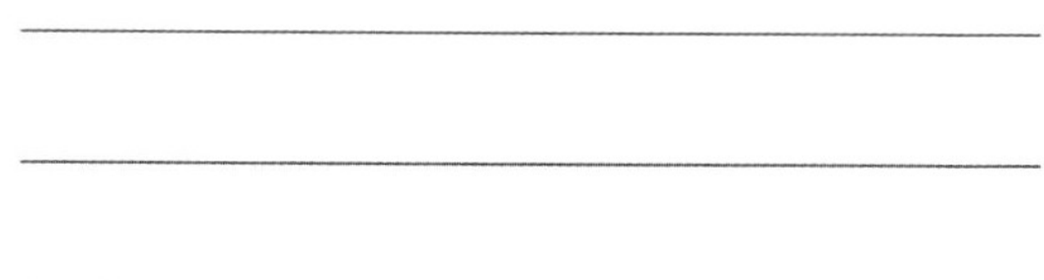

9 ABC are the corners of an isosceles triangle. Its vertical height is 12 cm and its base (AC) is 23 cm. Calculate its perimeter.

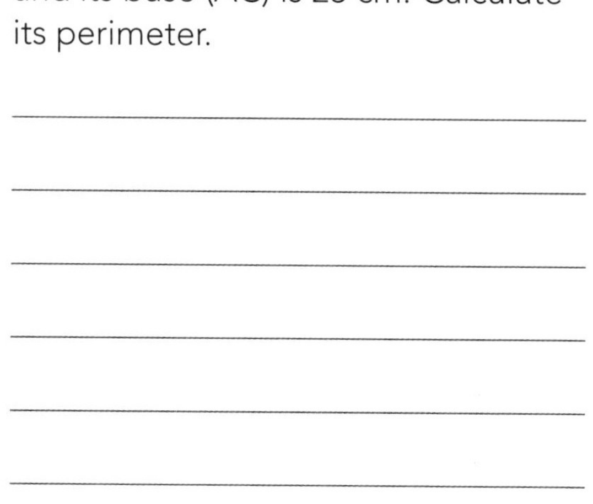

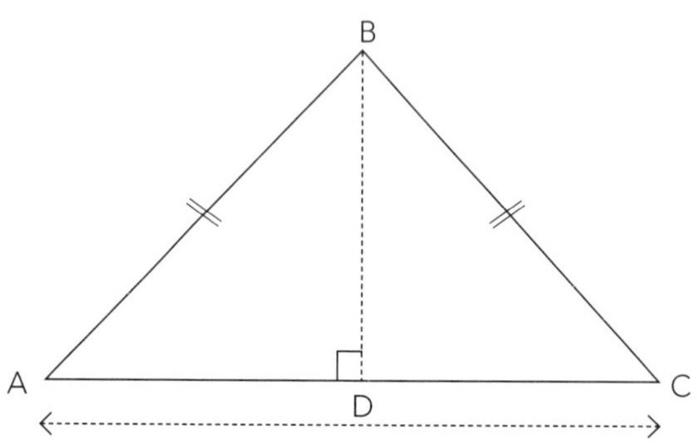

 ISBN: 9780170447577

Finding the lengths of short sides

Example: Calculate the length of b.

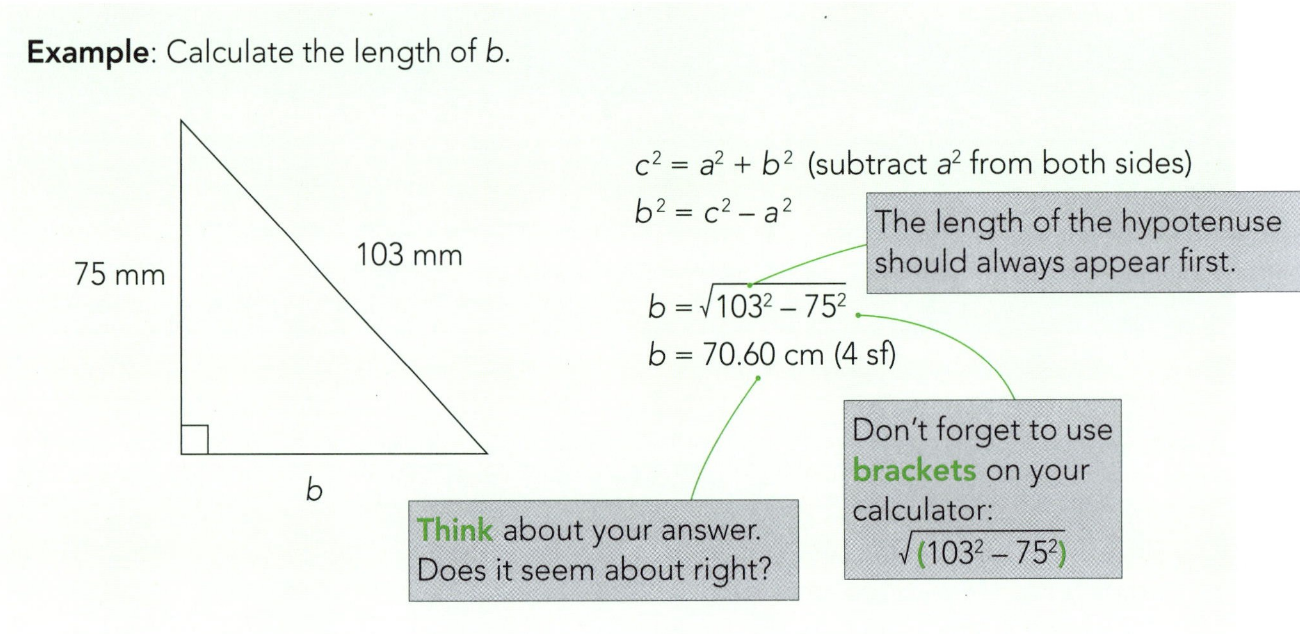

Calculate the unknown length of each triangle. Round your answers to **4 sf**.

1

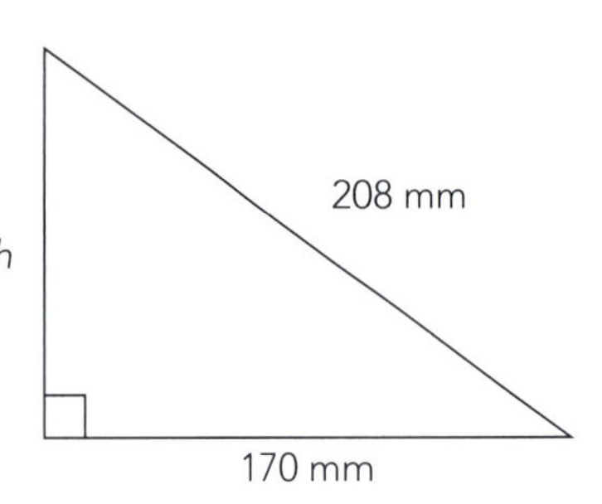

2

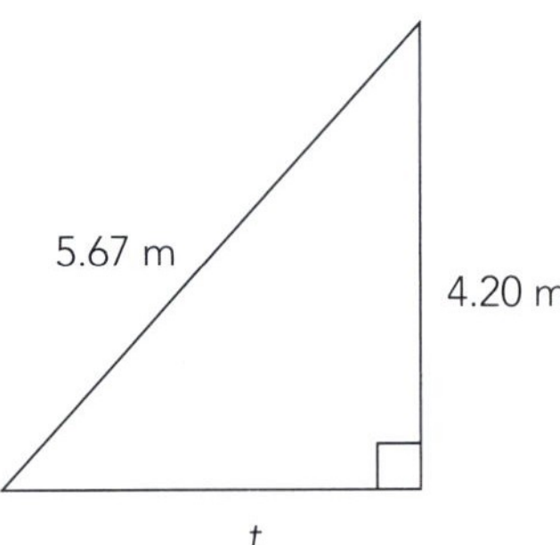

3

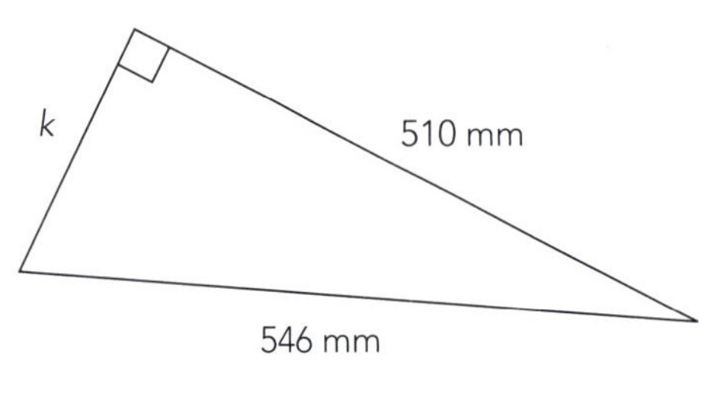

4

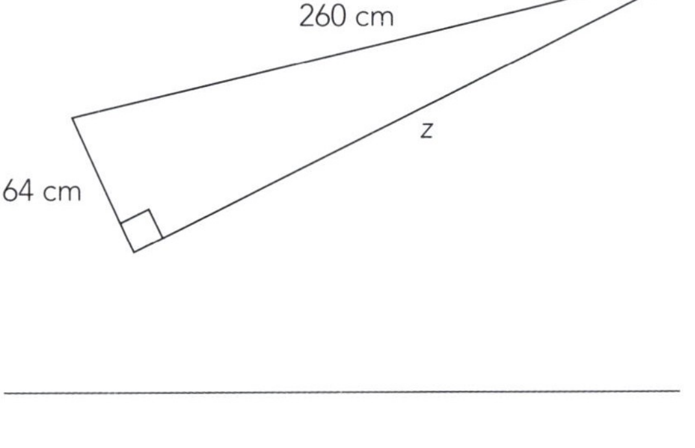

ISBN: 9780170447577

5

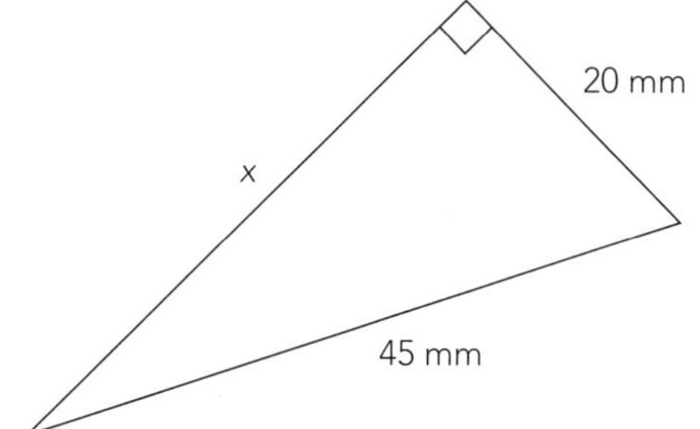

6

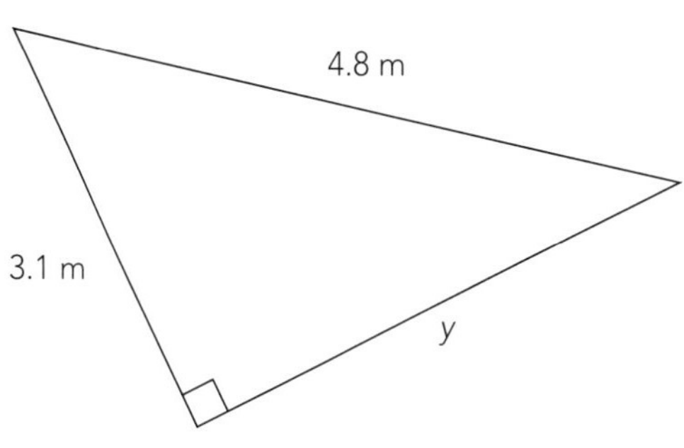

7 ABCD are the corners of a trapezium. Three sides are 1.5 m, 1.2 m and 1.6 m. Calculate the length of the fourth side (BC).

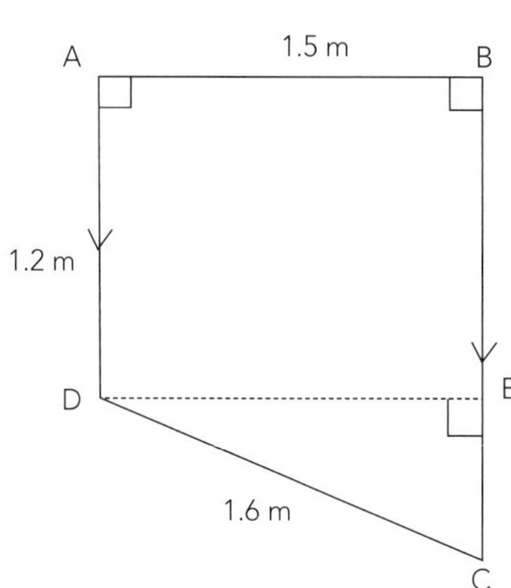

8 ABCD are the corners of a rectangle. Its short side is 45 cm and its diagonal is 100 cm. Calculate its perimeter.

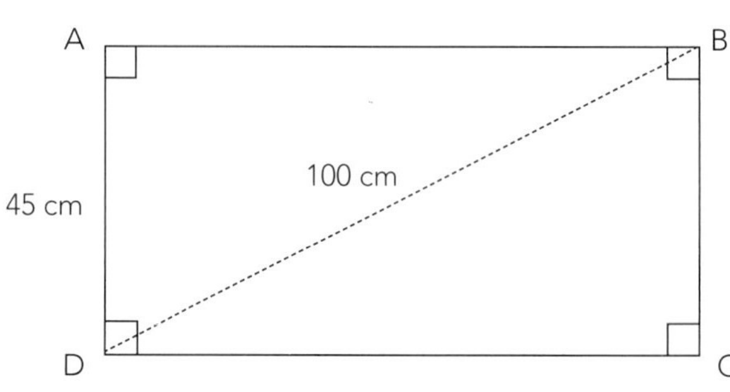

 ISBN: 9780170447577

Mixing it up

Calculate the unknown length of each triangle. Round your answers to **4 sf**.

1

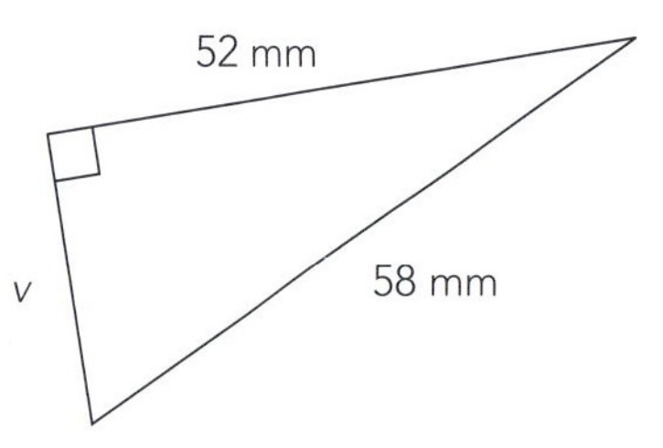

2

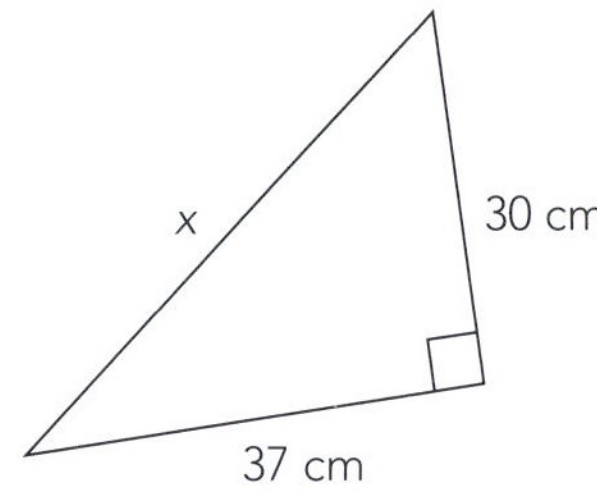

3

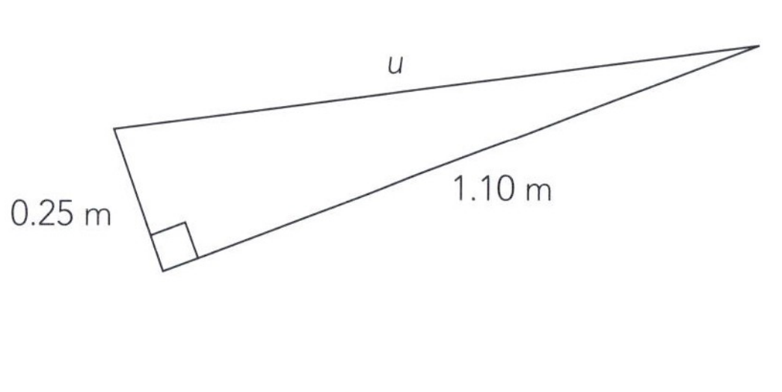

4

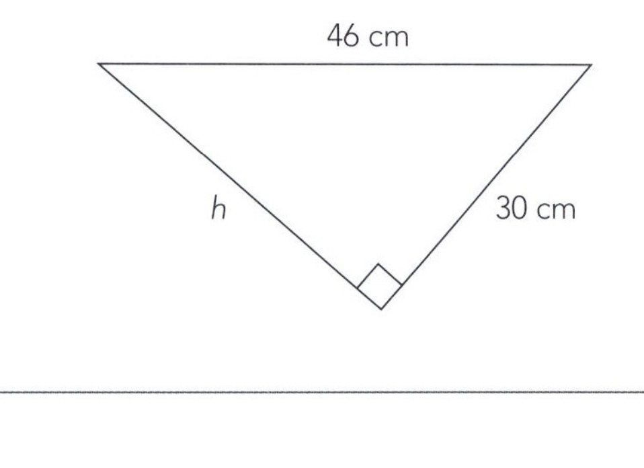

Mixing the theorem of Pythagoras with geometry

Answer the following questions. In each case, show your reasoning.

1 ABC are the corners of an equilateral triangle with sides of 14 cm. Calculate its vertical height, DC.

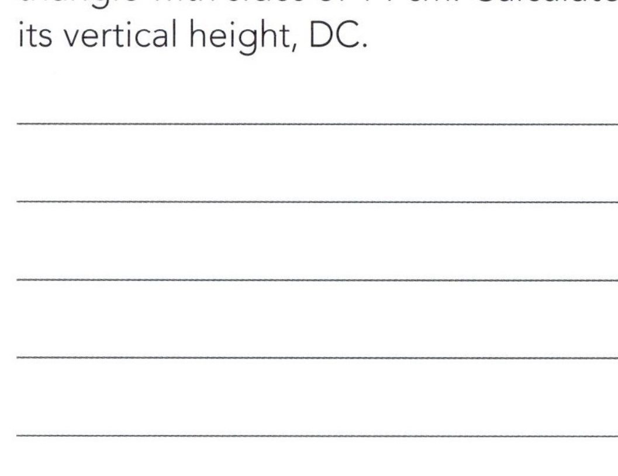

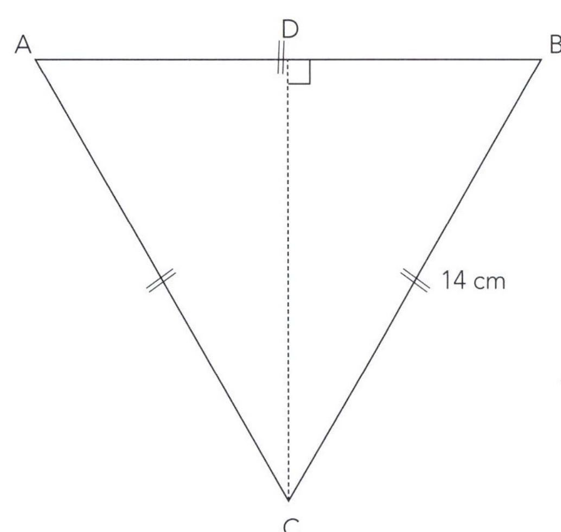

2 ABCD are the corners of a rhombus with sides of 93 mm. If BD is 87 mm, calculate the length of the diagonal AC.

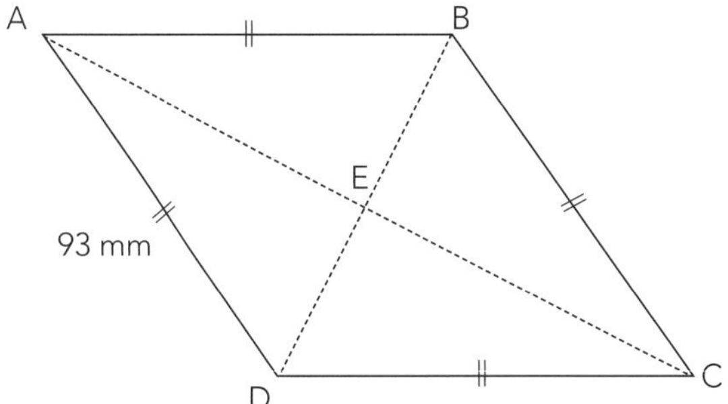

3 ABCD are the corners of a kite. Its sides are 107 mm and 150 mm long. Its width (AC) is 163 mm. Calculate its height (BD).

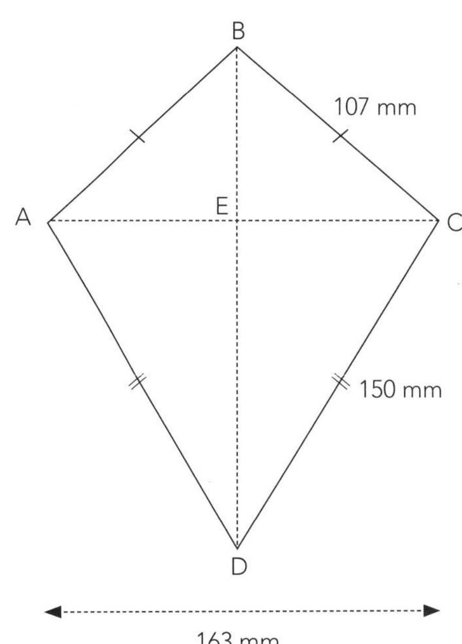

4 ABCD are the corners of an arrowhead. AB and BC are perpendicular. The long sides of the arrowhead are 90 mm long, and line DE is 20 mm. Calculate the length of short sides (AD and DC).

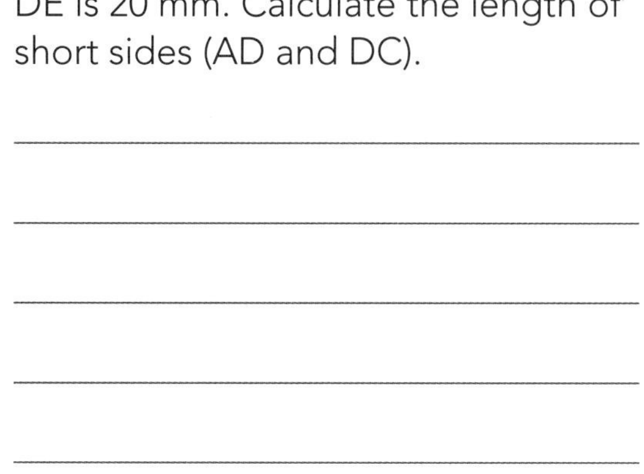

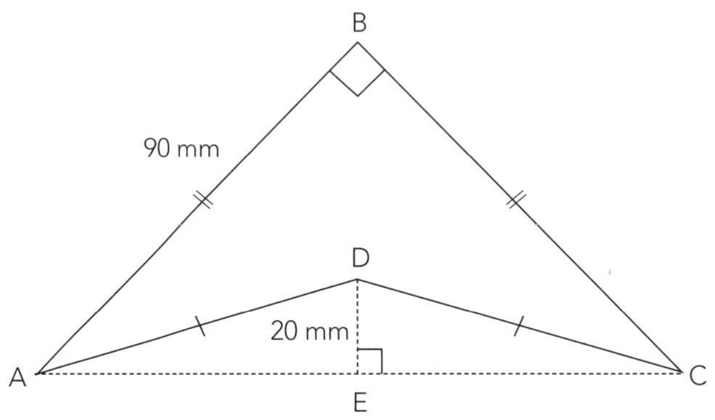

 ISBN: 9780170447577

5 ABCD are the corners of an isosceles trapezium. Calculate the vertical height (AE) of the trapezium.

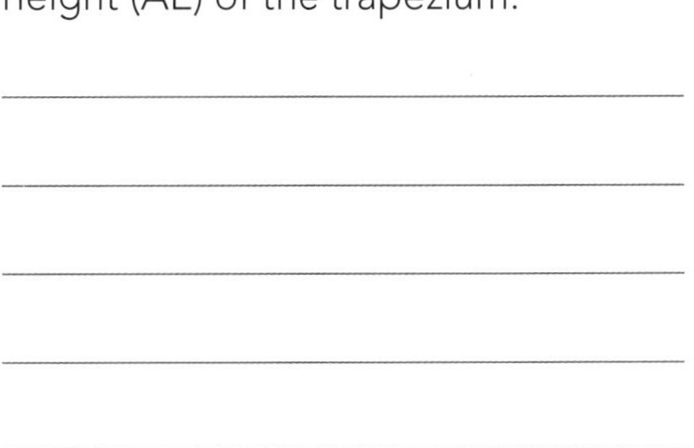

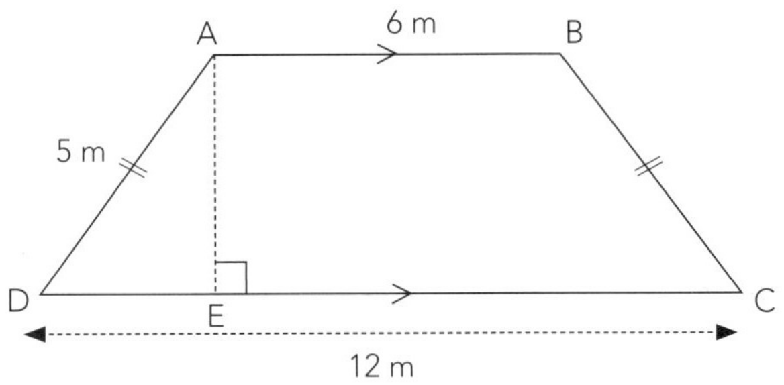

6 The diagonal of a square is 100 mm long. Calculate the length of its sides.

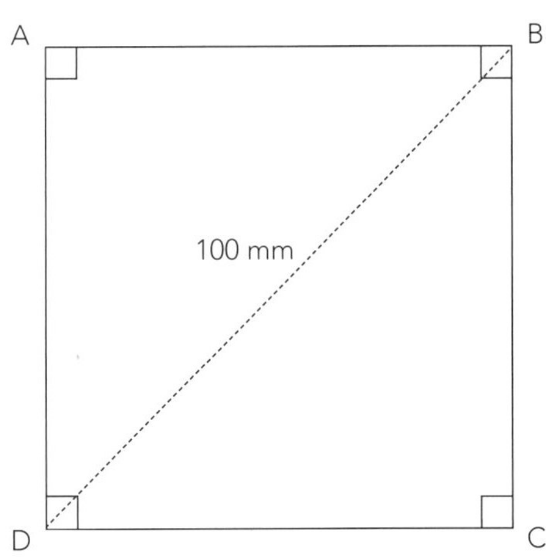

7 ABCD are the corners of a rectangle. Its diagonal is 100 mm long. Its width is twice its height. Calculate its height and width.

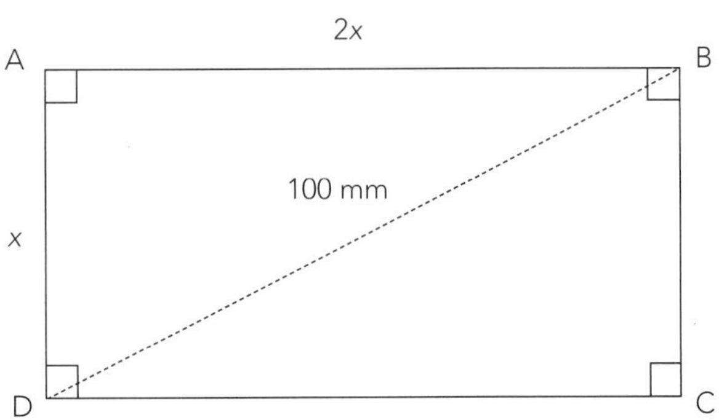

ISBN: 9780170447577

8 ABCD is an arrowhead. Its width is 140 mm and its long sides are 92 mm. The point D bisects its vertical height (BE). Calculate the length of its short sides (AD and DC).

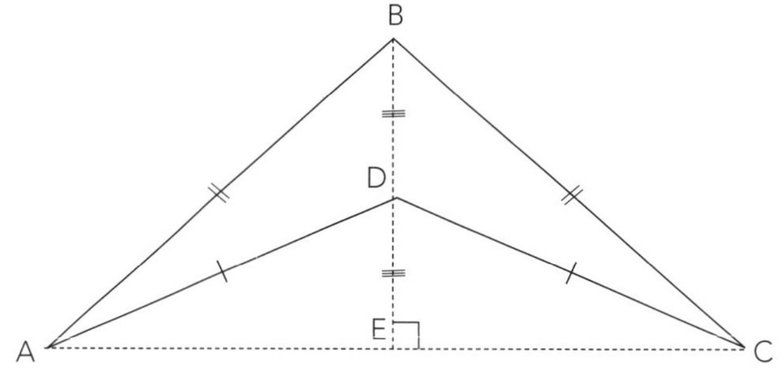

9 ABCD are the corners of a kite. Its short sides (AB and BC) are 57 mm. Angle ABC is a right angle. Calculate the lengths of its long sides (AD and CD).

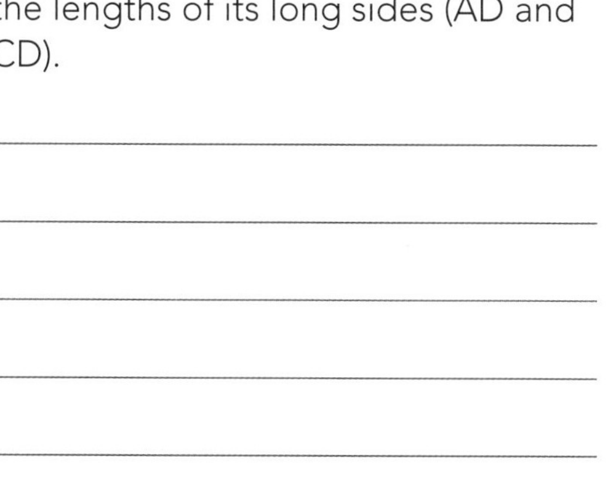

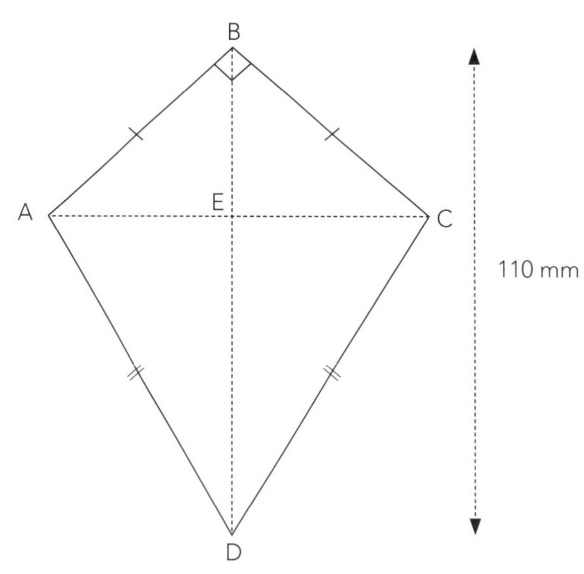

10 A rhombus is made up of two equilateral triangles ABC and ADC whose sides are *x* cm long. The long diagonal of the rhombus (BD) is 20 cm. Calculate the value of *x*.

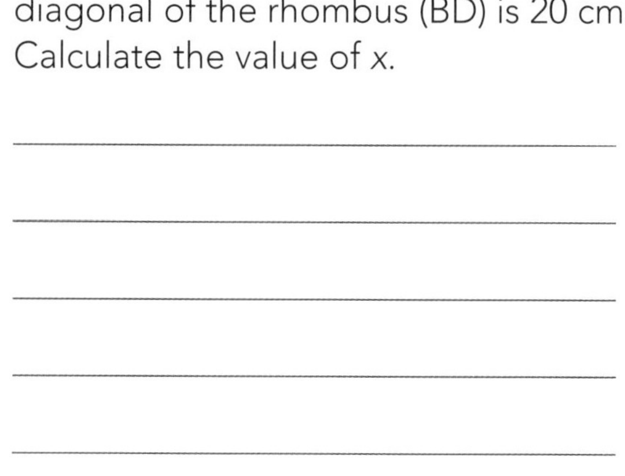

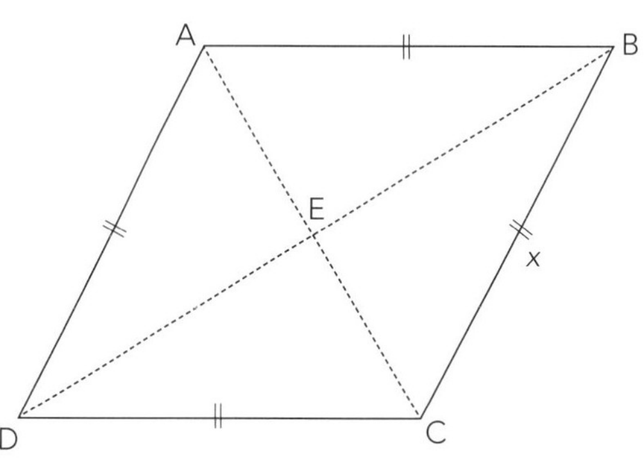

 ISBN: 9780170447577

11 **a** Show that the length of line $a = \sqrt{2}$.

b Find the lengths of lines b, c and d. Write your answers as surds (with a $\sqrt{\ }$ sign).

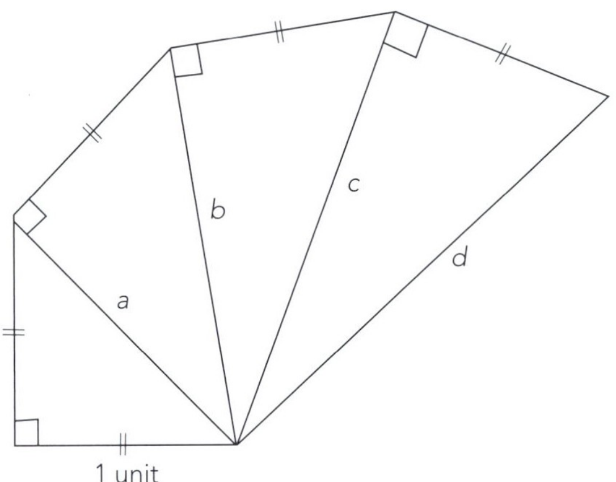

A little bit of history

- Triangle ADE in question 5 (page 57) has sides that are exactly 3, 4 and 5 units long.
- (3, 4, 5) is known as a **Pythagorean triple** — groups of three integers for which $a^2 + b^2 = c^2$.
- There are many others, e.g. (5, 12, 13), (8, 15, 17), (7, 24, 25).
- The Egyptians used the 3, 4, 5 triangle to construct accurate right angles. At exactly equal intervals, they tied 13 knots in a length of rope:
- They then stretched the rope so it was tight and used the knots to form a (3, 4, 5) triangle, and thus a perfect right angle.

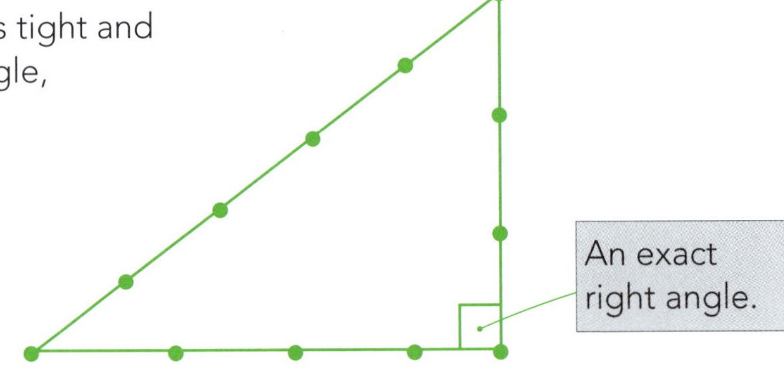

- Consequently, Egyptian surveyors were known as '**rope stretchers**'.

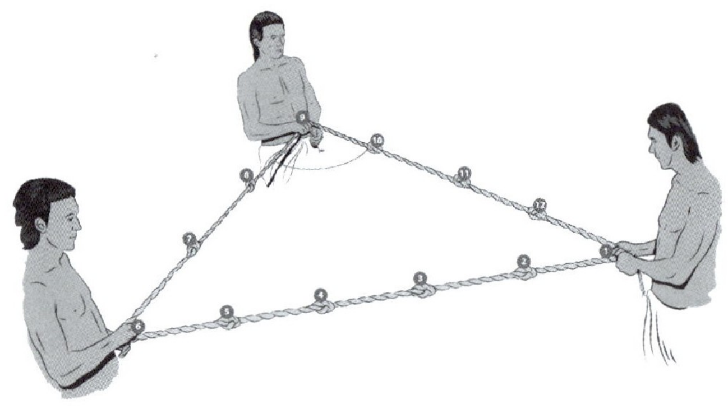

Trigonometry

What is trigonometry?

Consider the lengths of the shadows cast by a tree, a goal post and a person at a particular time of day.

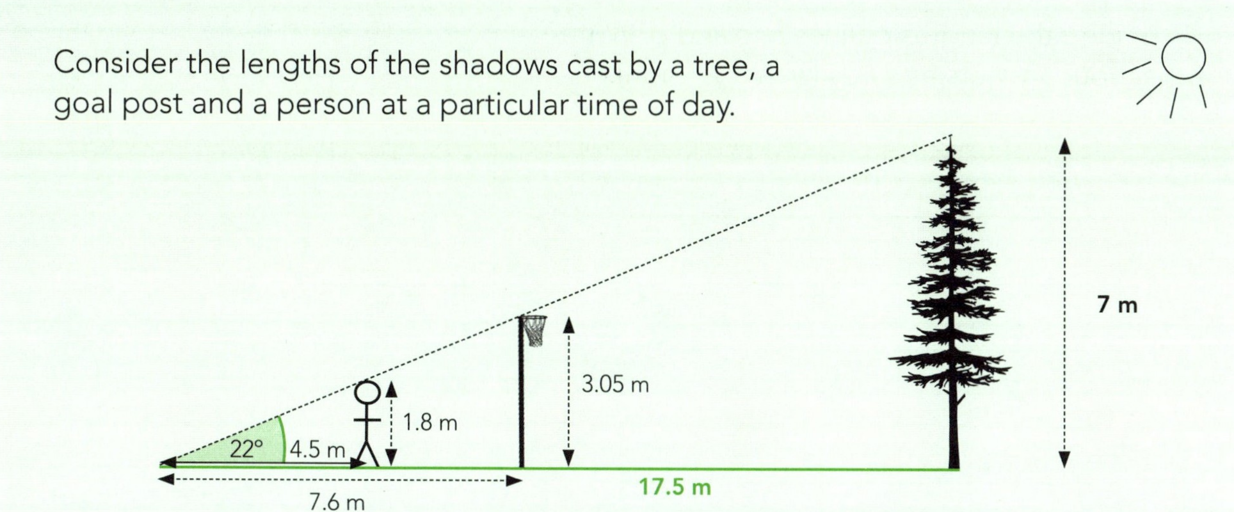

For each, calculate the ratio of their height to the length of the shadow.

For the tree: Ratio $= \dfrac{\text{height of tree}}{\text{length of its shadow}}$

$= \dfrac{7}{17.5}$

$= 0.40$ (2 dp)

For the goal post: Ratio $= \dfrac{\text{height of goal post}}{\text{length of its shadow}}$

$= \dfrac{\quad}{\quad}$

$=$ ________ (2 dp)

For the person: Ratio $= \dfrac{\text{height of person}}{\text{length of their shadow}}$

$= \dfrac{\quad}{\quad}$

$=$ ________ (2 dp)

- Notice that the ratios are ____________________.
- Because the angle between the sun's rays and the ground (22°) is the same for all three shadows, the triangles in the diagram are **similar**.
- For any given angle, these ratios in right-angled triangles are fixed.
- **Trigonometry is the use of these ratios to calculate the lengths of unknown sides and angles.**
- These ratios are stored in your calculator.
- In this case, tan 22° = 0.404.

ISBN: 9780170447577

More about trigonometry

- Trigonometry is used for calculating lengths and angles in **right-angled triangles**.
- Unlike calculations using the theorem of Pythagoras, an **angle must be involved**.

Before you begin a calculation involving trigonometry, you must **label the sides of the triangle**.

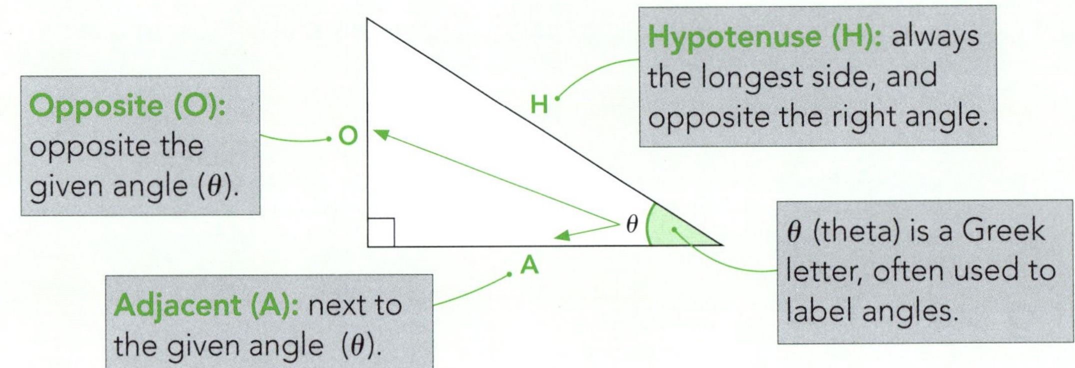

Label the sides of the following triangles with H, O and A.

1 θ

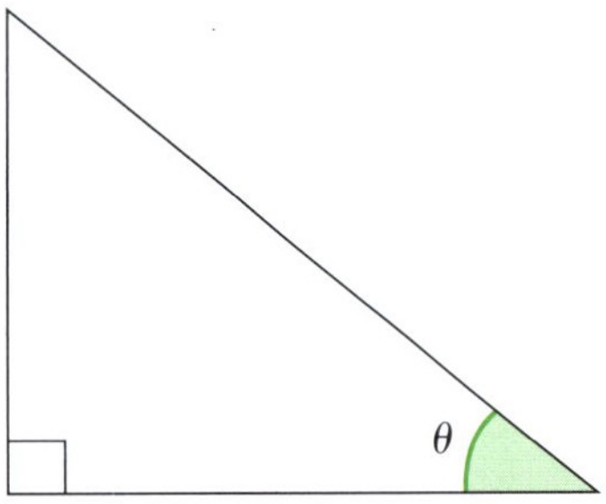

2 θ

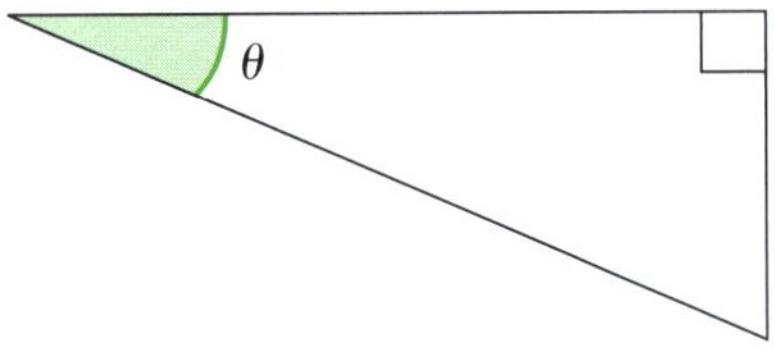

3 θ

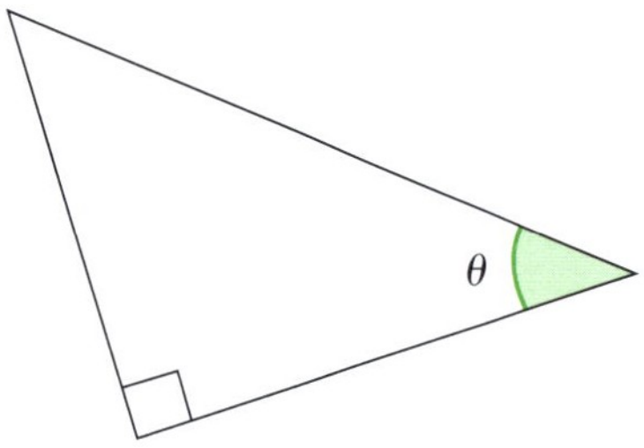

4 θ

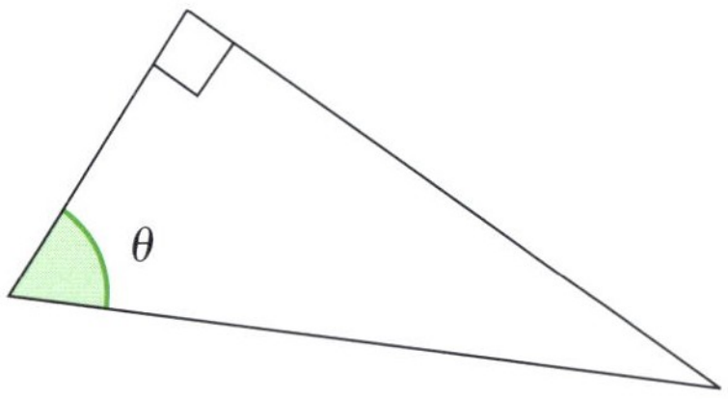

5 θ

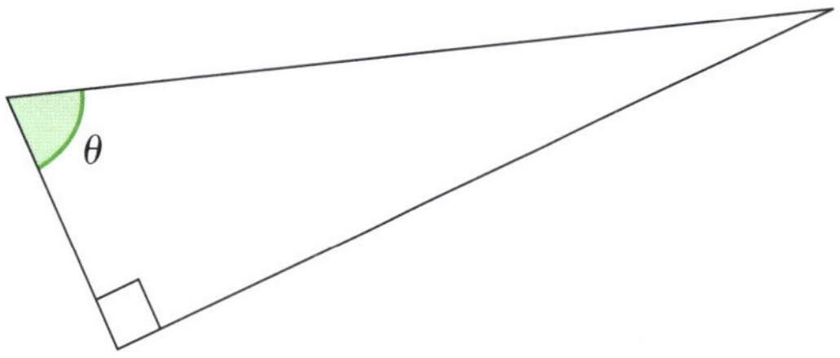

6 θ

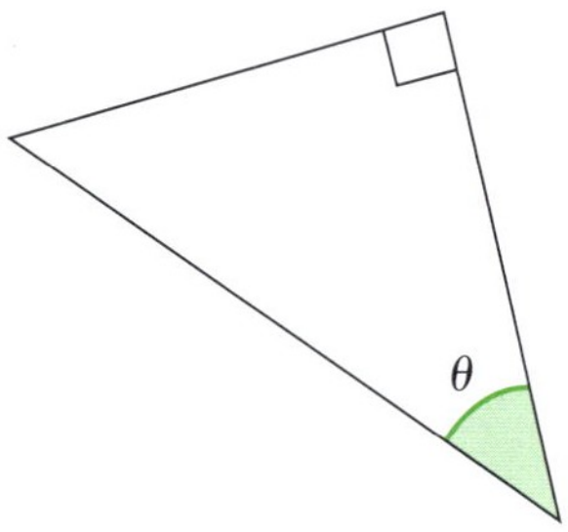

ISBN: 9780170447577

SOHCAHTOA

- You need to know about three trigonometrical functions: **sin** θ (sine)
  cos θ (cosine)
  tan θ (tangent).
- These are the rules in trigonometry:

$$\sin\theta = \frac{O}{H} \qquad \cos\theta = \frac{A}{H} \qquad \tan\theta = \frac{O}{A}$$

- Organising SOHCAHTOA into triangles can help you remember how to use it:

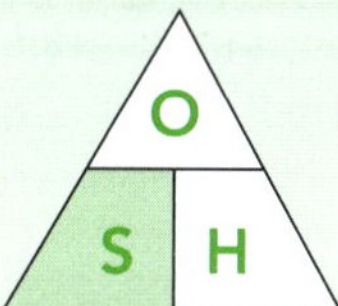

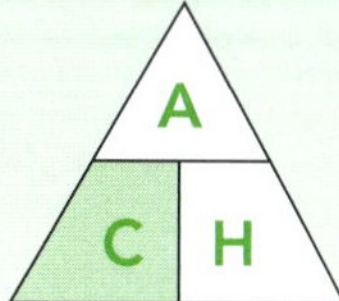

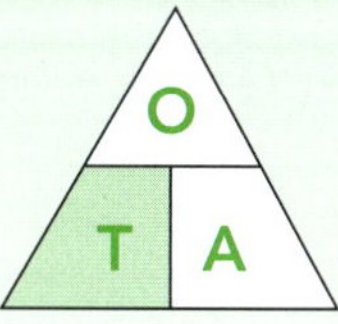

Finding sides using sine

Examples:

1 Calculate the length marked *y*.

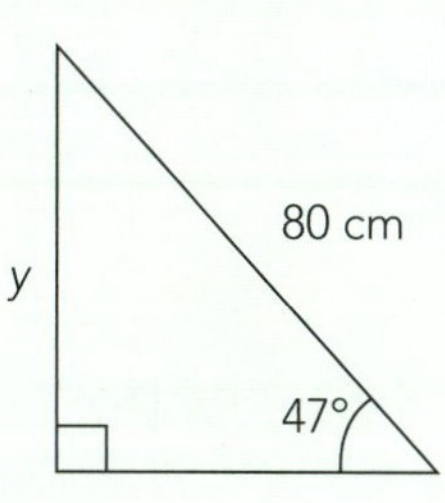

Step 1: Label the sides **that are involved** with A, O and H.

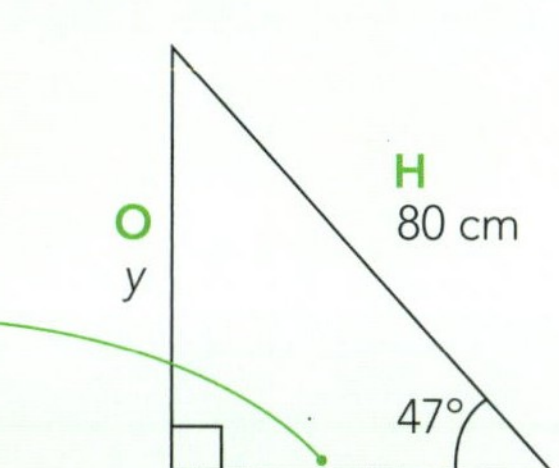

We don't know the length of this side. Nor do we need to know it.

Step 2: The labelled sides are **O** and **H**, so write out the triangle involving these:

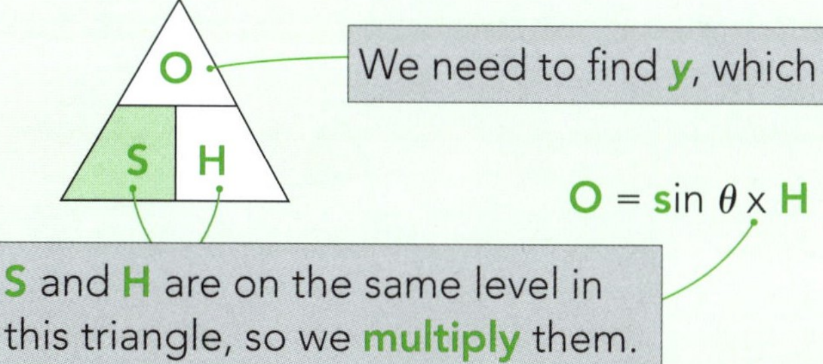

We need to find **y**, which is the **O**pposite side.

$O = \sin\theta \times H$

S and **H** are on the same level in this triangle, so we **multiply** them.

Step 3: Substitute the numbers and calculate the answer.

$O = \sin 47° \times 80$

$O = y = 58.51$ cm (4 sf)

Enter 'sin 47° **=** x 80', otherwise you will get 'sin(47° x 80)'.

You will find sin, cos and tan functions on your calculator. Before you use these, **check that your calculator is set to degrees (DRG or D)**.

Step 4: **Think** about your answer — does it seem about right? The hypotenuse is 80 cm, so 58.51 cm is reasonable for one of the shorter sides. ✓

ISBN: 9780170447577

2 Calculate the length marked y.

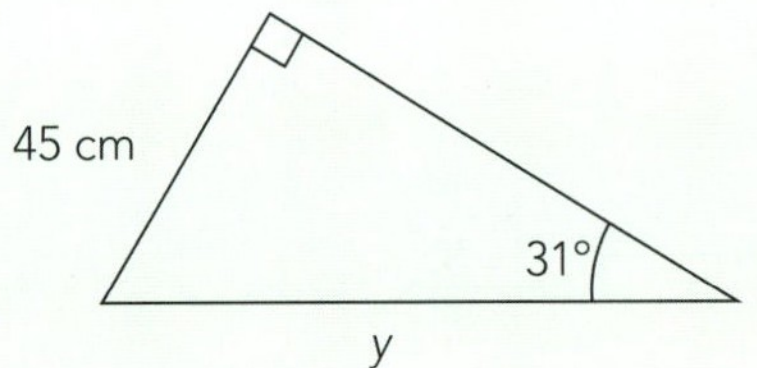

Step 1: Label the sides **that are involved** with A, O and H.

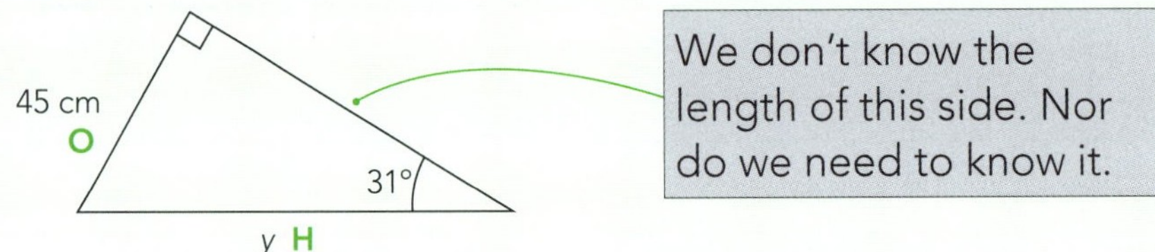

Step 2: The labelled sides are **O** and **H**, so write out the triangle involving these:

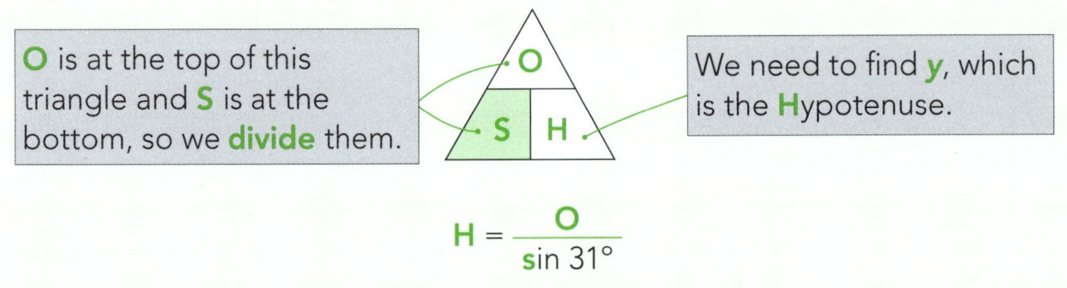

$$H = \frac{O}{\sin 31°}$$

Step 3: Substitute the numbers and calculate the answer.

$$H = \frac{45}{\sin 31°}$$

$$H = y = 87.37 \text{ cm (4 sf)}$$

Step 4: **Think** about your answer — does it seem about right?

y is the hypotenuse, so we would expect it to be longer than 45 cm. ✓

Handy hint

When checking your answers, remember that in any triangle:

- the **longest side** is always opposite the **biggest angle**
- the **shortest side** is always opposite the **smallest angle**.

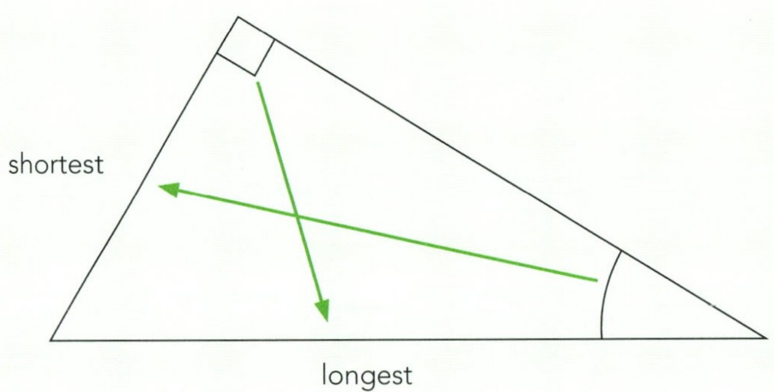

ISBN: 9780170447577

Use trigonometry to calculate the unknown length of each triangle. Round your answers to 4 sf.

1

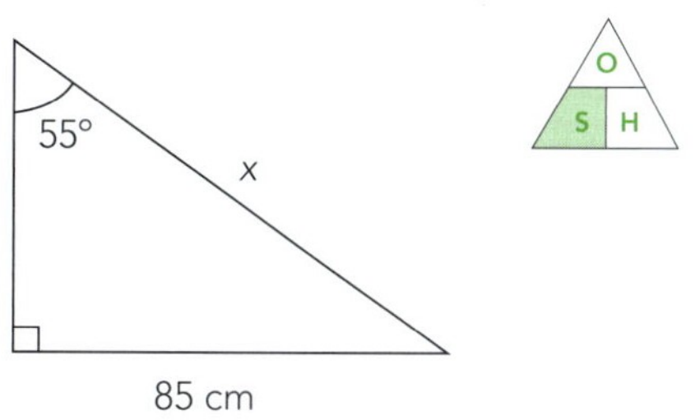

2

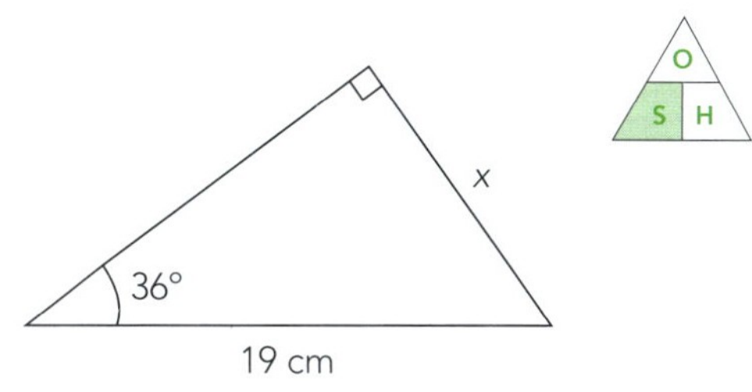

3

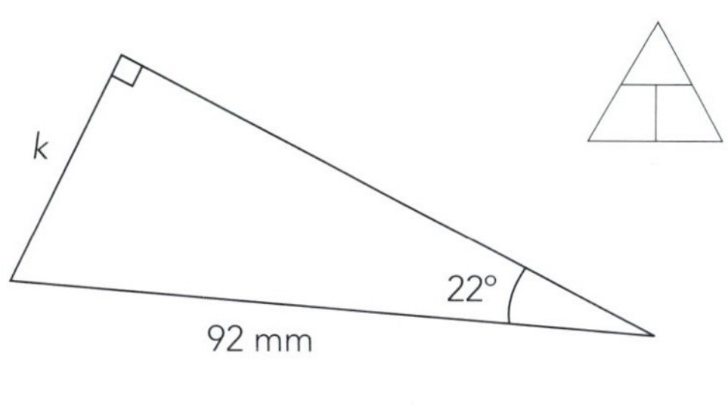

4

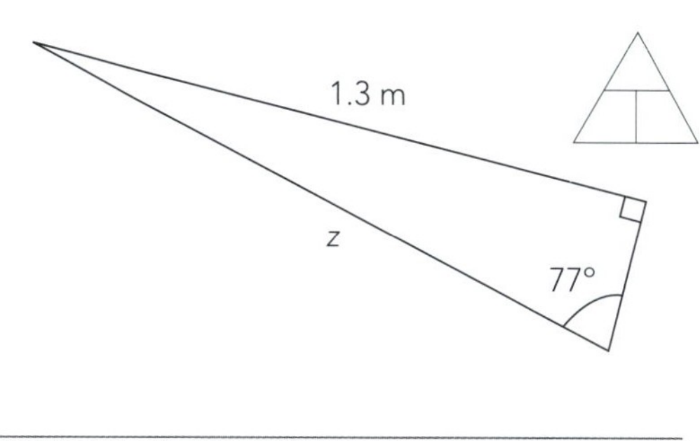

5

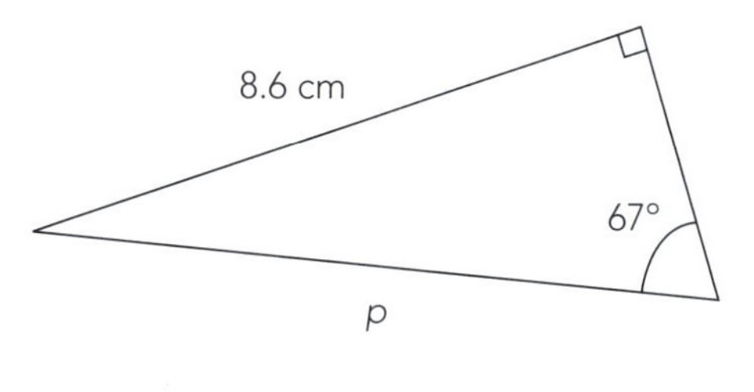

6

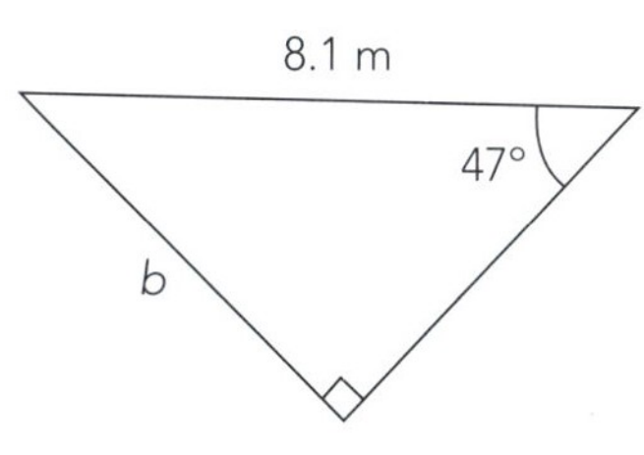

7

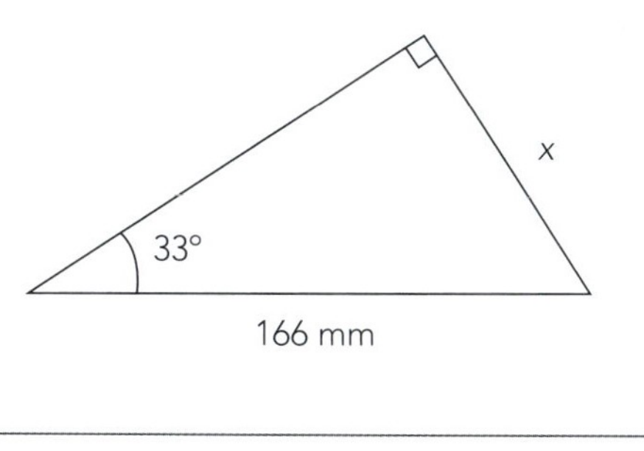

8

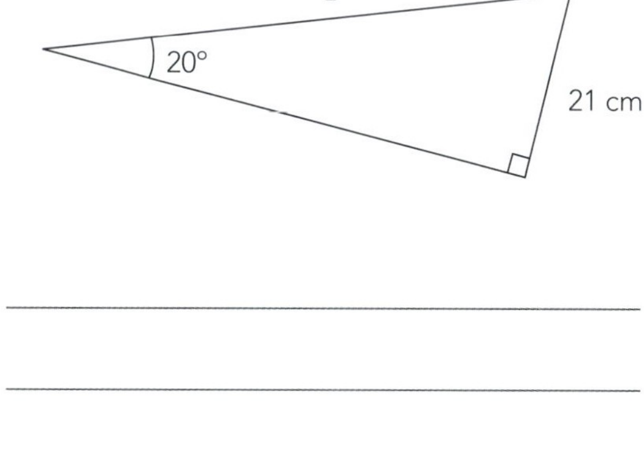

 ISBN: 9780170447577

Finding sides using cosine and tangent

- You can use the same steps along with these to find the lengths of right-angled triangle sides using cosines and tangents.

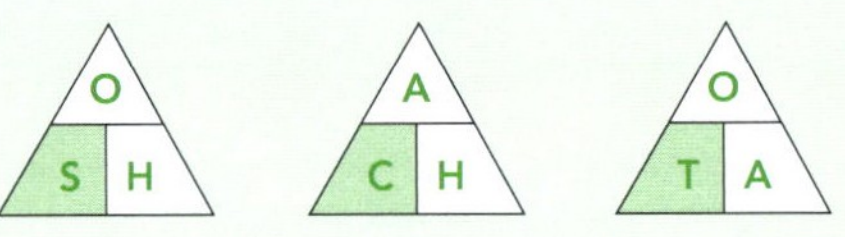

Examples:

1 Calculate the length marked *y*.

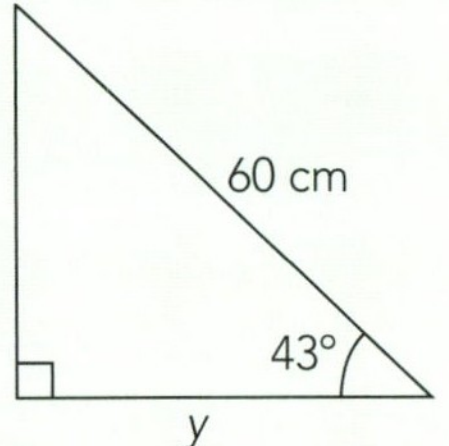

Step 1: Label the sides **that are involved** with A, O and H.

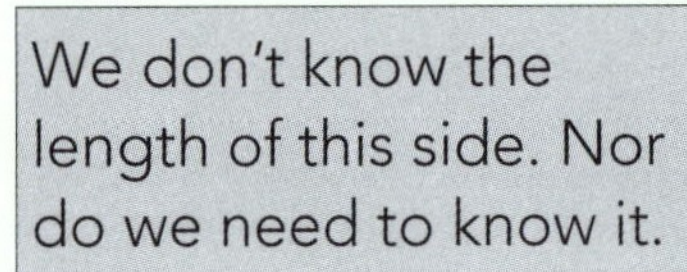

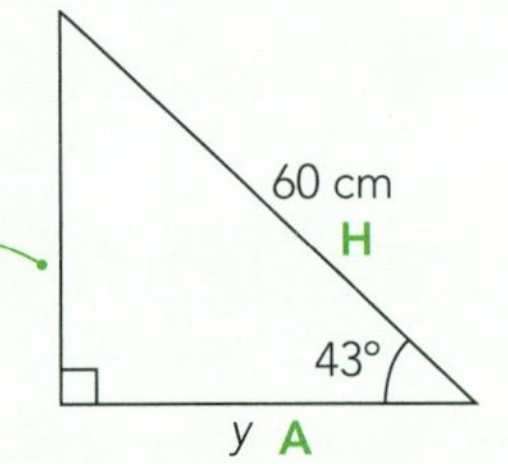

Step 2: The labelled sides are **A** and **H**, so write out the triangle involving these:

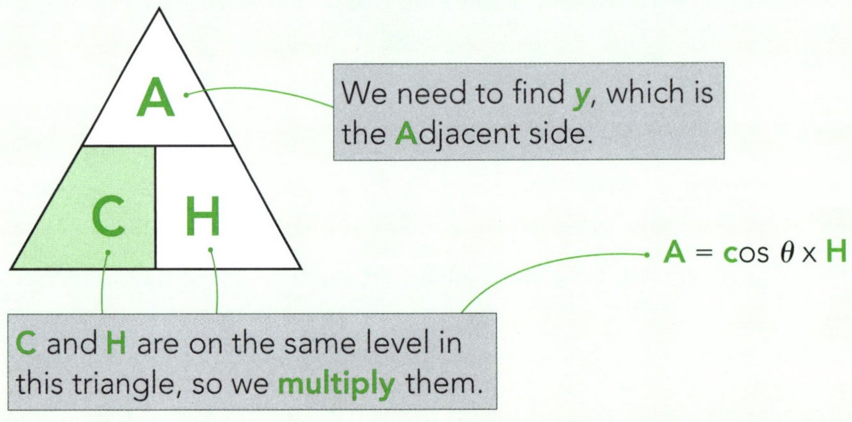

$A = \cos\theta \times H$

Step 3: Substitute the numbers and calculate the answer.

A = cos 43° x 60

A = *y* = 43.88 cm (4 sf)

Step 4: **Think** about your answer — does it seem about right?

The hypotenuse is 60 cm, so 43.88 cm is reasonable for one of the shorter sides. ✓

2 Calculate the length marked y.

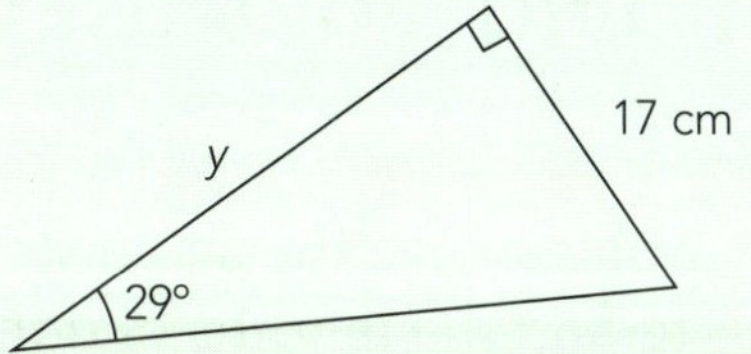

Step 1: Label the sides **that are involved** with A, O and H.

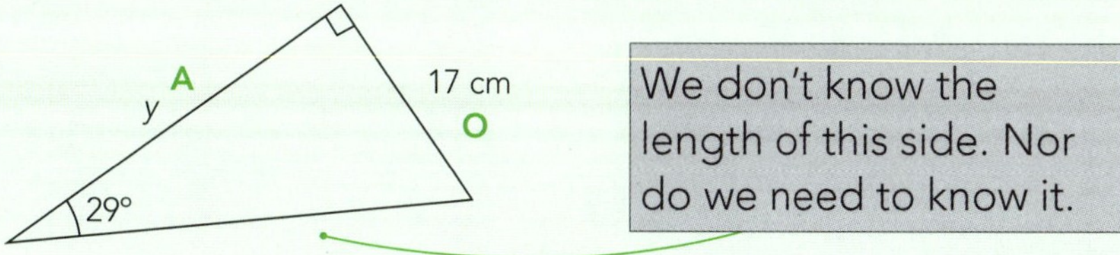

Step 2: The labelled sides are **O** and **A**, so write out the triangle involving these:

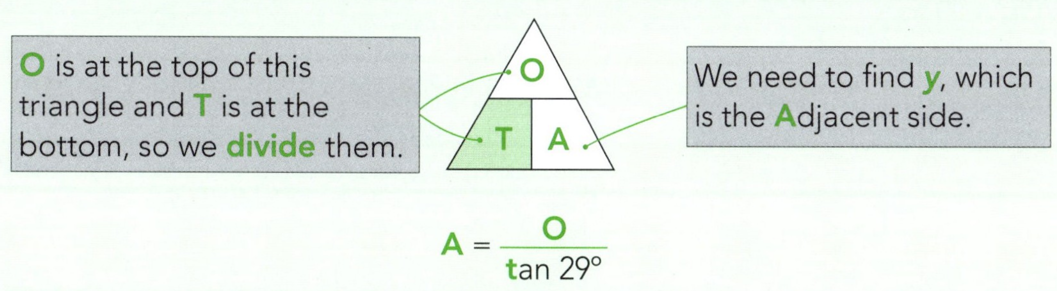

$$A = \frac{O}{\tan 29°}$$

Step 3: Substitute the numbers and calculate the answer.

$$A = \frac{17}{\tan 29°}$$

$A = y = 30.67$ cm (4 sf)

Step 4: **Think** about your answer — does it seem about right?

O = 17 cm is opposite the smallest angle, so we would expect x to be longer than 17 cm. ✓

Use trigonometry to calculate the unknown length of each triangle. Round your answers to **4 sf**.

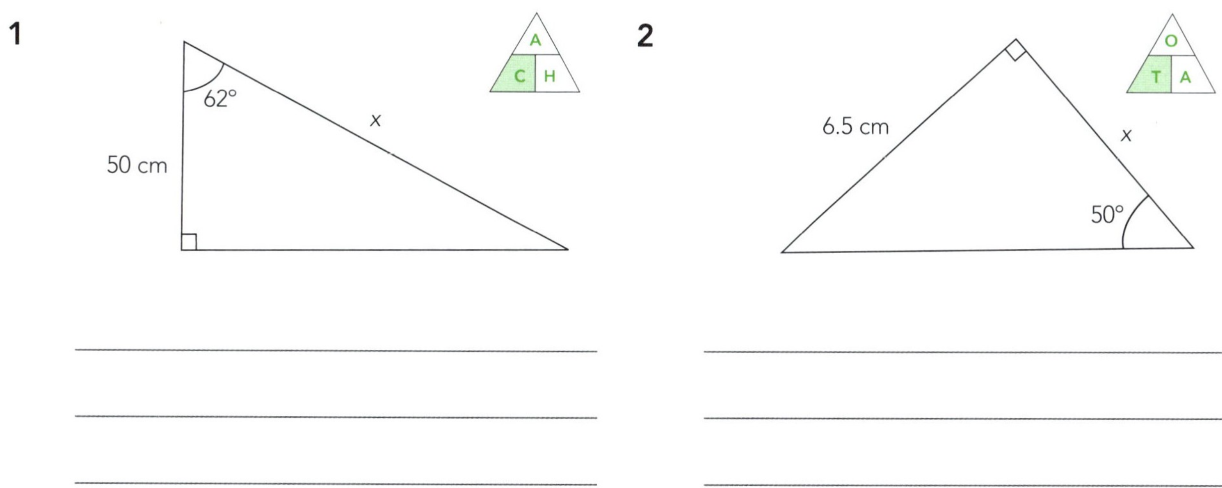

 ISBN: 9780170447577

3

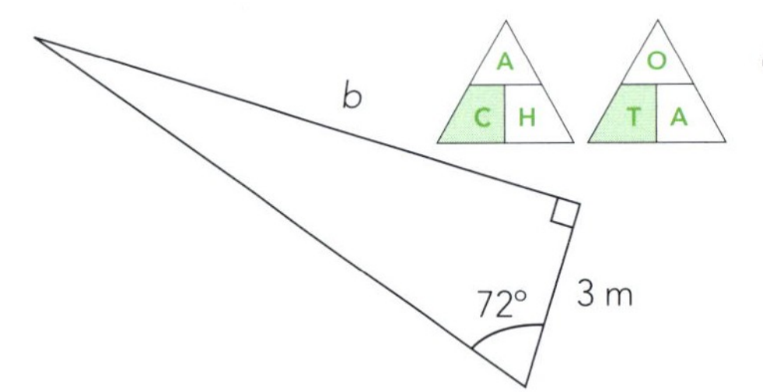

4

A
C H
O
T A

56°
115 mm
p

5

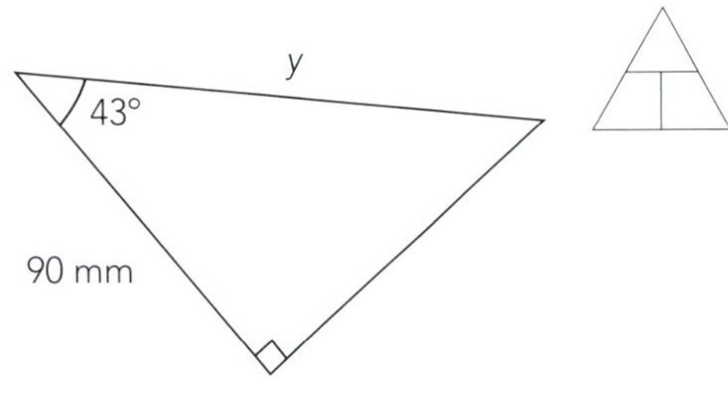

6

8 m
h
47°

7

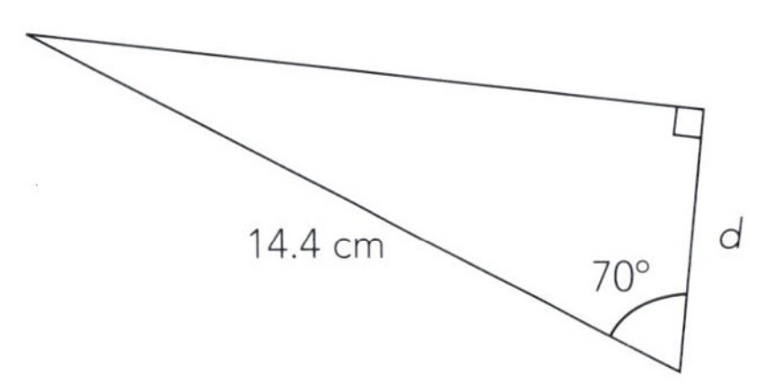

8

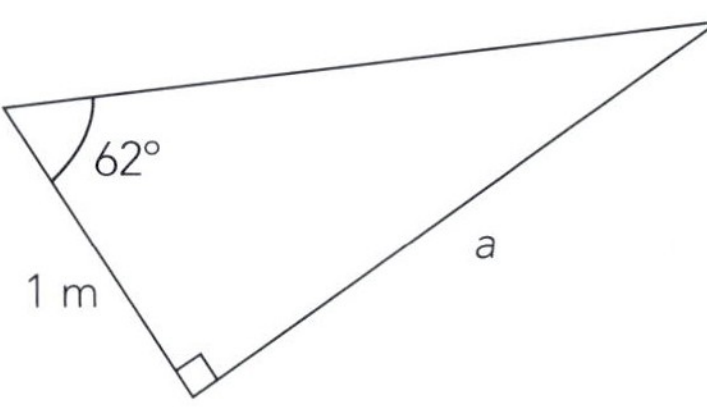

9

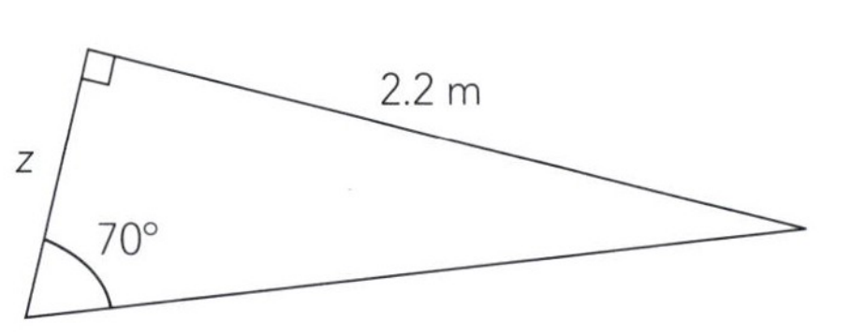

10

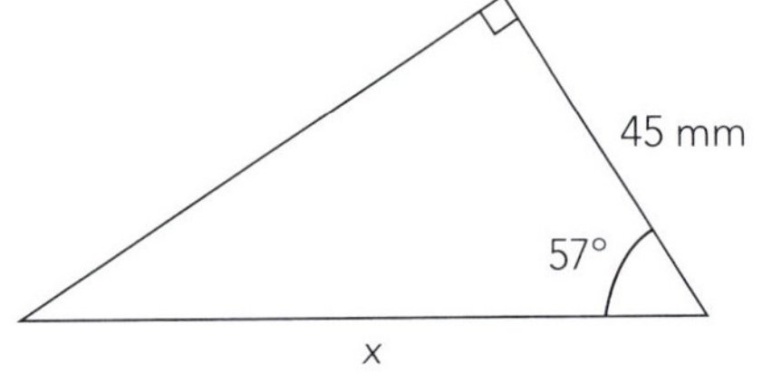

ISBN: 9780170447577

Mixing it up

Use trigonometry to calculate the unknown length of each triangle. Round your answers to 4 sf.

1

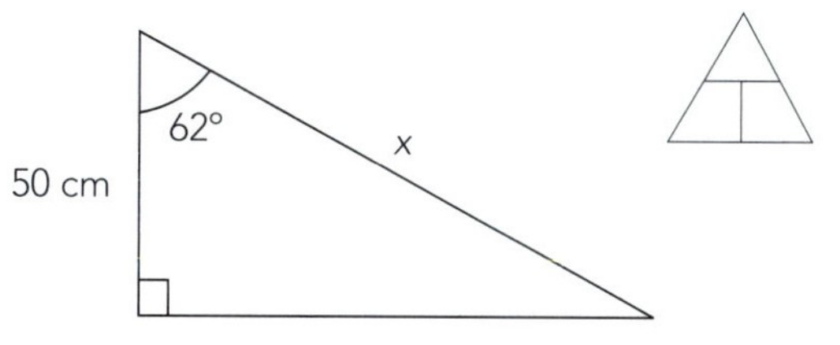

2

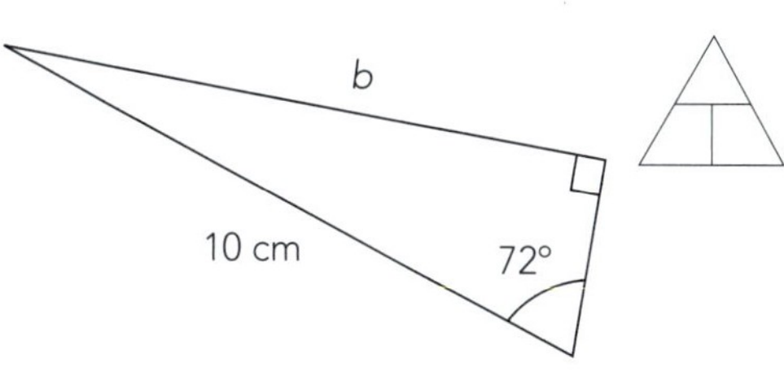

3

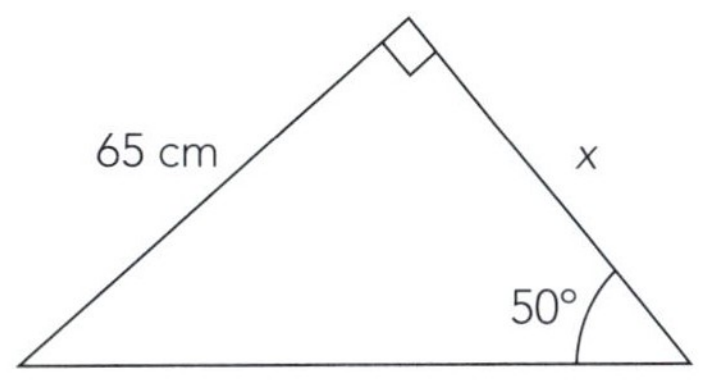

4

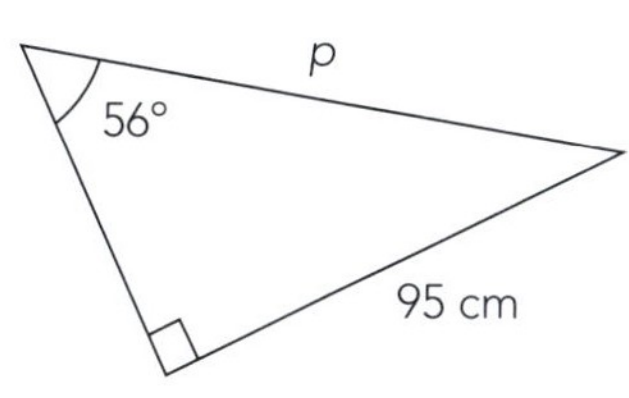

5

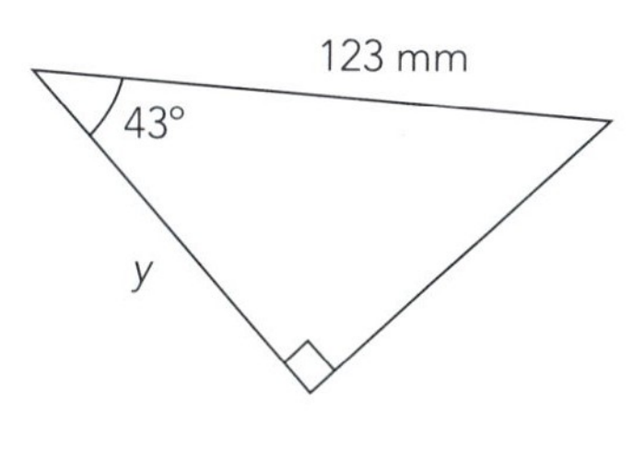

6

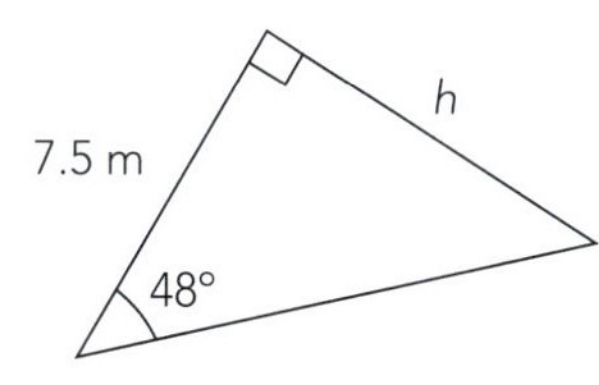

7

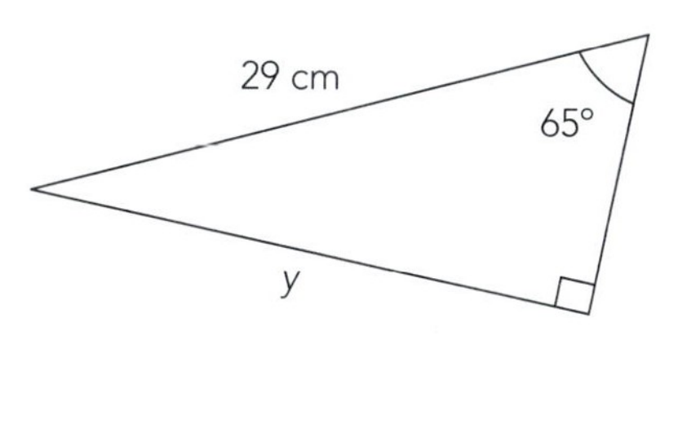

8

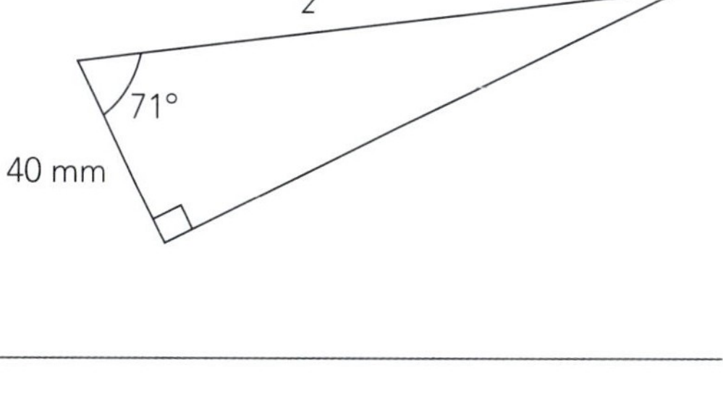

 ISBN: 9780170447577

Finding angles using sine

- You can also use similar steps along with these to find the **angles** in right-angle triangles.

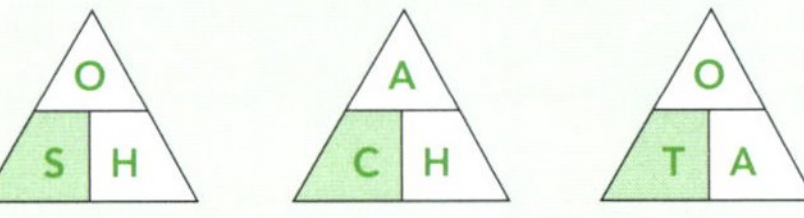

Examples:

1 Calculate the size of angle b.

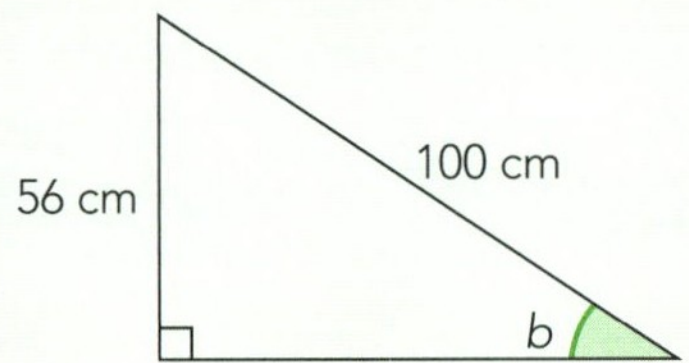

Step 1: Label the sides **that are involved** with A, O and H.

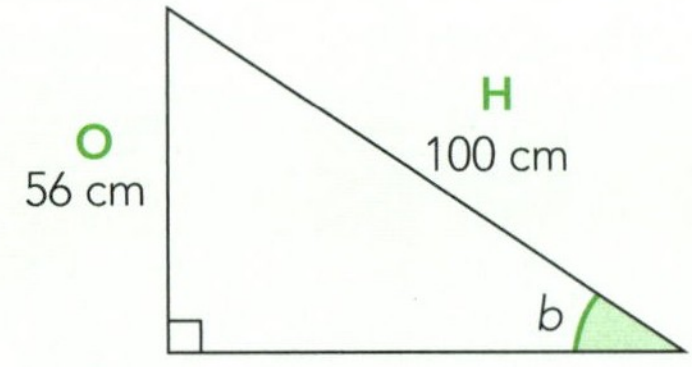

Step 2: The labelled sides are **O** and **H**, so write out the triangle involving these:

We need to find **angle *b***, so we write an expression for **sin *b***.

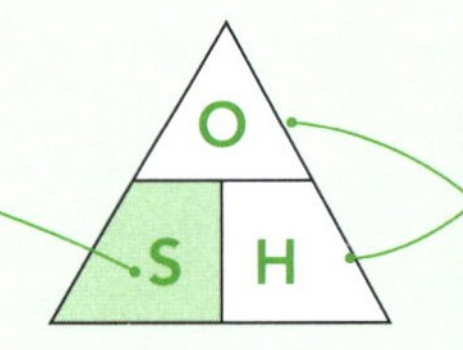

O is at the top of this triangle and **H** is at the bottom, so we **divide** them.

$$\sin b = \frac{O}{H}$$

Step 3: Substitute the numbers and calculate the answer.

$$\sin b = \frac{56}{100}$$

'undo' sin

$$b = \sin^{-1}\left(\frac{56}{100}\right)$$

'undo' sin

$$b = 34.1° \text{ (1 dp)}$$

Angles are such small units of measure, that usually it is sensible to round them to just **1 dp**.

In order to find b, we need to '**undo**' the sine of b.

As with any equation, we must do the **same to both sides**.

To '**undo**' a sine, cosine or tangent, you use the 'shift' (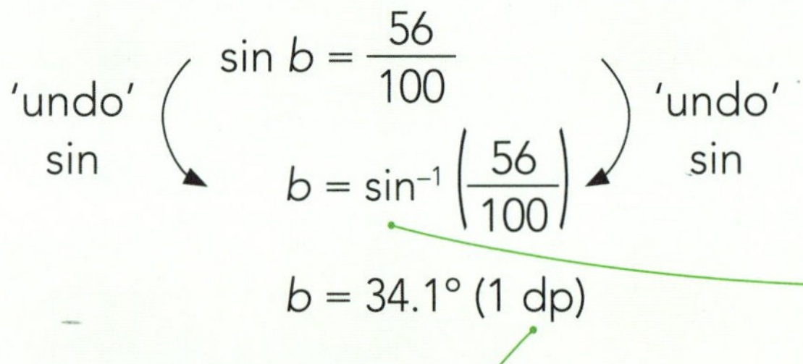) or the '2nd F' (2ndF) buttons before you press the sine, cosine or tangent buttons. Don't forget the brackets.
Note: if you get an 'error' message, check that your fraction is the right way up.

Step 4: **Think** about your answer — does it seem about right?

$b = 34.1°$ is opposite the shortest side, so we would expect b to be less than 45° ✓

Use your 'inverse sin' button ($\sin^{-1}$) to find the answers to the following. Round the answers to 1 dp.

1 If $\sin\theta = 0.5$, then $\theta =$ ______________

2 If $\sin\theta = 0.95$, then $\theta =$ ______________

3 If $\sin\theta = 0.\dot{6}$, then $\theta =$ ______________

4 If $\sin\theta = \frac{3}{4}$, then $\theta =$ ______________

5 If $\sin\theta = \frac{27}{42}$, then $\theta =$ ______________

6 If $\sin\theta = \frac{7}{53}$, then $\theta =$ ______________

Use trigonometry to calculate the unknown angle in each triangle. Round your answers to 1 dp.

7

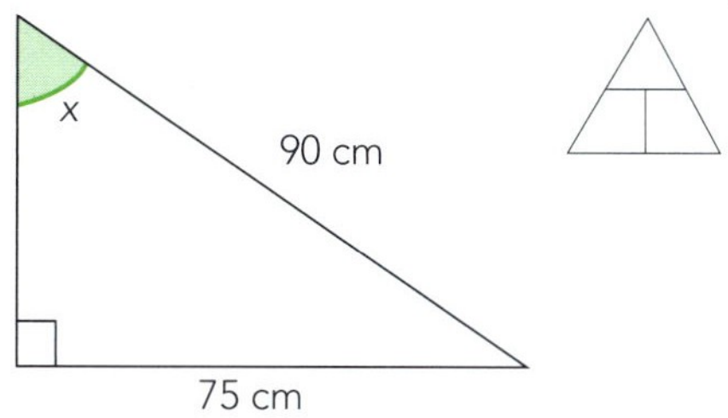

____

____

____

8

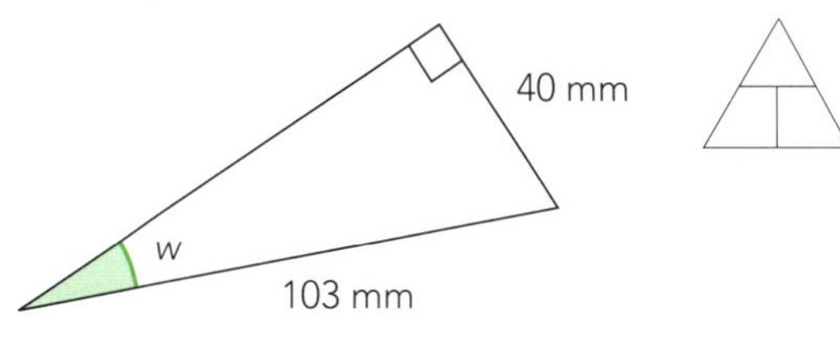

____

____

____

9

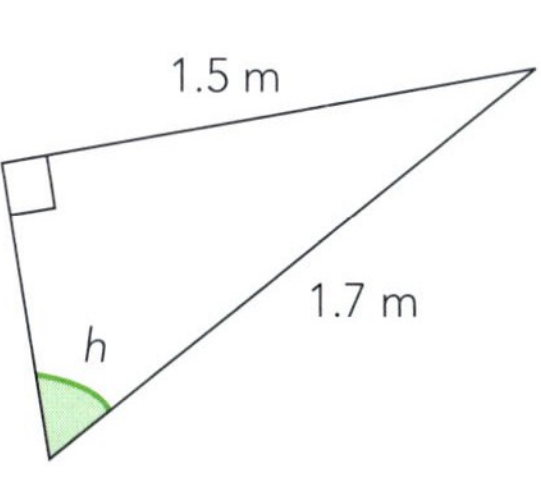

____

____

____

10

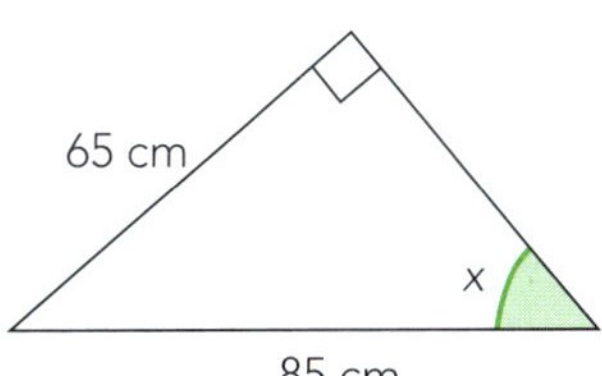

____

____

____

11

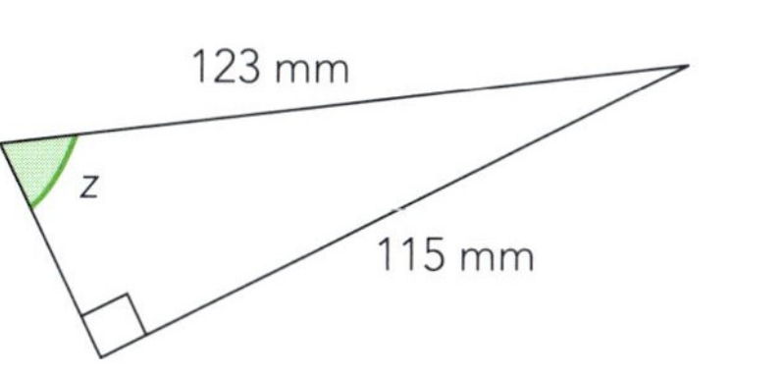

____

____

____

12

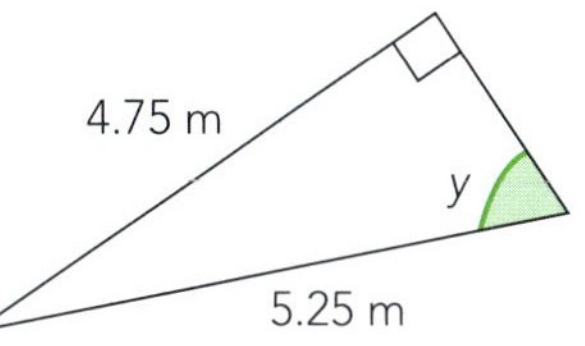

____

____

____

 ISBN: 9780170447577

Finding angles using cosine and tangent

- You can use the same steps to find angles in right-angled triangles using cosine and tangent.

Examples:

1 Calculate the size of angle θ.

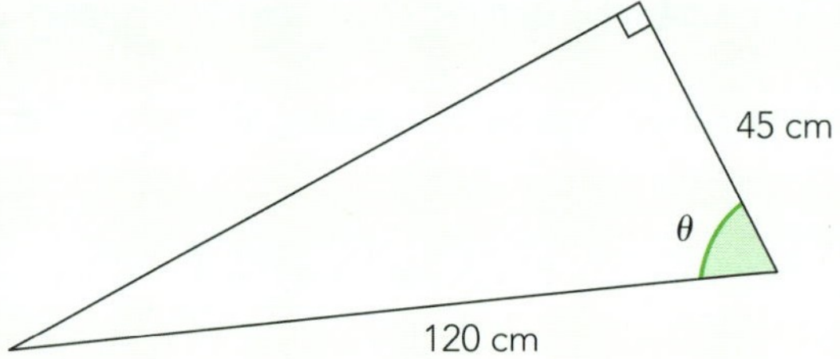

Step 1: Label the sides **that are involved** with A, O and H.

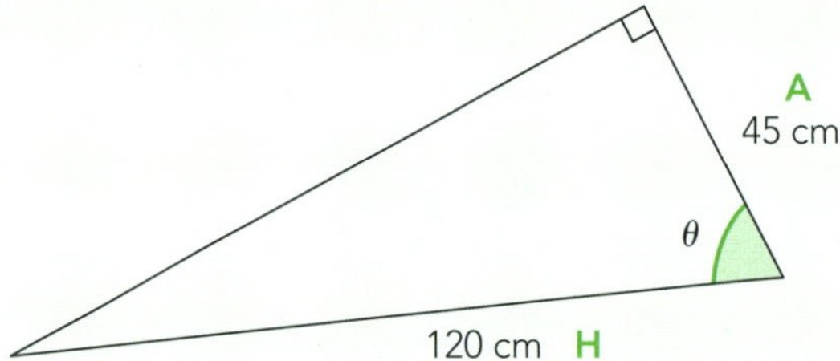

Step 2: The labelled sides are **A** and **H**, so write out the triangle involving these:

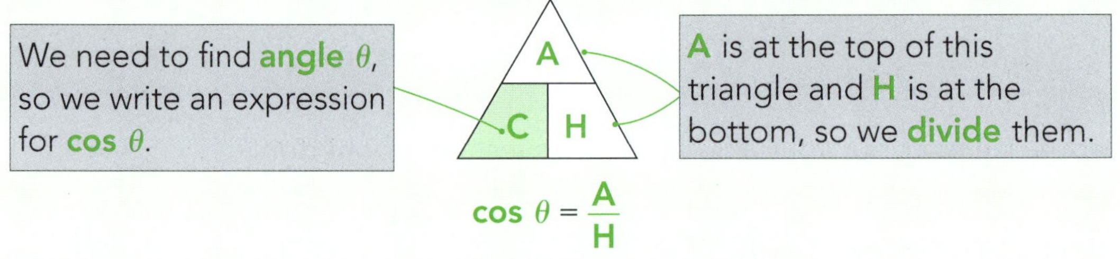

$$\cos\theta = \frac{A}{H}$$

Step 3: Substitute the numbers and calculate the answer.

'undo' cos

$$\cos\theta = \frac{45}{120}$$

$$\theta = \cos^{-1}\left(\frac{45}{120}\right)$$

$$\theta = 68.0° \text{ (1 dp)}$$

'undo' cos

Step 4: **Think** about your answer — does it seem about right?

$\theta = 68.0°$ is opposite the longer side (not counting the hypotenuse), so we would expect θ to be more than 45° ✓

ISBN: 9780170447577

2 Calculate the size of angle y.

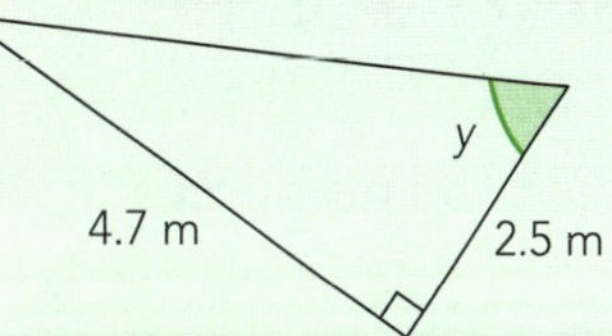

Step 1: Label the sides **that are involved** with A, O and H.

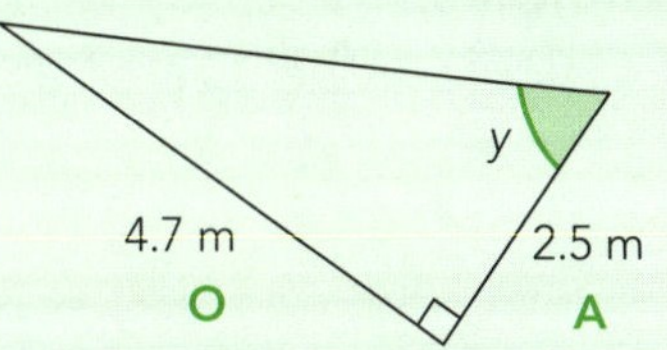

Step 2: The labelled sides are **O** and **A**, so write out the triangle involving these:

We need to find **angle *y***, so we write an expression for **tan *y***.

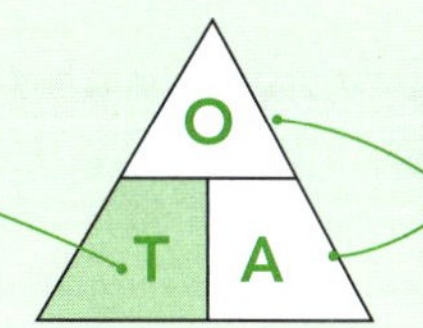

O is at the top of this triangle and **A** is at the bottom, so we **divide** them.

$$\tan y = \frac{O}{A}$$

Step 3: Substitute the numbers and calculate the answer.

$$\tan y = \frac{4.7}{2.5}$$

'undo' tan ⟶ 'undo' tan

$$y = \tan^{-1}\left(\frac{4.7}{2.5}\right)$$

$$y = 62.0° \text{ (1 dp)}$$

Step 4: **Think** about your answer — does it seem about right?

$y = 62.0°$ is opposite the longer side (not counting the hypotenuse), so we would expect y to be more than 45° ✓

Use your 'inverse cos' button ($\cos^{-1}$) or 'inverse tan' button ($\tan^{-1}$) to find the answers to the following. Round the answers to 1 dp.

1 If $\cos\theta = 0.5$, then $\theta =$ ______________

2 If $\tan\theta = 1$, then $\theta =$ ______________

3 If $\tan\theta = 4.9$, then $\theta =$ ______________

4 If $\cos\theta = \frac{3}{7}$, then $\theta =$ ______________

5 If $\tan\theta = \frac{19}{11}$, then $\theta =$ ______________

6 If $\cos\theta = \frac{75}{118}$, then $\theta =$ ______________

  ISBN: 9780170447577

Use trigonometry to calculate the unknown angle in each triangle. Round your answers to 1 dp.

7

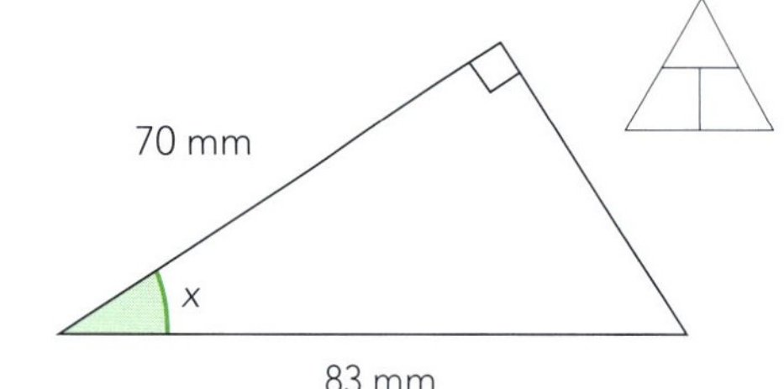

8

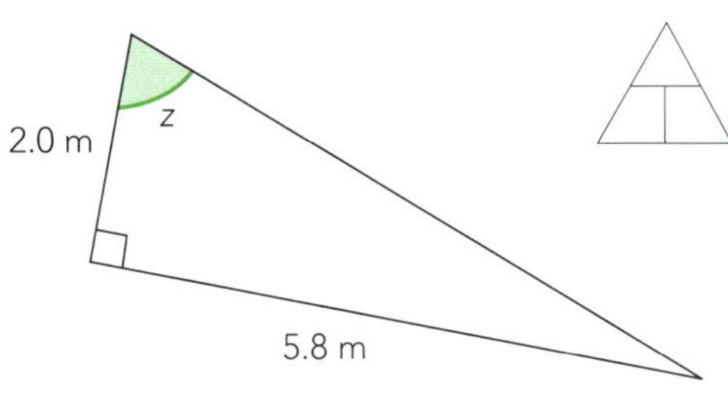

9

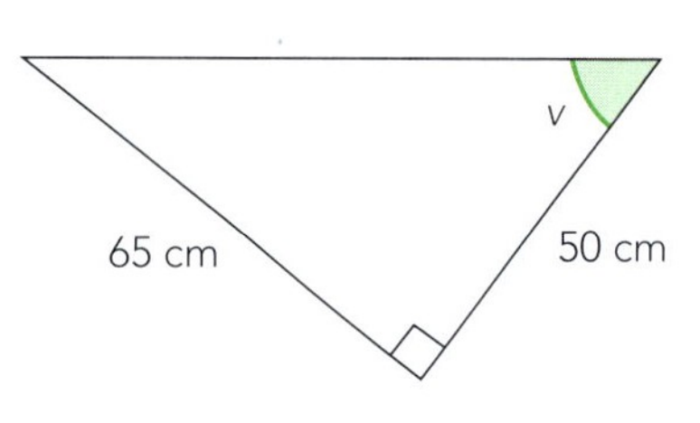

10

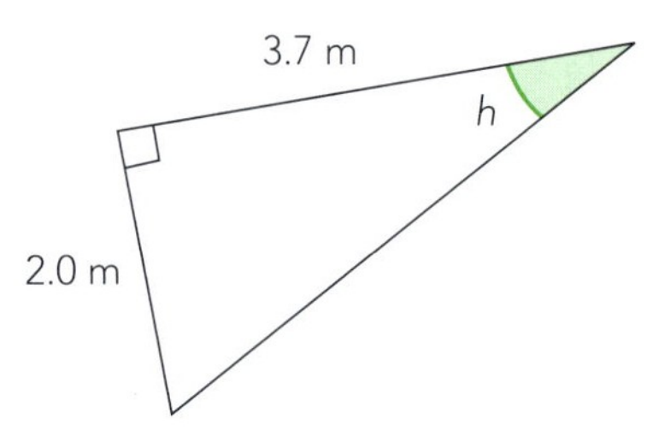

11

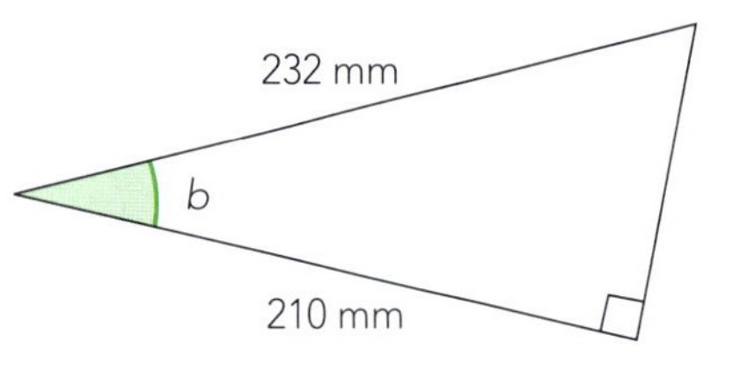

12

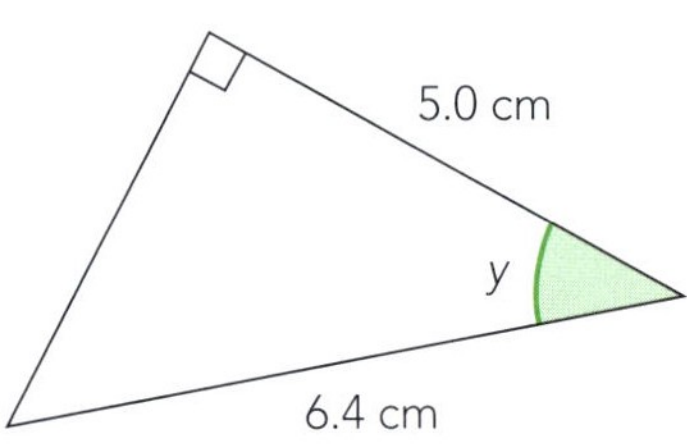

13

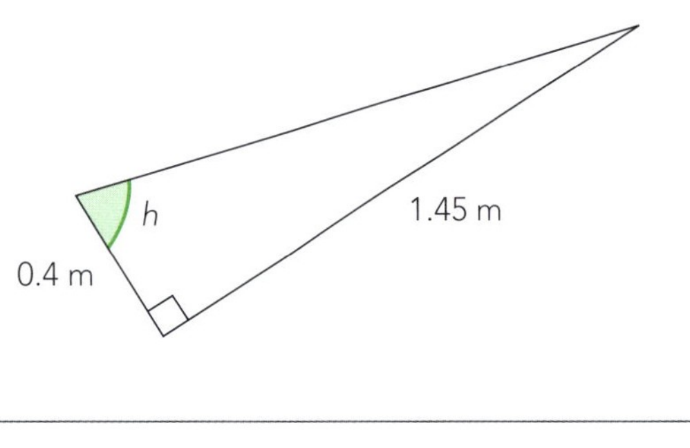

14

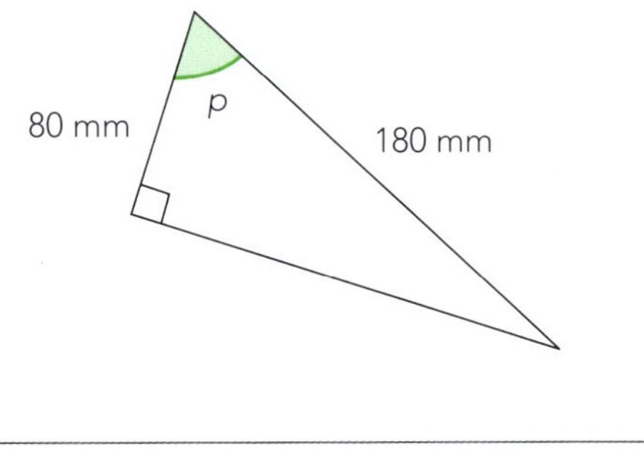

ISBN: 9780170447577

Mixing trigonometry with geometry

- Some problems require you to do several trigonometrical calculations. It is best to do your calculations **all together** and **round only at the end** in order to avoid rounding errors.
- Sometimes this is difficult, in which case round the intermediate answers to **at least one more significant figure** than that required in the answer.

Example: Calculate the total height (CE) for the figure on the right.

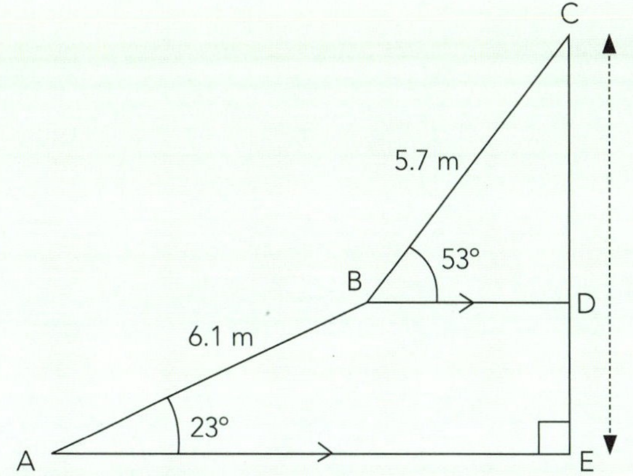

Separate calculations:

CD = 5.7 sin 53°
= 4.55 m (2 dp)

DE = 6.1 sin 23°
= 2.38 m (2 dp)

∴ CE = 4.55 + 2.38
= 6.9**3** m (2 dp)

Combined calculation:

CE = 5.7 sin 53° + 6.1 sin 23°
= 6.9**4** m (2 dp)

This is a **more accurate** answer because the rounding was done **only once**, and at the **end** of the calculation.

Answer the following questions. In each case, show your reasoning.

1 ABCD is a rhombus. Its sides are 10 cm. Angle ACD = 29°. Calculate the lengths of its diagonals.

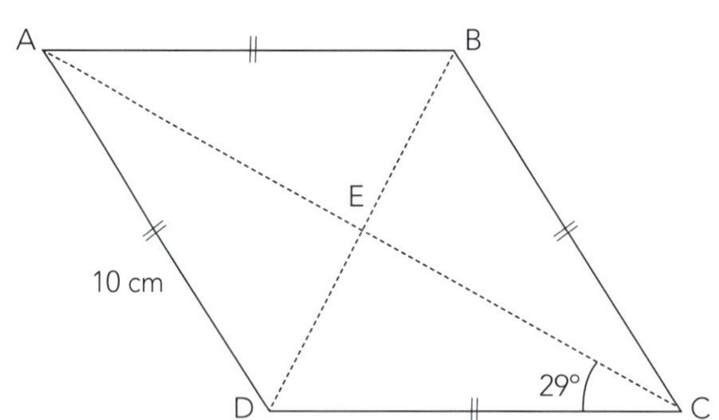

2 ABC and ABD are both right-angled triangles. AB is 59 cm, CD is 50 cm, and angle ADC is 29°. Calculate the size of angle ACB.

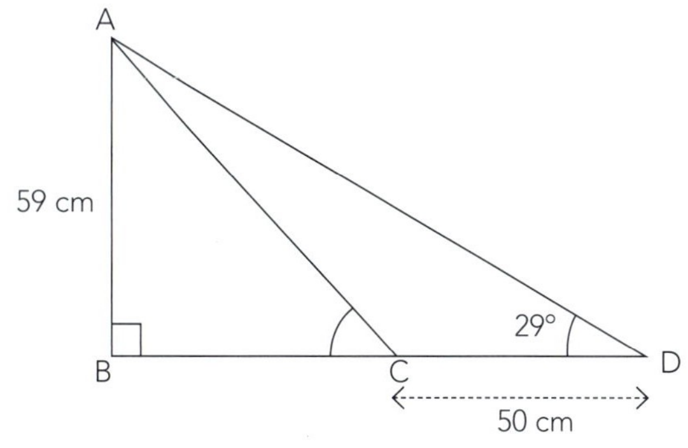

ISBN: 9780170447577

3 The width (BC) of triangle ABC is twice its height. Calculate the size of angle ACB.

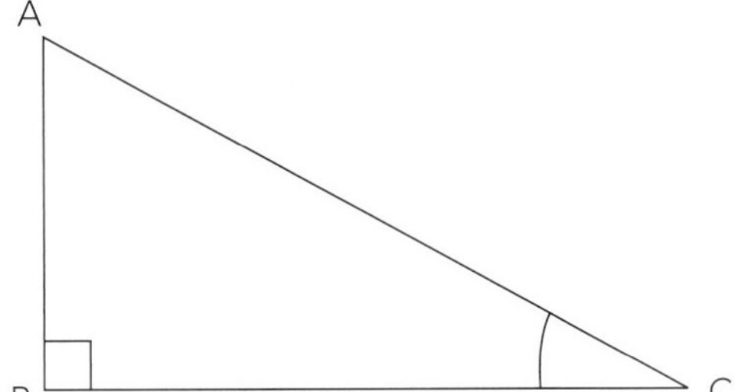

4 ABC is a right-angled triangle whose vertical height is BD. DC is 40 mm long. Calculate the length of AB.

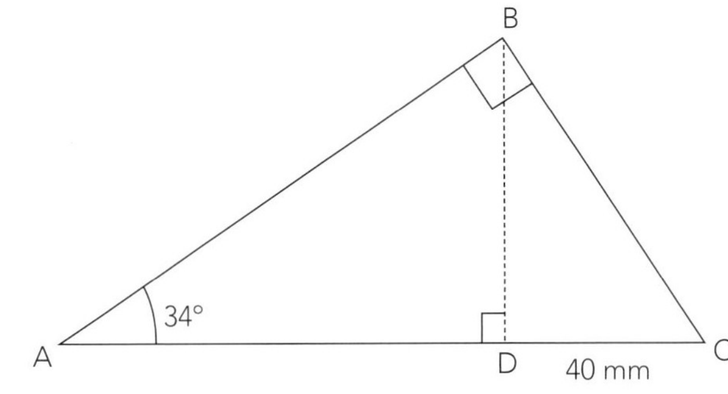

5 **a** Triangle ABC is right angled, and angle ACB is 52°. The line ED is parallel to BC. AE is 110 mm long. BC is 150 mm long. Calculate the length of EB.

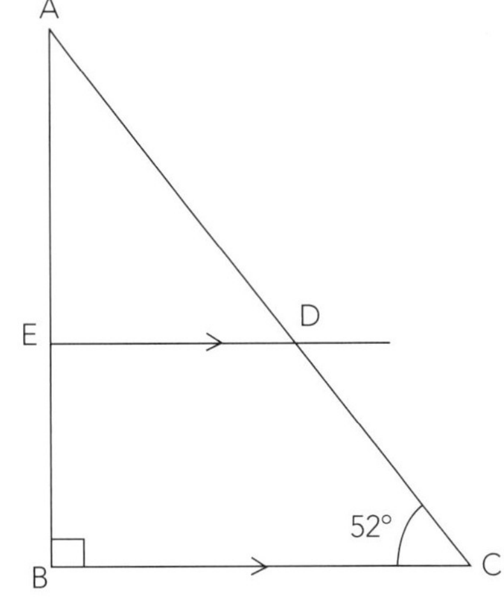

b Calculate the length of DC.

6 ABCD is a quadrilateral. AB is 172 mm, CD is 145 mm, and angle DAC is 54°. Triangle ABC is bisected by BE. Calculate the size of angle BCD.

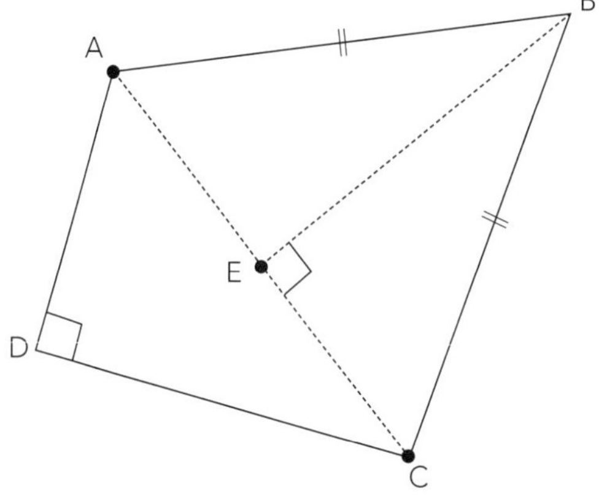

7 ACDE is a quadrilateral. AE is parallel to BD. Angle AED is 119°, ED is 51.5 m, CD is 78.3 m, and angle BDC is 27°. Calculate the length of AC.

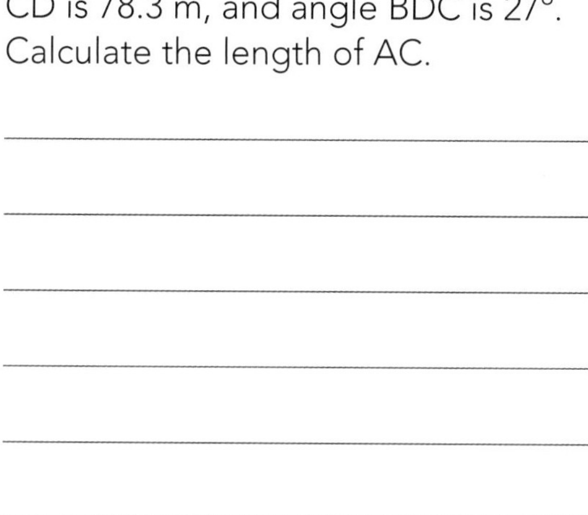

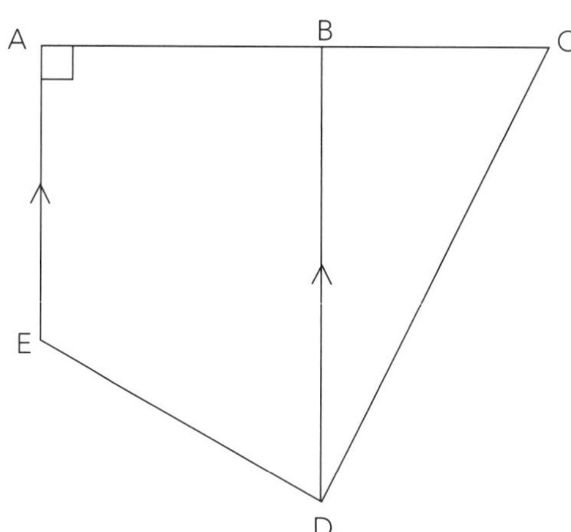

8 ABCD is an arrowhead. AC is 100 mm, BD is 65 mm, and angle DCE = 31°. Calculate the size of angle BCD.

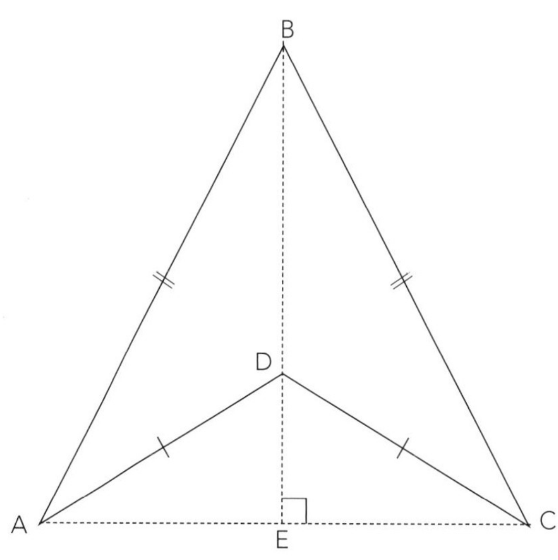

 ISBN: 9780170447577

Geometry and ϕ (phi), the golden ratio

- **Fibonacci** (pronounced *fib-on-arch-ee*), known by several other names such as Leonardo of Pisa, was an **Italian** who lived in the **12th century**.
- He published a book on how to do calculations which included a section on what is now called the Fibonacci sequence.
- The golden ratio (phi) can be derived from this sequence.

The golden ratio, ϕ

Here are the first 18 terms of the Fibonacci sequence.

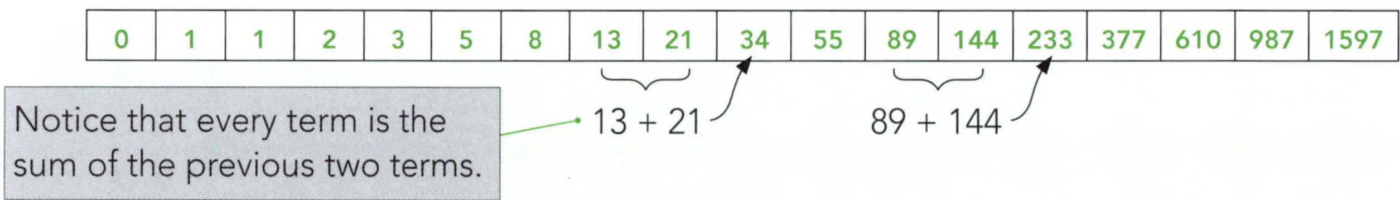

Notice that every term is the sum of the previous two terms.

Calculate the values of the ratios formed by dividing each of the last six terms above by their previous terms. Round your answers to 5 dp.

$\frac{144}{89}$ = ____________

$\frac{233}{144}$ = ____________

$\frac{377}{233}$ = ____________

$\frac{610}{377}$ = ____________

$\frac{987}{610}$ = ____________

$\frac{1597}{987}$ = ____________

What do you notice about the last two values?

____

____

The actual value the ratios are approaching is 1.618033988749897...

- This is an irrational number with special meaning, like π.
- It is called **phi**, and has the symbol ϕ.
- **1.618033988749897...** is also called the **golden ratio**.

What the ratio looks like:

ISBN: 9780170447577

The weird mathematical properties of phi

1 $\frac{1}{1.6180339\ldots} = 0.6180339\ldots$ or $\frac{1}{\phi} = \phi - 1$ or $\boldsymbol{\phi = 1 + \frac{1}{\phi}}$

In other words, the reciprocal of ϕ is one less than itself.

Find this relationship on the diagram at the bottom of the page.

2 Consider a right-angled triangle with sides ϕ, $\sqrt{\phi}$ and 1:

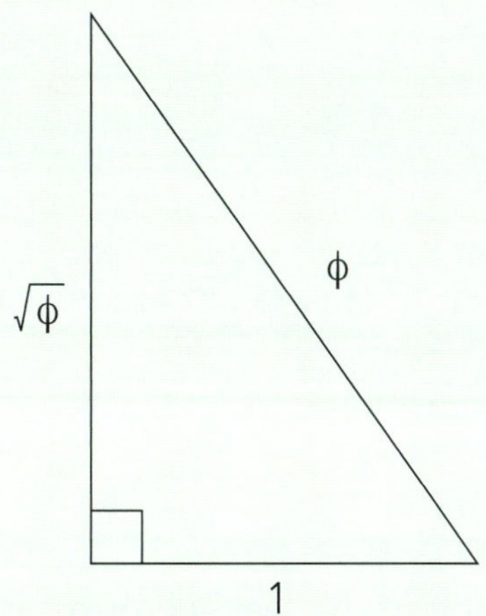

By Pythagoras: $\phi^2 = (\sqrt{\phi})^2 + 1^2$

$\therefore\ \boldsymbol{\phi^2 = \phi + 1}$

In other words, the square of ϕ is one more than itself.

Find this relationship on the diagram at the bottom of the page.

3 Using a little algebra:

We know that $\phi^2 = \phi + 1$.

Multiply both sides by ϕ: $\phi^3 = \phi^2 + \phi$.

Find this relationship on the diagram below.

Putting these together:

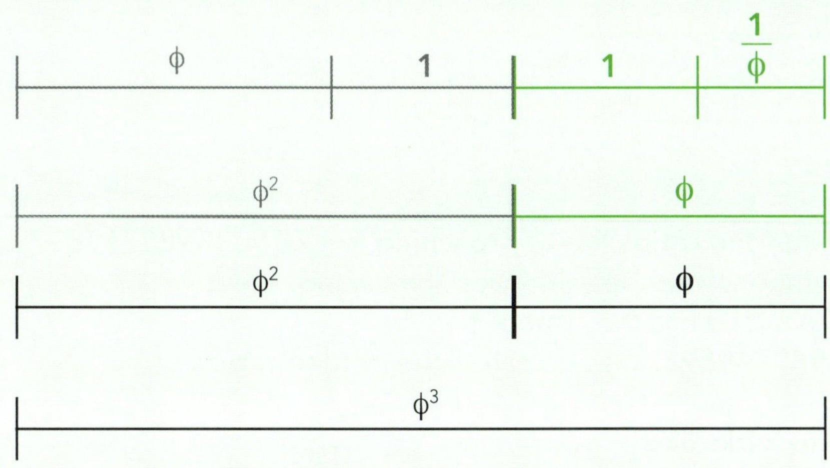

 ISBN: 9780170447577

Construction of a golden rectangle

Step 1: Draw a square with sides 2 units long and bisect the base.

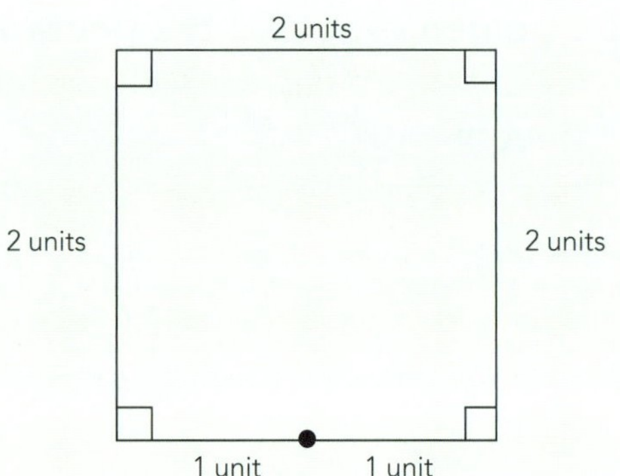

Step 2: Draw a line between the midpoint of the base (A) and the top corner of the square (B).

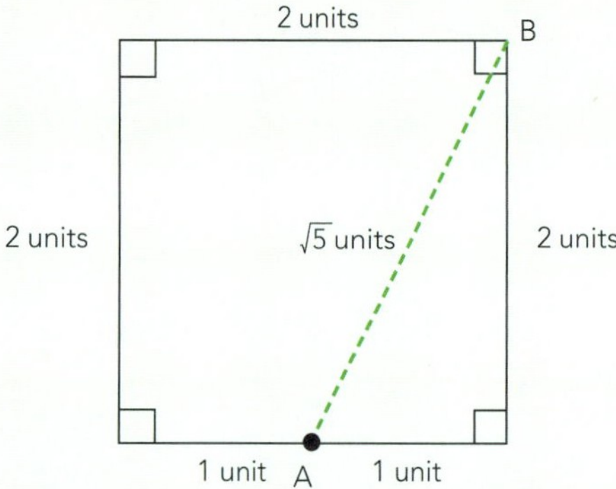

By Pythagoras:

Length of diagonal $= \sqrt{2^2 + 1^2}$

$= \sqrt{5}$

Step 3: Draw an arc with centre A and radius $\sqrt{5}$. Extend the base of the square to meet the arc at C.

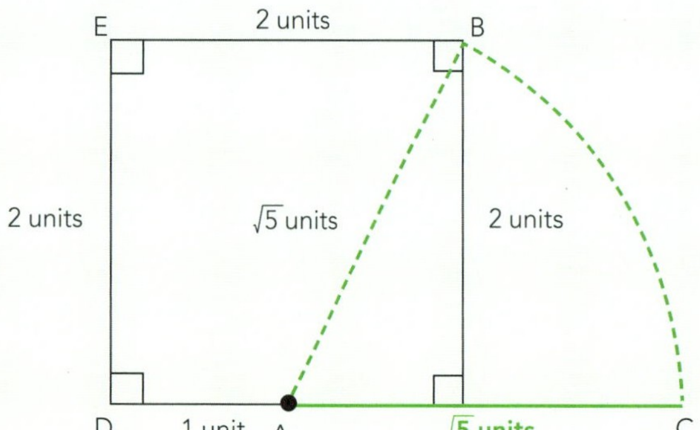

Length of DC $= 1 + \sqrt{5}$

Ratio of ED:DC $= 2:(1 + \sqrt{5})$

$= 1:\dfrac{1 + \sqrt{5}}{2}$

$= 1:1.61803...$

$= 1:\phi$

Step 4: Construct a rectangle with base DC and height DE.

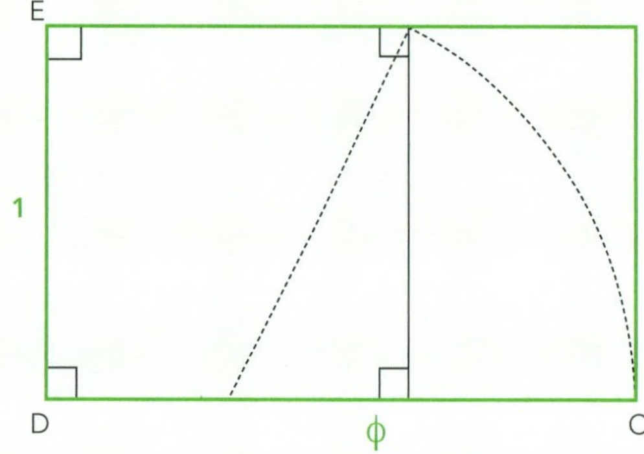

A golden rectangle.

ISBN: 9780170447577

The golden ratio and the pentagram

- A pentagram can be constructed by joining the corners of a regular pentagon with straight lines.

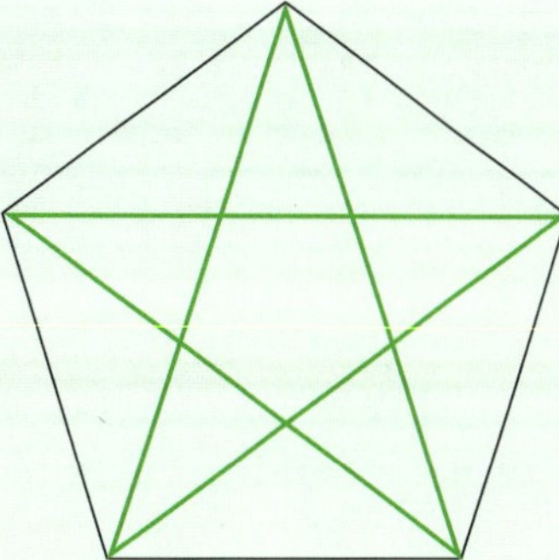

- This symbol has been used for several thousand years in association with many religious and mystical beliefs.

Angles and lengths in a pentagram

1 Consider just the top part of a pentagram.

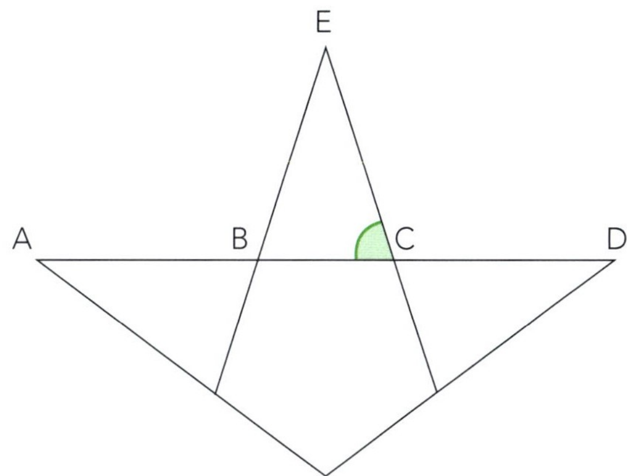

Explain why angle BCE = 72°.

____

____

____

2 Consider just the triangle BEC.
Let EB = EC = 1 unit
Let FE be the perpendicular bisector of BC.

Use trigonometry to calculate the length of FC.

____

____

____

∴ BC = ______________

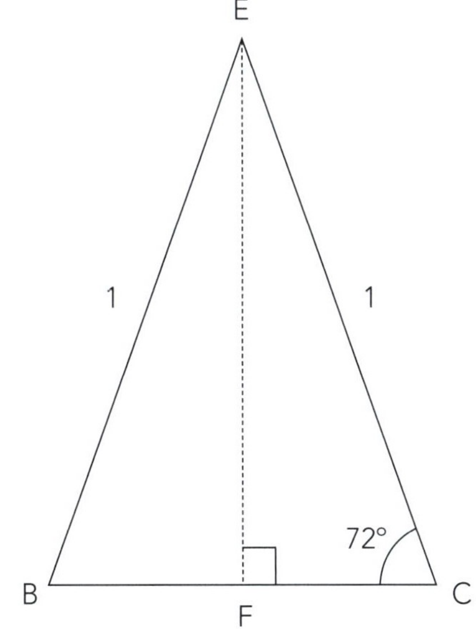

ISBN: 9780170447577

3 Write down the following lengths.

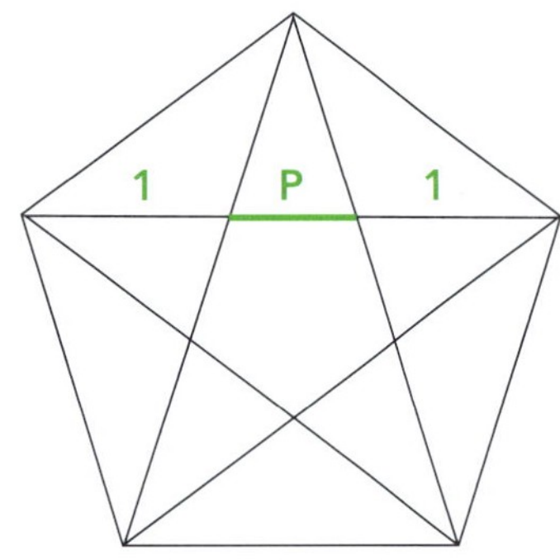

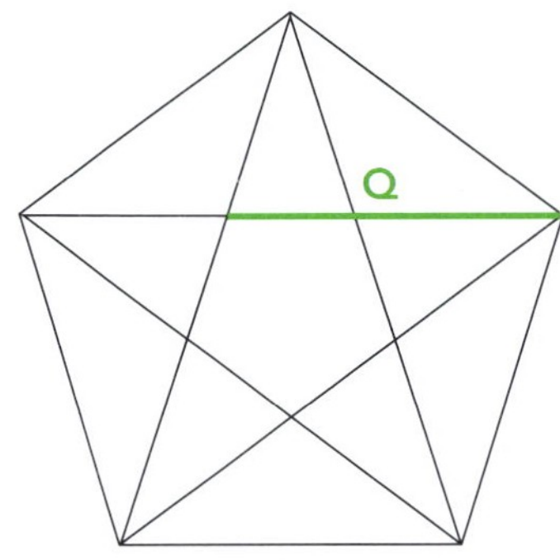

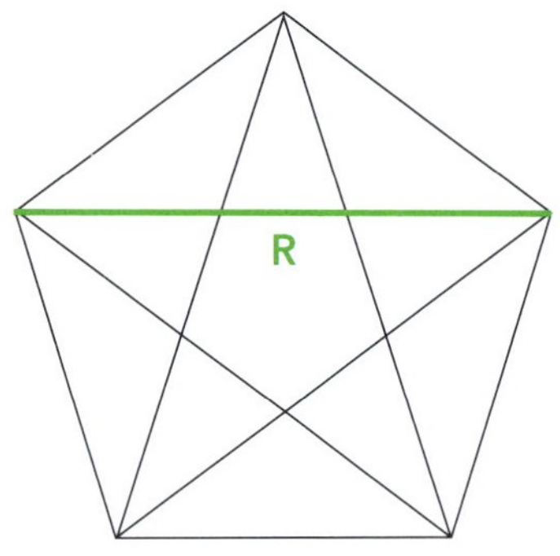

P = ______________ Q = ______________ R = ______________

4 Calculate the ratios of each of the following pairs of lengths.

a

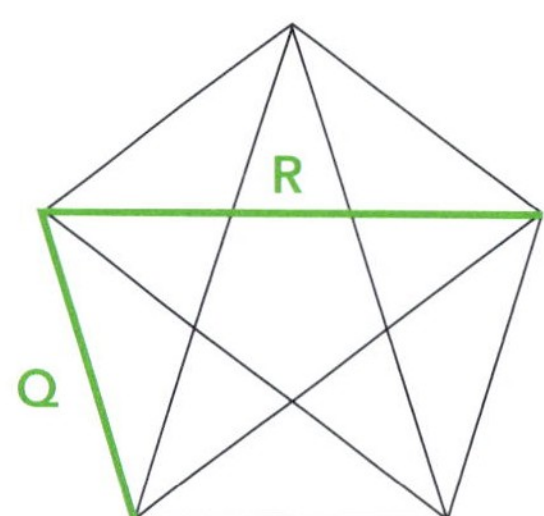

$\frac{R}{Q}$ = ______________

= ______________

b

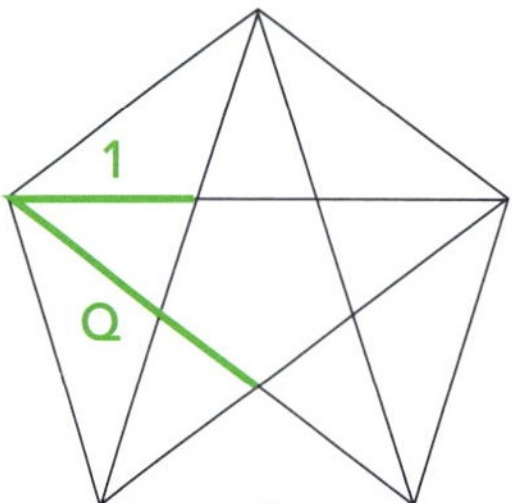

$\frac{Q}{1}$ = ______________

= ______________

c

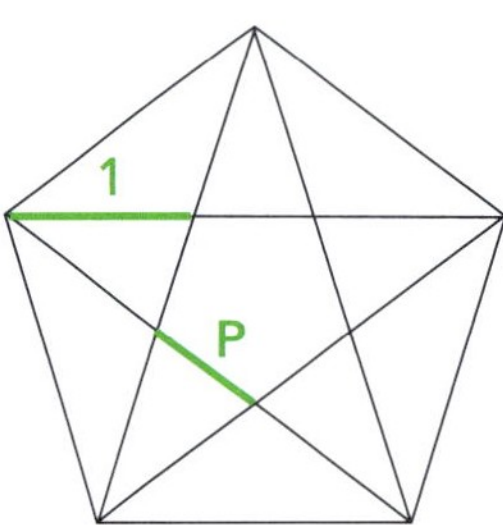

$\frac{1}{P}$ = ______________

= ______________

5 Complete the following sentence.

In a pentagram, the length of many line segments are in the ______________________

______________________ to many other lengths.

ISBN: 9780170447577

Revision 1

1 Calculate the missing angles and write the reasons where indicated. If your reasons are different from those in the answers, check them with your teacher.

a

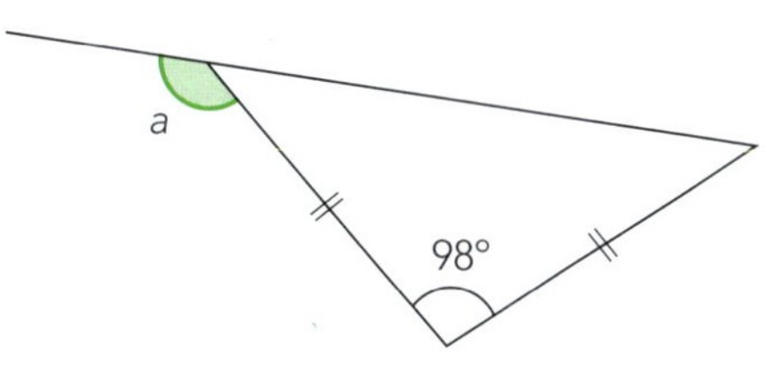

Reason:

b

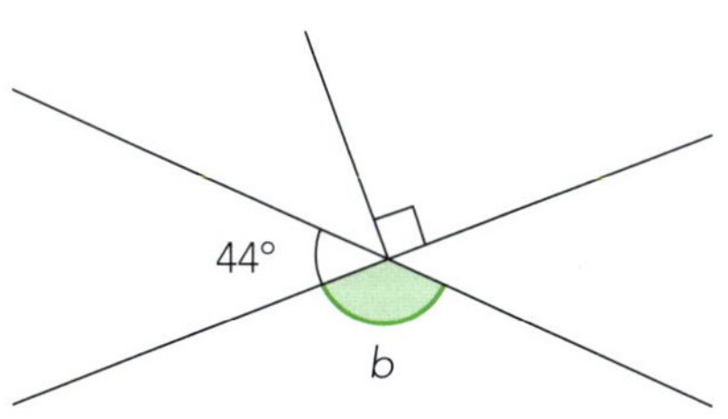

Reason:

c

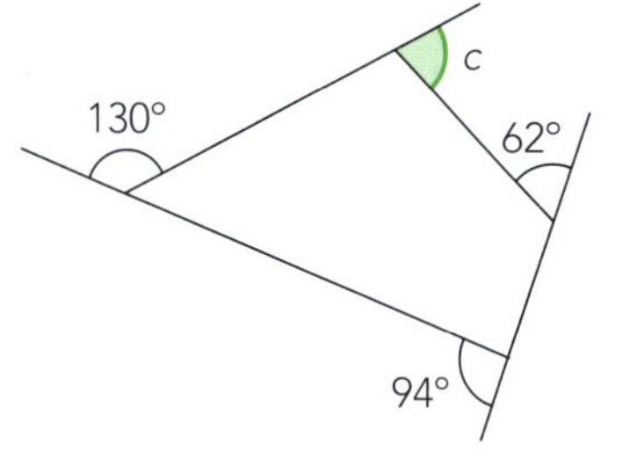

d

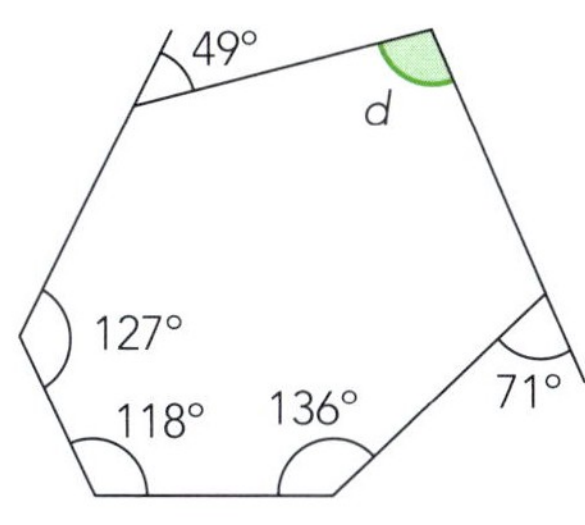

e

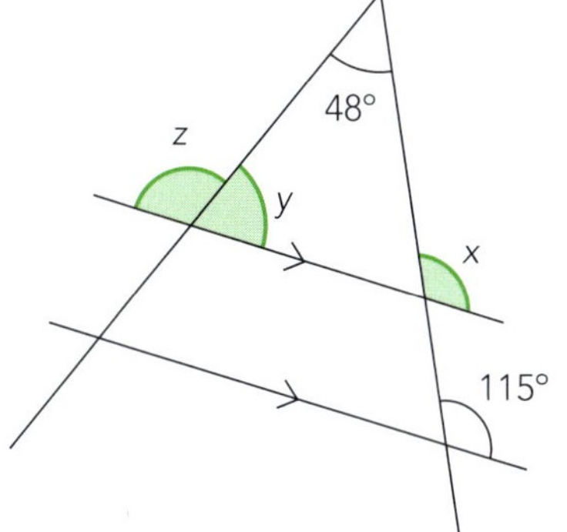

$x =$ ______ Reason:

$y =$ ______ Reason:

$z =$ ______ Reason:

Calculate the value of x.

f

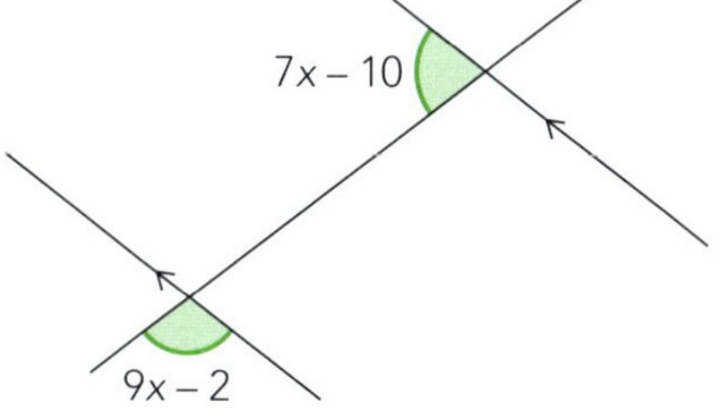

g

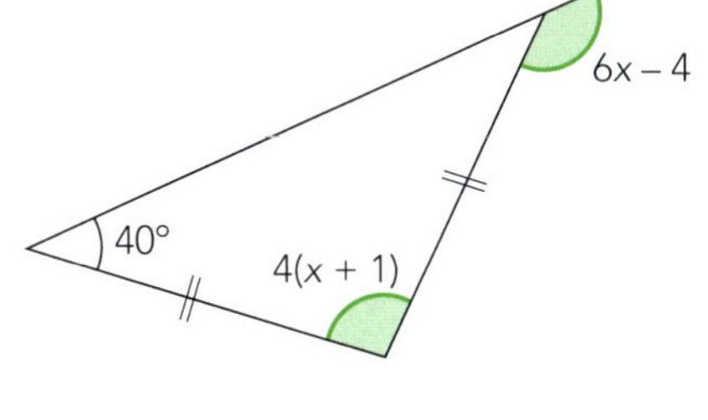

 ISBN: 9780170447577

2 Use this map to answer the following questions. The horizontal gridlines are 110 km apart.

a Circle the most likely bearing for a line from Auckland to Rotorua. 110° 140° 170°

b What would you find at at 37.7°S 174.8°E? ______________________

c Write the grid reference for Rotorua. ______________________

d Estimate the direct distance between Auckland and Tauranga.

In km: ______________

In NM: ______________

e Sketch the locus of all the points that are within 100 km of Auckland.

3 Reflect the figure in the mirror line. Label any invariant points.

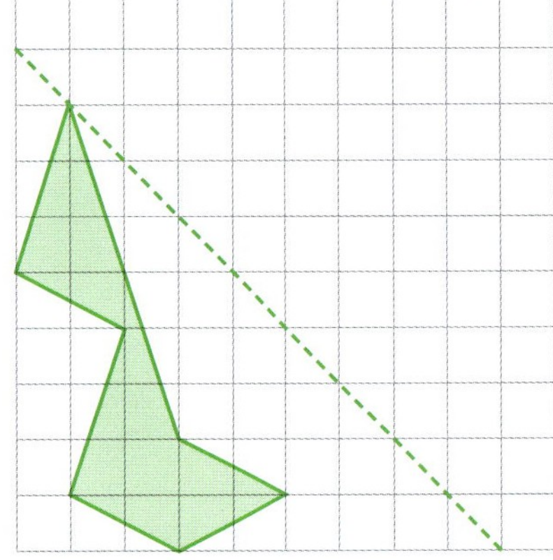

4 Write the orders of rotational and line symmetry for this image.

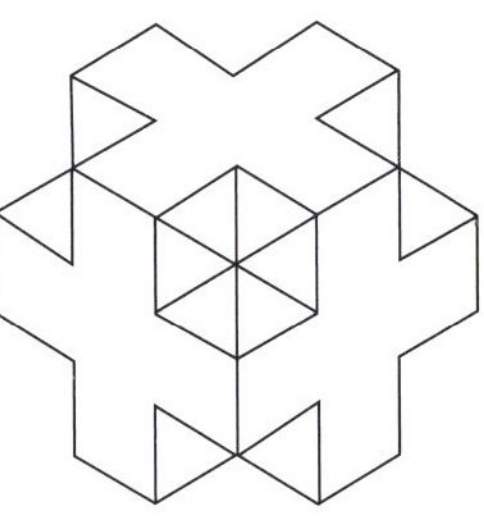

Order of rotational symmetry = ______

Order of line symmetry = ______

ISBN: 9780170447577

5 Find the centre of enlargement for this image.

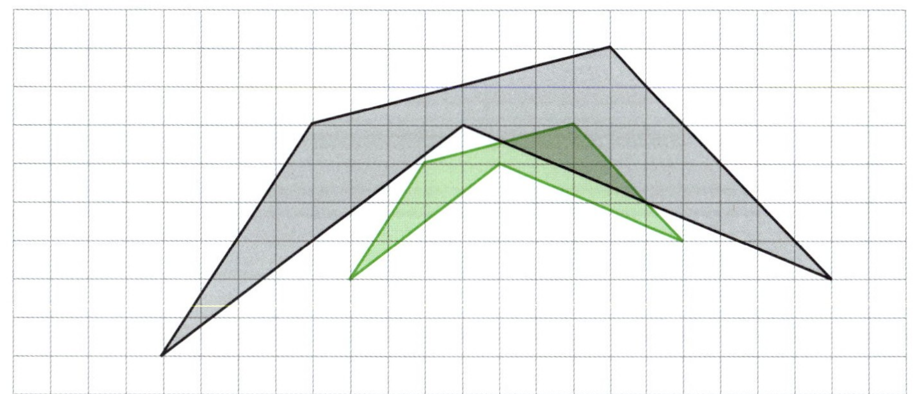

6 Use the theorem of Pythagoras to calculate the unknown sides in this figure. Round your answers to 1 dp.

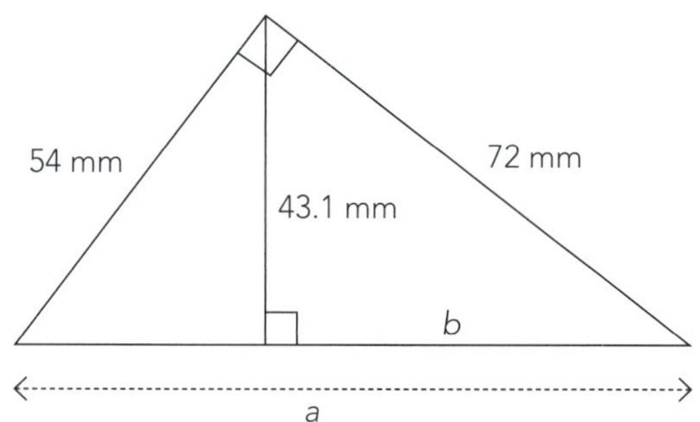

a ______________________

____

b ______________________

____

7 Use trigonometry to calculate the unknown sides and angles labelled *c*, *d*, *e* and *f*. Round your answers to 1 dp.

a

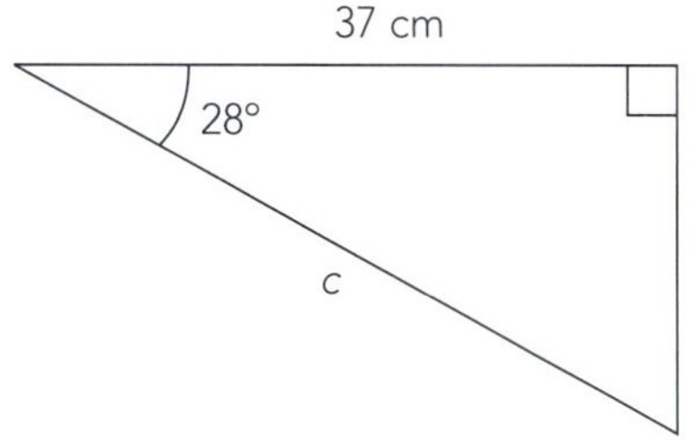

____

____

b

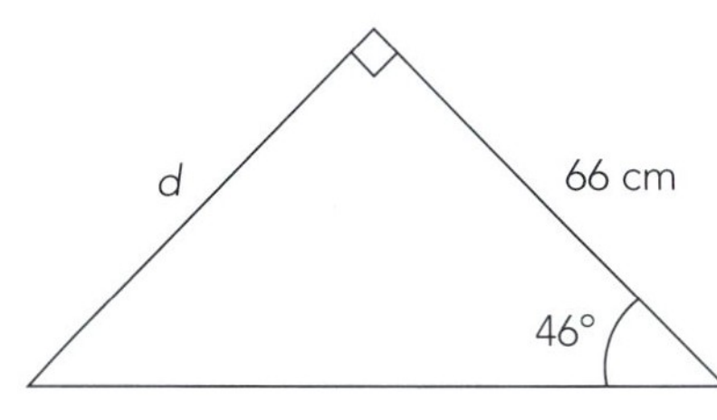

____

____

c

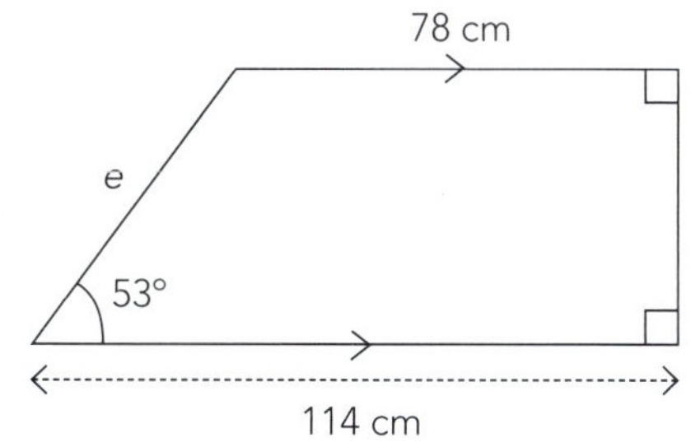

____

____

d

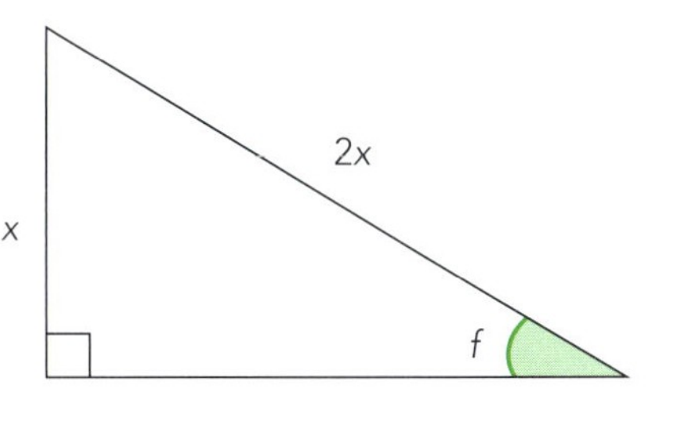

____

____

 ISBN: 9780170447577

Revision 2

1 Calculate the missing angles and write the reasons where indicated. If your reasons are different from those in the answers, check them with your teacher.

a

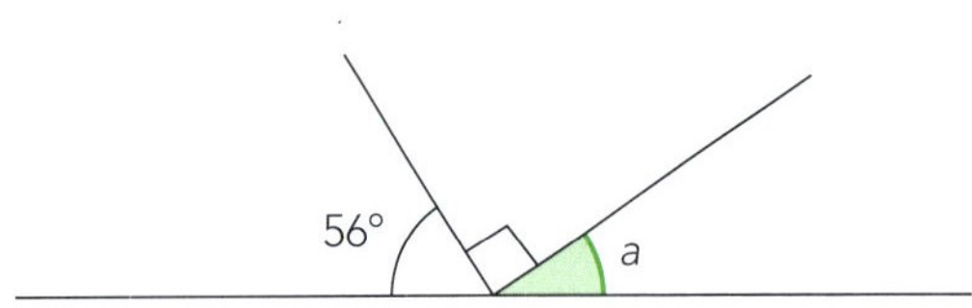

____

Reason: ______________________

b

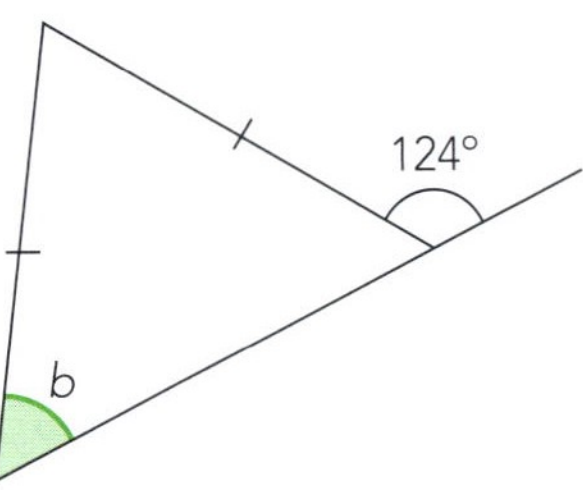

____

Reason: ______________________

c

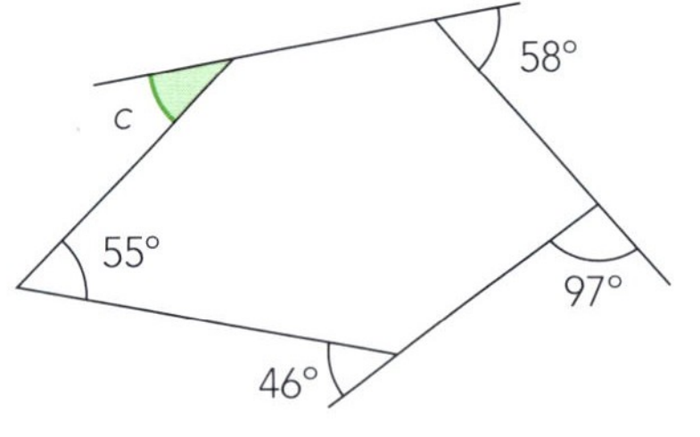

____

____

d

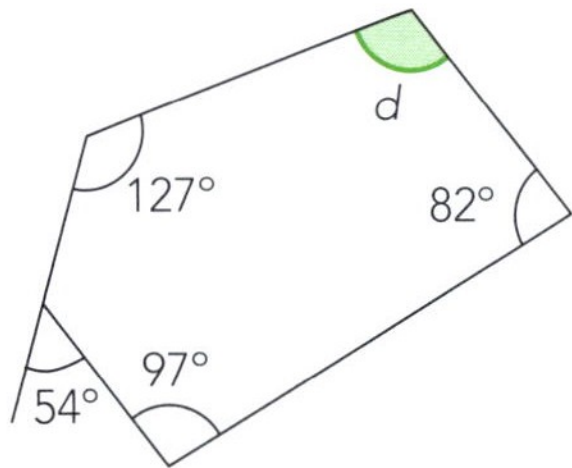

____

____

e

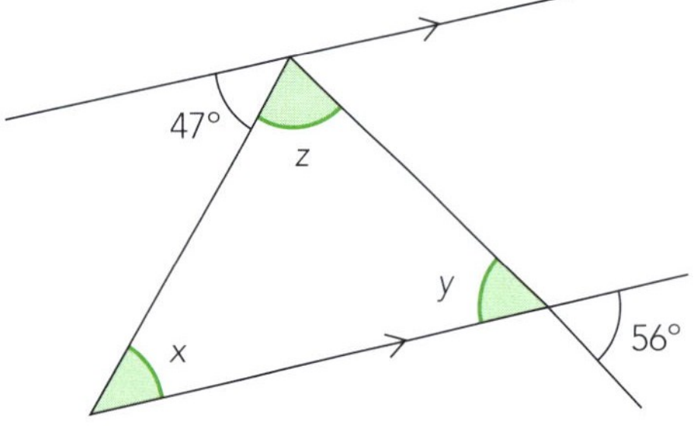

$x =$ ______ Reason: ______________________

$y =$ ______ Reason: ______________________

$z =$ ______ Reason: ______________________

Calculate the value of x.

f

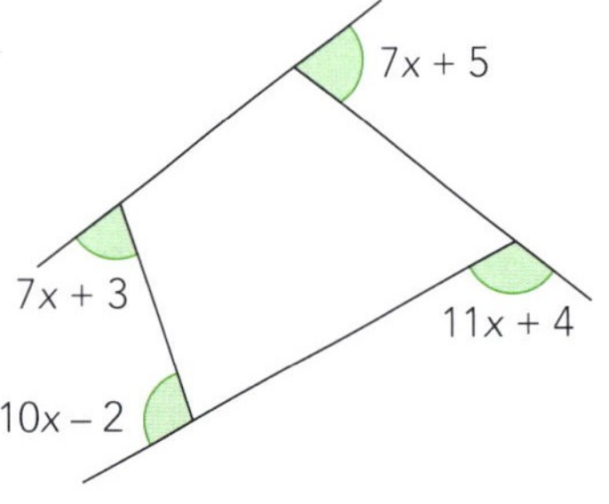

____

____

____

g

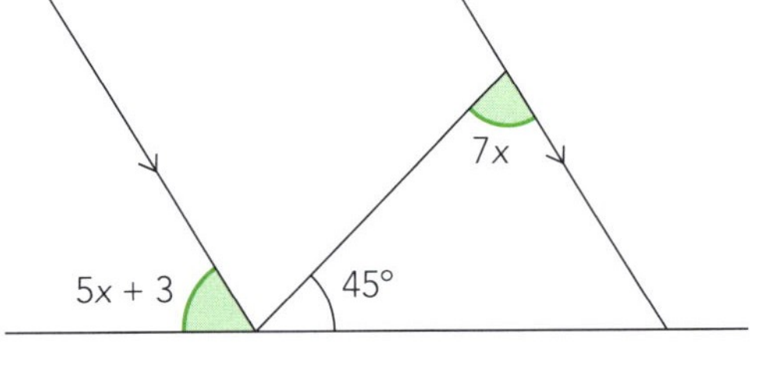

____

____

____

ISBN: 9780170447577

2 Use this map to answer the following questions. The horizontal gridlines are 120 km apart.

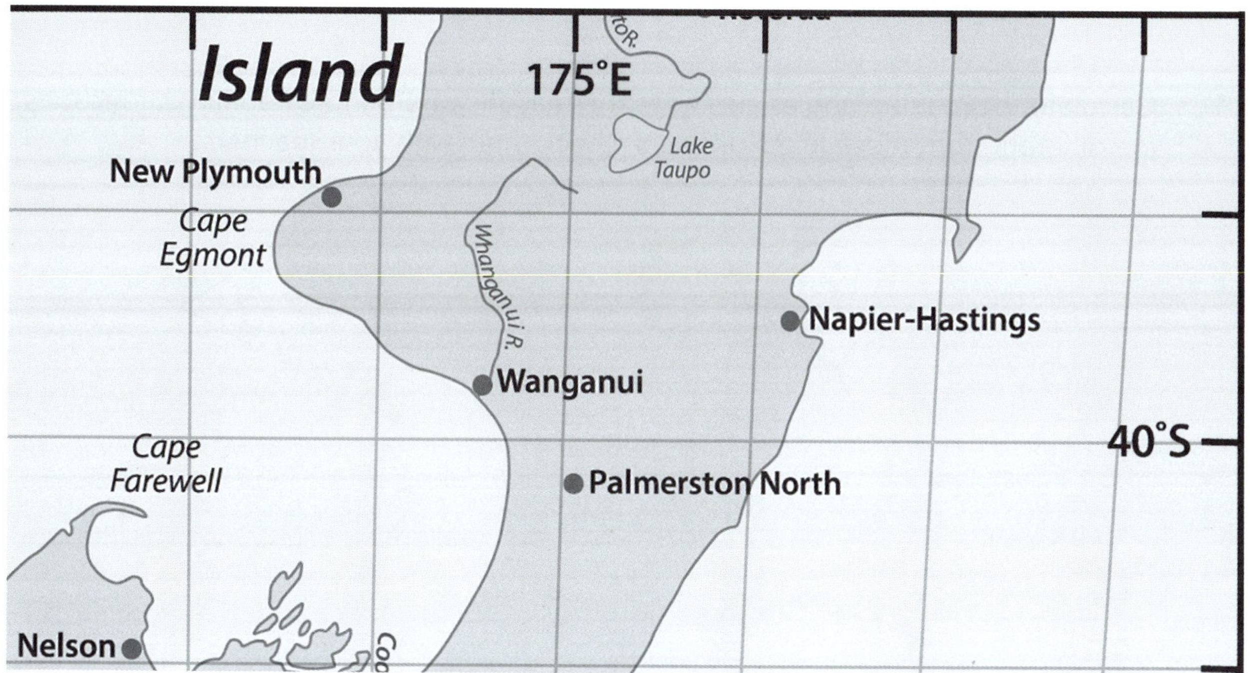

a Circle the most likely bearing for a line from Palmerston North to Nelson. 280° 220° 250°

b What would you find at at 40.9°S 172.7°E? ______________________

c Write the grid reference for Napier-Hastings. ______________________

d Estimate the direct distance between between Nelson and Napier-Hastings.

In km: ______________

In NM: ______________

e Sketch the locus of all the points that are equidistant from Nelson and New Plymouth.

3 Write the vector for this translation. The original figure is green.

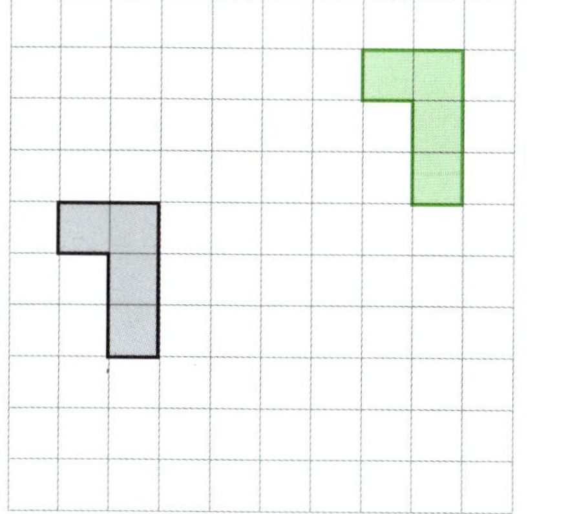

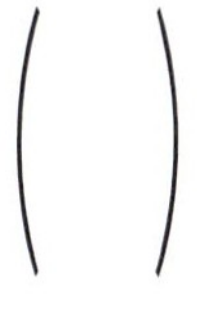

4 Write the orders of rotational and line symmetry for this image.

Order of rotational symmetry = ______

Order of line symmetry = ______

 ISBN: 9780170447577

5 Enlarge this triangle by a scale factor of $\frac{3}{2}$.

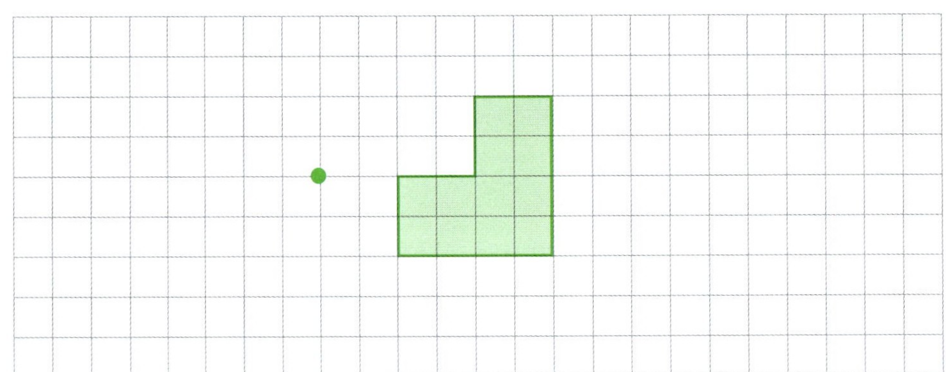

6 Use the theorem of Pythagoras to calculate the unknown lengths in this kite. Round your answers to 1 dp.

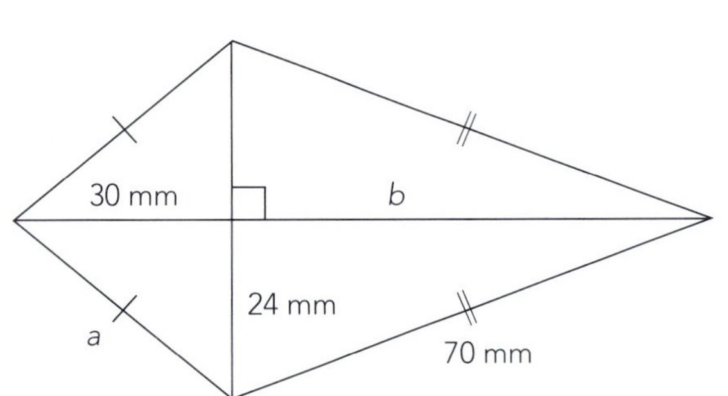

a ______________________

____

b ______________________

____

7 Use trigonometry to calculate the unknown sides and angles labelled *c*, *d*, *e* and *f*. Round your answers to 1 dp.

a

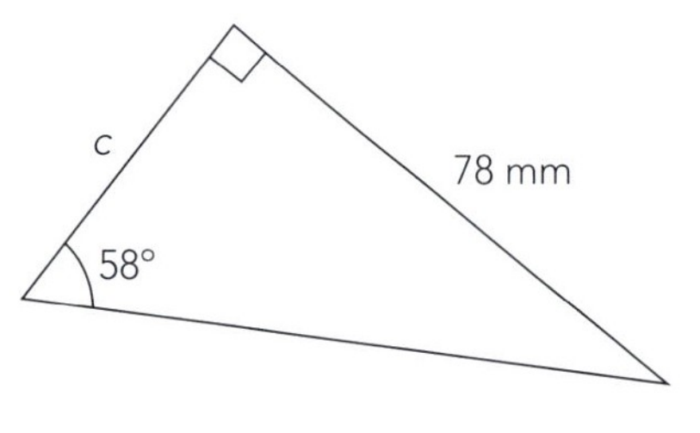

____

____

b

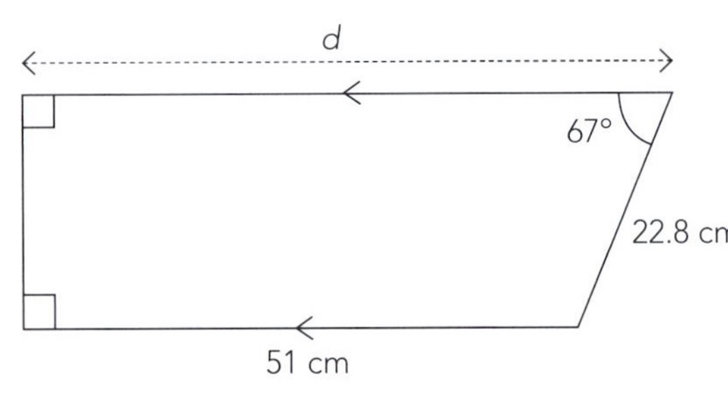

____

____

c

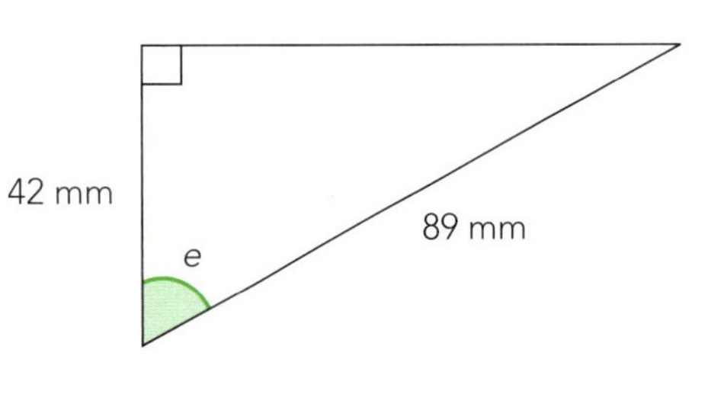

____

____

d

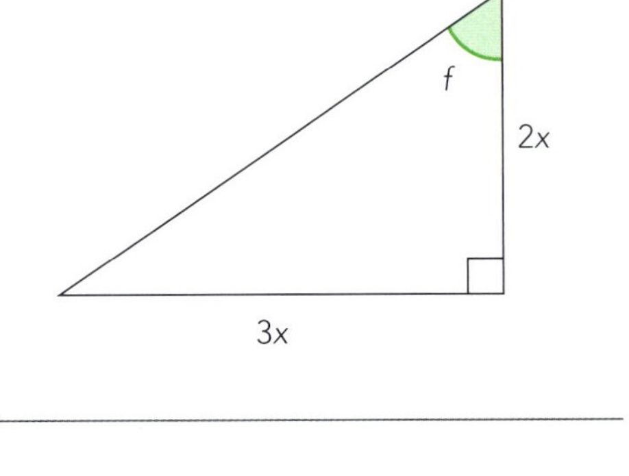

____

____

ISBN: 9780170447577

Answers

Angles (pp. 6–16)

Angles revision (pp. 6–7)

1 $x = 55°$
Vert opp ∠s = 180°.
2 $a = 38°$
∠s in a Δ = 180°.
3 $z = 58°$
∠s in a Δ = 180°.
4 $g = 76°$
∠s on a line add to 180°.
5 $d = 157°$
∠s on a point add to 360°.
6 $f = 98°$
ext ∠ of Δ = into opp ∠s.
7 $x = 144°$
∠s in a Δ = 180° and ext ∠s of Δ = into opp ∠s.
8 $b = 33°$
∠s at a point add to 360° and vert opp ∠s.

Polygons (pp. 8–11)

Exterior angles

1 $y = 107°$
2 $z = 109°$
3 $a = 120°$
4 $h = 60°$
5 $p = 55°$
6 $x = 118°$
7 $m = 46°$
8 $y = 49°$
9 $g = 132°$
10 $h = 128.6°$

Interior angles

1 $a = 82°$
2 $c = 108°$
3 $g = 123°$
4 $x = 119°$
5 $m = 144°$
6 $d = 309°$
7 $b = 18°$
8 $f = 51°$

Parallel lines (pp. 12–13)

1 $a = 24°$
Co-int ∠s add to 180°, ∥ lines.
2 $x = 111°$
Alt ∠s =, ∥ lines.
3 $y = 109°$
Corr ∠s =, ∥ lines.
4 $z = 71°$
Alt ∠s =, ∥ lines and ∠s on a line add to 180°.
5 $b = 56°$
Alt ∠s =, ∥ lines and ∠s in a Δ = 180°.
6 $d = 337°$
Many possibilities. Check with your teacher.
7 $t = 258°$
Co-int ∠s add to 180°, ∥ lines and ∠s at a point add to 360°.
8 $p = 112°$
Many possibilities. Check with your teacher.

Algebra and angles (pp. 14–16)

1 $x = 20°$
2 $x = 60°$
3 $x = 15°$
4 $x = 14°$
5 $x = 50°$
6 $x = 10°$
7 $x = 28°$
8 $x = 61°$
9 $x = 15°$
10 $x = 32°$
$y = 16°$
11 $x = 30°$
12 $x = 5°$

Position and orientation (pp. 17–37)

Direction: bearings (pp. 17–18)

1 238°
2 153°
3 031°
4 257°
5 061°
6 103°
7 321°
8 293°
9

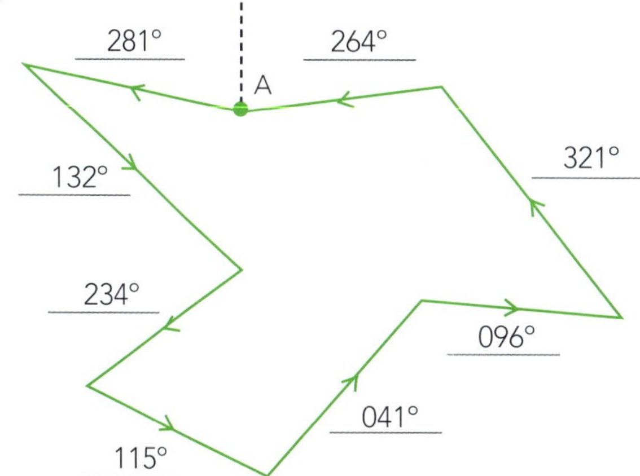

Using a protractor to find bearings (pp. 19–22)

1 Bearing: 150°
Distance: 180 km
2 Bearing: 225°
Distance: 560 km
3 Bearing: 010°
Distance: 60 km
4 Bearing: 210°
Distance: 310 km
5 Bearing: 035°
Distance: 680 km
6 Bearing: 065°
Distance: 510 km
7 Bearing: 220°
Distance: 1020 km
8 Bearing: 295°
Distance: 260 km
9 Bearing: 150°
Distance: 140 km
10 Bearing: 030°
Distance: 220 km
11 Bearing: 330°
Distance: 240 km
12 Bearing: 085°
Distance: 350 km
13 The Trio Islands (Kuru Pongi)
14 Turner Peak

ISBN: 9780170447577

15 The Haystack (Moturaka)
16 Ninepin Rock
17 Kaitira (East Entry Point)
18 Takapōtaka Attempt Hill
19 Anatakupu Island

Location: loci (pp. 23–27)

1 a

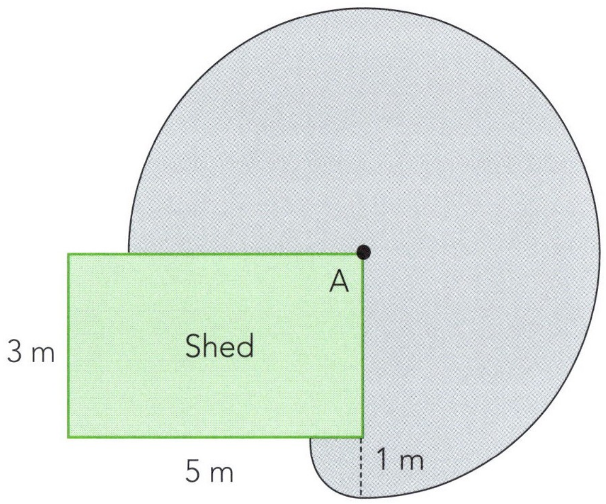

3 m
A
Shed
5 m
1 m

b

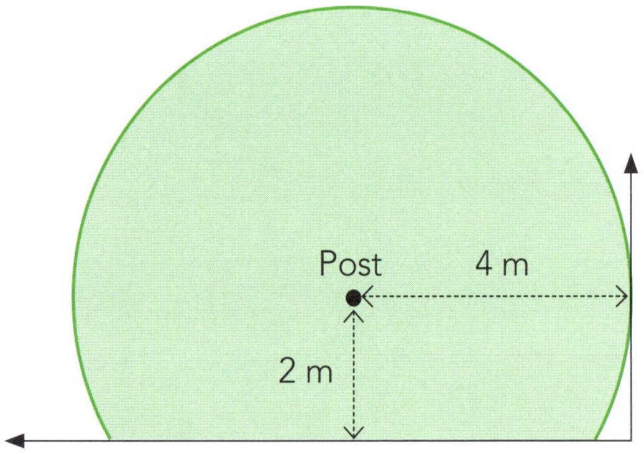

Post
4 m
2 m

c

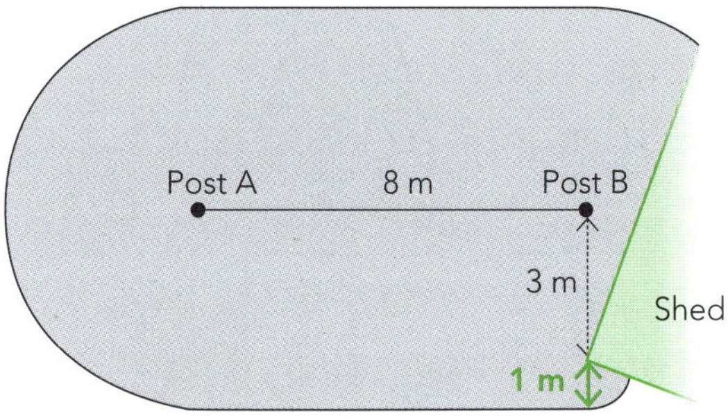

Post A
8 m
Post B
3 m
Shed
1 m

2

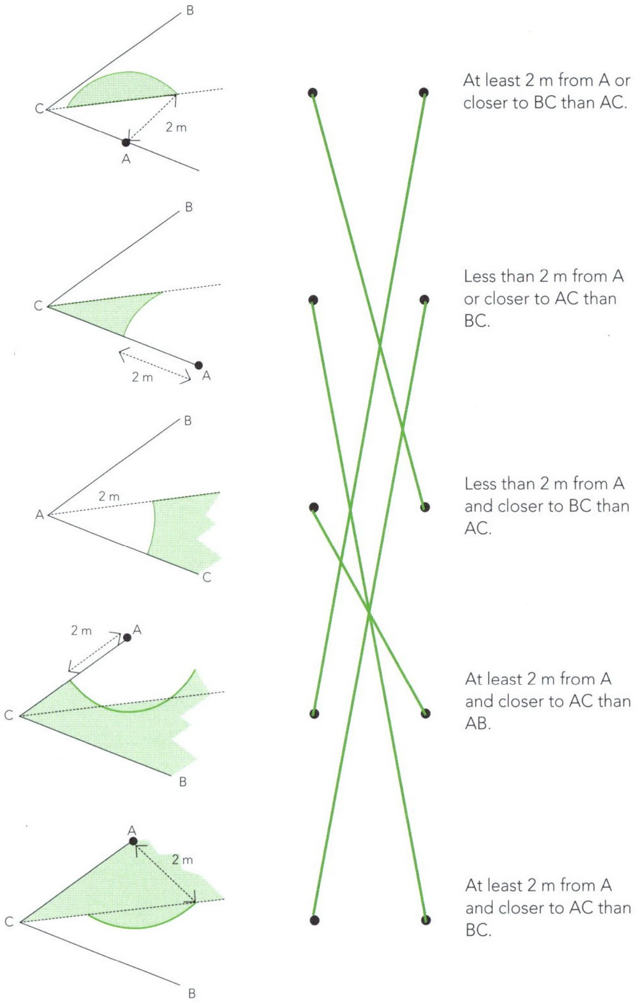

At least 2 m from A or closer to BC than AC.

Less than 2 m from A or closer to AC than BC.

Less than 2 m from A and closer to BC than AC.

At least 2 m from A and closer to AC than AB.

At least 2 m from A and closer to AC than BC.

3 **a** E **b** F
c H **d** A
e B **f** D
g G **h** I
i C

Distances: scales on maps and diagrams (pp. 28–33)

1 1 cm ≡ 100 m **2** 1 cm ≡ 10 km
3 1 cm ≡ 2 m **4** 1 cm ≡ 250 m
5 1 cm ≡ 0.2 mm **6** 1 cm ≡ 0.005 mm ≡ 5 μm (microns)
7 1325 m **8** 900 m
9 25 m **10** 71 m

Accept answers that are ± 0.5 km

11 **a** 30 km **b** 34.5 km
c 17.5 km **d** 57.5 km
e 13.5 km **f** 37.5 km

Accept answers that are ± 0.1 m

12 **a** 2.0 m x 3.4 m **b** 6.9 m
c 2.1 m

Accept answers that are ± 0.5 mm

13 **a** 3 mm **b** 0.7 mm
c 2.55 mm (accept 2.4 or 2.7)

ISBN: 9780170447577

Navigation (pp. 34–37)

1 55° S 70° W
2 40° S 170° E
3 50° N 0° W or E
4 43° S 147° E
5 80° S 45° W
6 9° N 78° E
7 33° S 18° E
8

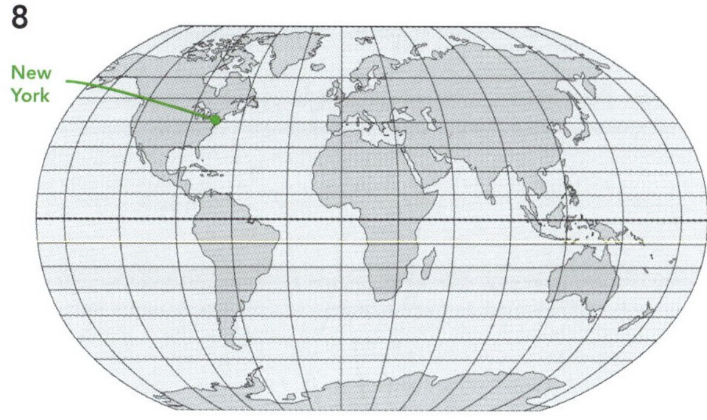

9 Dunedin
10 East Cape
11 New Plymouth
12 Cape Reinga

Allow 0.1° either side of these answers.

13 36.8°S 174.4°E
14 40.9°S 172.7°E
15 46.3°S 168.6°E
16 37.7°S 175.6°E
17 Because degrees of longitude differ depending on how close they are to the poles. Degrees of latitude are always the same size.

Allow 5NM either side of the answers.

18 60 NM
19 260 NM
20 170 NM
21 330 NM

Transformation geometry (pp. 38–48)

Rotation

	Invariant
Size	✓
Shape	✓
Orientation	✓

Enlargement

	Invariant
Size	✗
Shape	✓
Orientation	✓

1 Enlargement
2 None
3 Reflection, rotation

Revision of translation, reflection and rotation (pp. 40–41)

1 **a** $\begin{pmatrix} -7 \\ 3 \end{pmatrix}$ **b** $\begin{pmatrix} 4 \\ -2 \end{pmatrix}$

2 $\begin{pmatrix} -3 \\ -4 \end{pmatrix}$

3

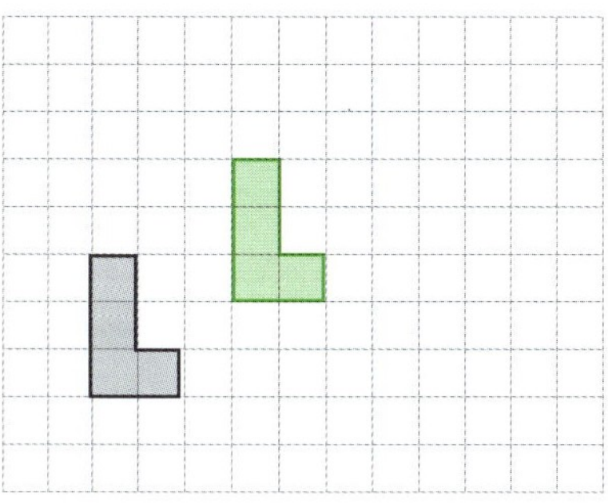

4 **a**

b

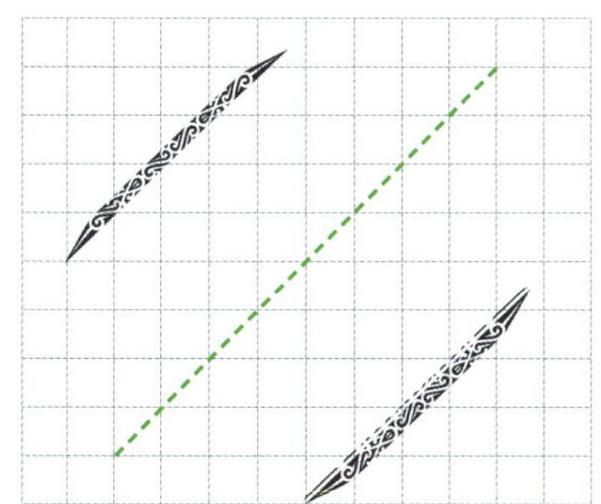

5

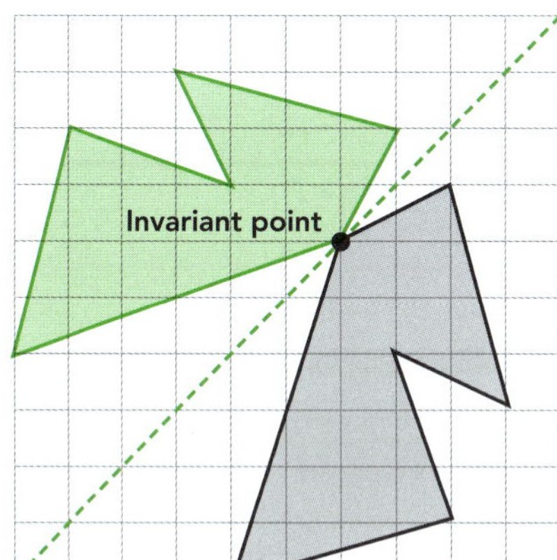

6

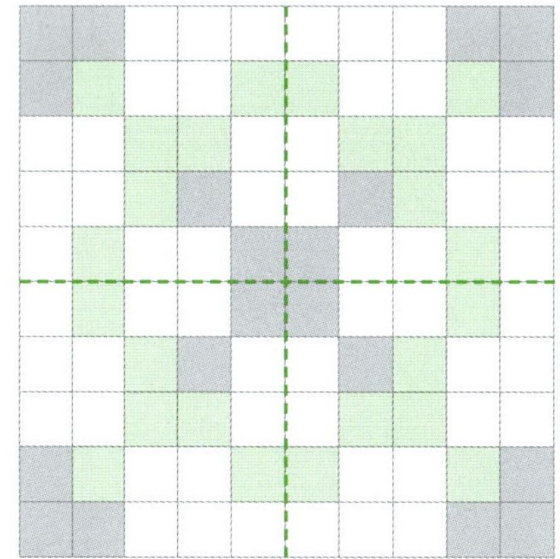

 ISBN: 9780170447577

7 a Order of line symmetry = 2
b Order of line symmetry = 4

8 a Angle of rotation = 225°
b Angle of rotation = 315°

9 a

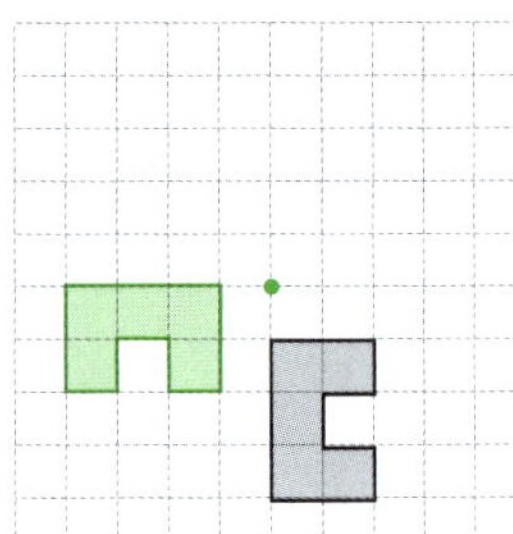

b

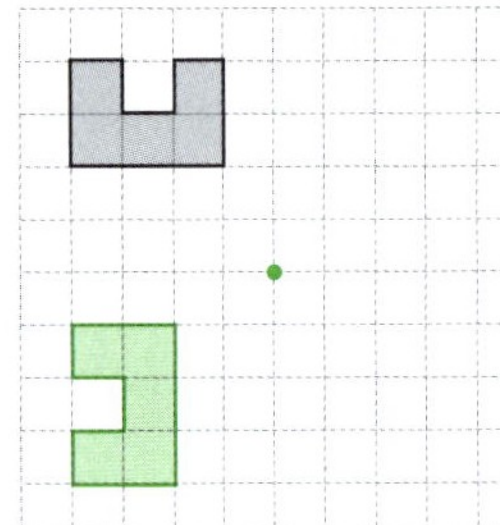

10 a Order of rotational symmetry = 4
b Order of rotational symmetry = 1

Challenge (p. 42)

You may find different letters.

1 Letter(s): A
Transformation: Reflection

2 Letter(s): H
Transformation: Rotation, order of symmetry 2

3 Letter(s): NZ
Transformation: Rotation, order of symmetry 4

4 Letter(s): L
Transformation: Translation

5 Letter(s): C
Transformation: Rotation, order of symmetry 4

6 Letter(s): TH
Transformation: None

7 Letter(s): HK
Transformation: Rotation, order of symmetry 2

8 Letter(s): NZ
Transformation: Rotation, order of symmetry 3

9 Letter(s): IXK
Transformation: Reflection

10 Letter(s): WM
Transformation: Rotation, order of symmetry 2

Enlargement (pp. 42–48)

Scale factor

1 scale factor = $\frac{3}{2}$

scale factor = $\frac{1}{2}$

scale factor = 3

2 scale factor = $\frac{1}{3}$

scale factor = $\frac{4}{3}$

scale factor = $\frac{2}{3}$

3 scale factor = $\frac{1}{4}$

scale factor = $\frac{3}{2}$

scale factor = $\frac{1}{2}$

scale factor = 2

Finding the centre of enlargement

1 scale factor = 3

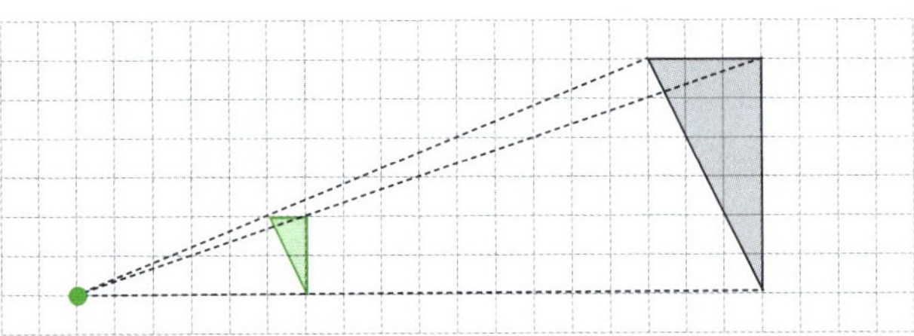

2 scale factor = $\frac{1}{2}$

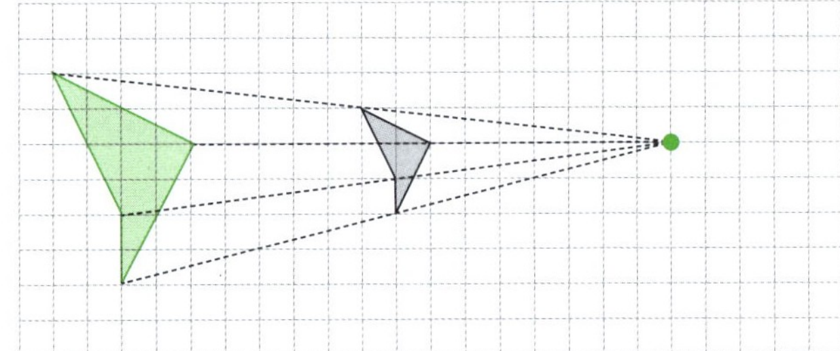

3 scale factor = $\frac{1}{4}$

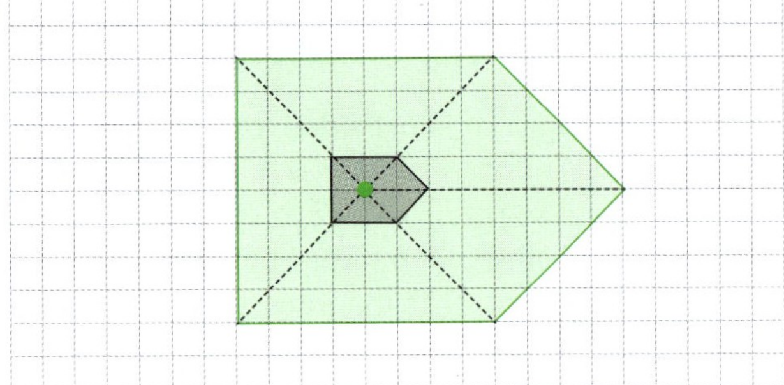

Drawing enlargements

1

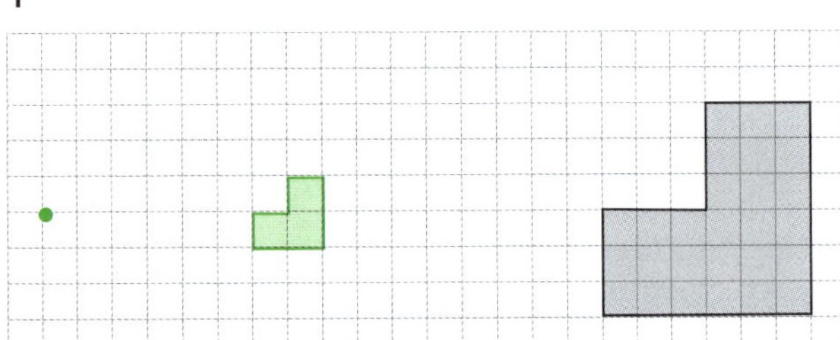

ISBN: 9780170447577

2

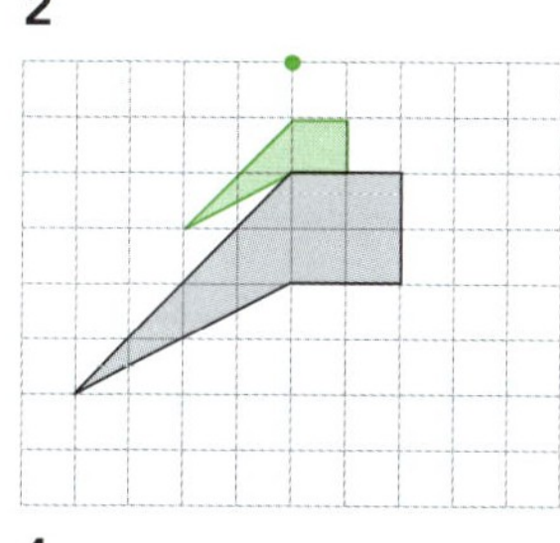

3

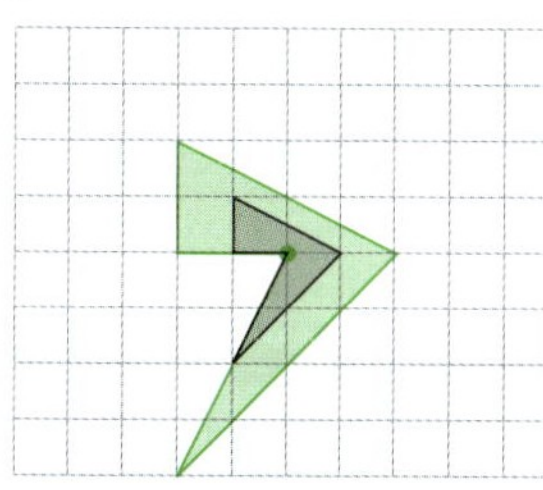

4

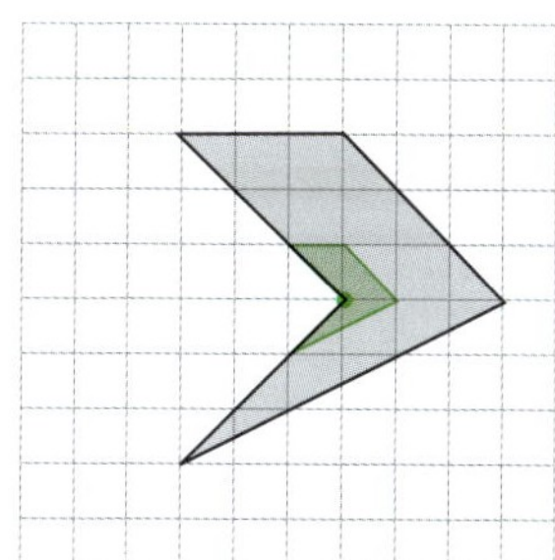

5

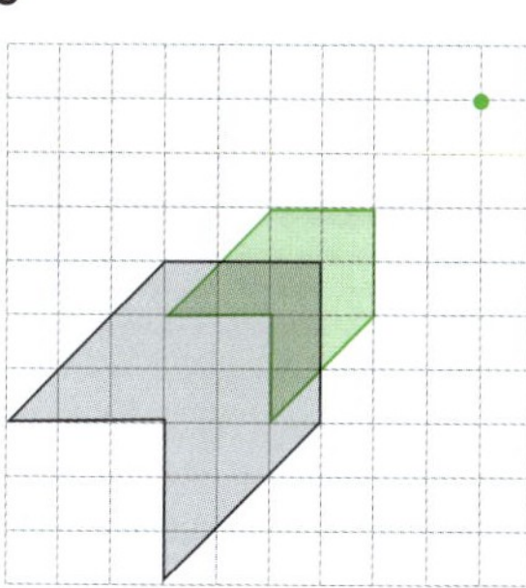

The theorem of Pythagoras (pp. 49–59)

Finding the length of the hypotenuse (pp. 50–52)

1 8.746 cm (4 sf) **2** 6.687 m (4 sf)
3 224.7 mm (4 sf) **4** 65.05 cm (4 sf)
5 926.5 mm (4 sf) **6** 93.41 cm (4 sf)
7 BC = 35 mm
CD = 61.03 mm (4 sf) (Pythagoras)
8 Diagonals = 14.14 cm (4 sf) (Pythagoras)
9 DC = 11.5 cm
AB = BC = 16.62 cm (4 sf) (Pythagoras)
Perimeter = 56.24 cm (4 sf)

Finding the length of short sides (pp. 53–54)

1 119.8 mm (4 sf) **2** 3.809 m (4 sf)
3 195.0 mm (4 sf) **4** 252.0 cm (4 sf)
5 40.31 mm (4 sf) **6** 3.665 m (4 sf)
7 CE = 0.5568 m (4 sf) (Pythagoras)
BC = 1.2 m + 0.5568 m
= 1.757 m (4 sf)
8 AB = 89.30 cm (4 sf) (Pythagoras)
Perimeter = 268.6 cm (4 sf)

Mixing it up (p. 55)

1 25.69 mm (4 sf) **2** 47.63 cm (4 sf)
3 1.128 m (4 sf) **4** 34.87 cm (4 sf)

Mixing the theorem of Pythagoras with geometry (pp. 55–59)

1 AB is bisected at point D, so DB = 7 cm.
DC = 12.12 cm (4 sf) (Pythagoras)
2 Diagonals intersect at right angles and bisect each other.
DE = 43.5 mm
AE = 82.20 mm (4 sf) (Pythagoras)
∴ AC = 164.4 mm (4 sf)
3 EC = 81.5 mm
BE = 69.33 mm (2 dp) (Pythagoras)
DE = 125.93 mm (2 dp) (Pythagoras)
BD = 125.93 mm + 69.33 mm
= 195.3 mm (4 sf)
4 AC = 127.28 mm (2 dp) (Pythagoras)
AE = 63.64 mm (2 dp)
AD = 66.71 mm (4 sf) (Pythagoras)
5 $DE = \frac{12-6}{2} = 3\text{m}$
AE = 4.000 m (4 sf) (Pythagoras)
6 $x^2 + x^2 = 100^2$
$x^2 = \frac{100^2}{2}$
$x = 70.71$ mm (4 sf)
7 $(2x)^2 + x^2 = 100^2$
$5x^2 = 100^2$
$x = \sqrt{\frac{100^2}{5}}$
Height = 44.72 mm (4 sf)
Width = 89.44 mm (4 sf)
8 BE = 59.70 mm (4 sf) (Pythagoras)
DE = 29.85 mm (4 sf)
AD = 76.10 mm (4 sf) (Pythagoras)
9 AC = 80.61 mm (4 sf) (Pythagoras)
∴ EC = 40.31 (4 sf) (symmetry)
EB = 40.31 mm (BD bisects the kite, so $\angle EBC = \angle ECB = 45° \Rightarrow \Delta BEC$ is isosceles)
∴ ED = 110 mm – 40.31 mm = 69.69 mm
Long sides = 80.51 mm (4 sf) (Pythagoras)
10 Diagonals intersect at right angles, and bisect each other.
∴ ΔBEC is right angled and $EC = \frac{x}{2}$
$x^2 = 10^2 + \left(\frac{x}{2}\right)^2$
$\frac{3x^2}{4} = 100$
$x = 11.55$ cm (4 sf)
11 **a** $a^2 = 1^2 + 1^2$
$a = \sqrt{2}$
b $b = \sqrt{3}, c = \sqrt{4}, d = \sqrt{5}$

Trigonometry (pp. 60–76)

What is trigonometry? (pp. 60–61)

For the goal post: $\text{Ratio} = \frac{\text{height of goal post}}{\text{length of shadow}}$
$= \frac{3.05}{7.6}$
$= 0.40$ (2 dp)

For the tree: $\text{Ratio} = \frac{\text{height of tree}}{\text{length of shadow}}$
$= \frac{1.8}{4.5}$
$= 0.40$ (2 dp)

- Notice that the ratios are the same (or equal).

ISBN: 9780170447577

1

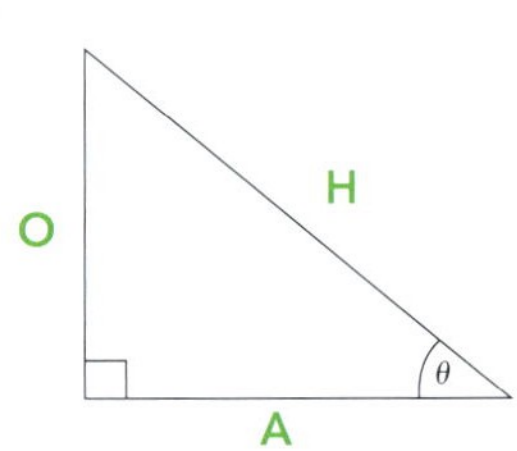

2

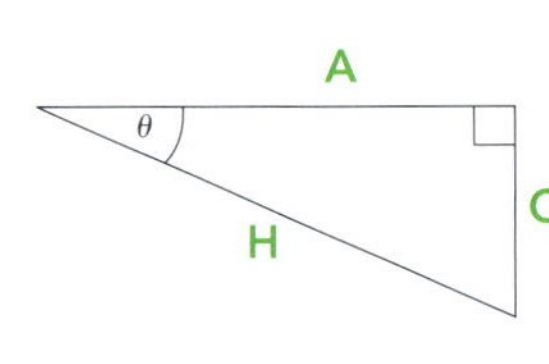

3

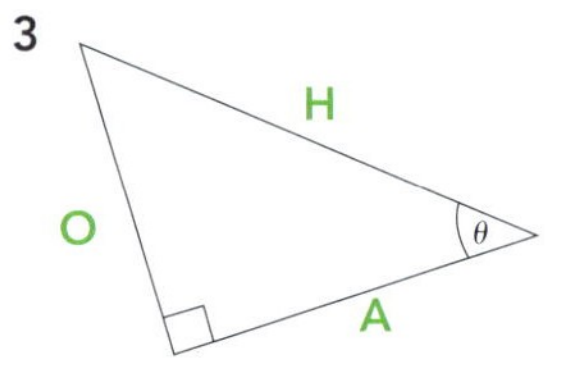

4

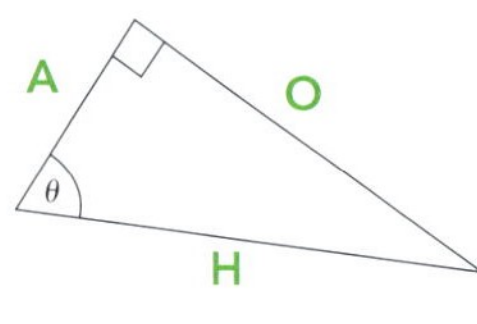

5

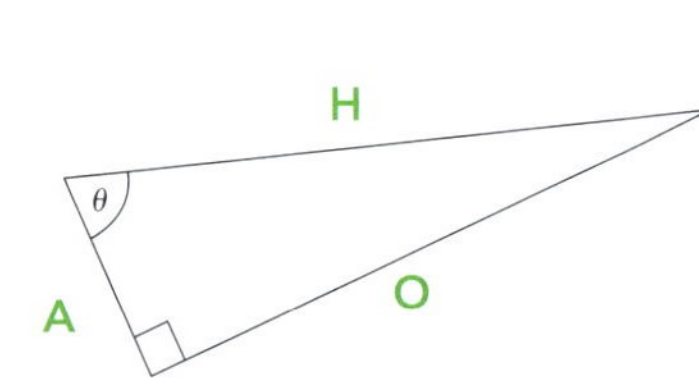

6

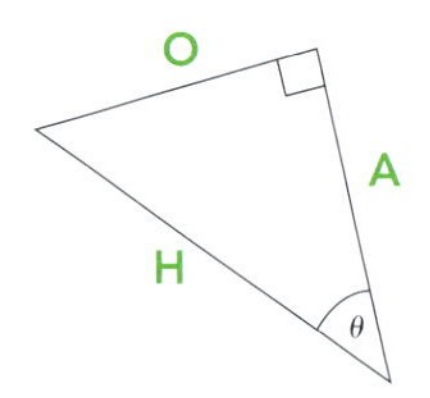

Finding sides using sine (pp. 62–64)

1 103.8 cm (4 sf) **2** 11.17 cm (4 sf)
3 34.46 mm (4 sf) **4** 1.334 m (4 sf)
5 9.343 cm (4 sf) **6** 5.924 m (4 sf)
7 90.41 mm (4 sf) **8** 61.40 cm (4 sf)

Finding sides using cosine and tangent (pp. 65–67)

1 106.5 cm (4 sf) **2** 5.454 cm (4 sf)
3 9.233 m (4 sf) **4** 64.31 mm (4 sf)
5 123.1 mm (4 sf) **6** 7.460 m (4 sf)
7 4.925 cm (4 sf) **8** 1.881 m (4 sf)
9 0.8007 m (4 sf) **10** 82.62 mm (4 sf)

Mixing it up (p. 68)

1 106.5 cm (4 sf) **2** 9.511 cm (4 sf)
3 54.54 cm (4 sf) **4** 114.6 mm (4 sf)
5 89.96 mm (4 sf) **6** 8.330 m (4 sf)
7 26.28 cm (4 sf) **8** 122.9 mm (4 sf)

Finding angles using sine (pp. 69–70)

1 30.0° **2** 71.8°
3 41.8° **4** 48.6°
5 40.0° **6** 7.6°
7 56.4° (1 dp) **8** 22.9° (1 dp)
9 61.9° (1 dp) **10** 49.9° (1 dp)
11 69.2° (1 dp) **12** 64.8° (1 dp)

Finding angles using cosine and tangent (pp. 71–73)

1 60.0° **2** 45.0°
3 78.5° **4** 64.6°
5 59.9° **6** 50.5°
7 32.5° (1 dp) **8** 71° (1 dp)
9 52.4° (1 dp) **10** 28.4° (1 dp)
11 25.2° (1 dp) **12** 38.6° (1 dp)
13 74.6° (1 dp) **14** 63.6° (1 dp)

Mixing trigonometry with geometry (pp. 74–76)

You may use different reasoning to get these answers.

1 Diagonals intersect at right angles and bisect each other.

$AC = 2(10 \cos 29°)$
$= 17.49$ cm (4 sf)
$DB = 2(10 \sin 29°)$
$= 9.696$ cm (4 sf)

2 $BD = \dfrac{59}{\tan 29°}$
$= 106.4$
$\angle ACB = \tan^{-1}\left(\dfrac{59}{106.4 - 50}\right)$
$= 46.3°$ (1 dp)

3 Let $BC = 2x$.
Then $AB = x$.
$\angle ACB = \tan^{-1}\left(\dfrac{x}{2x}\right)$
$= \tan^{-1}(0.5)$
$= 26.6°$ (1 dp)

4 $\angle BCD = 56°$ ($\angle$ sum Δ)
$BD = 40 \tan 56°$
$AB = \dfrac{40 \tan 56°}{\sin 34°}$
$= 106.1$ mm (4 sf)
or
$BC = \dfrac{40}{\cos 56°}$
$AB = \dfrac{40 \div \cos 56°}{\tan 34°}$
$= 106.1$ mm (4 sf)

5 **a** $AB = 150 \tan 52°$
$= 192.00$ mm (5 sf)
$\therefore$ EB = 82.00 mm (4 sf)

b $\angle ADC = \angle ACB$ (corr $\angle$s, $\parallel$ lines)
$AD = \dfrac{110}{\sin 52°}$
$= 139.59$ mm (5 sf)
$AC = \dfrac{150}{\sin 52°}$
$= 243.64$ mm (5 sf)
or
$AD = \sqrt{150^2 + 192^2}$
$= 243.64$ mm (5 sf)
$\therefore$ DC = 104.1 mm (4 sf)

ISBN: 9780170447577

6 $AC = \dfrac{145}{\sin 54°}$

$= 179.23$ mm (2 dp)

$\therefore$ EC = 89.615 (BE bisects isos Δ)

$\angle BCE = \cos^{-1}\left(\dfrac{89.615}{172}\right)$

$= 58.6°$ (1 dp)

ACE = 36° (∠ sum Δ)

$\therefore$ ∠BCD = 94.6° (1 dp)

7 ∠EDB = 61° (co-int ∠, ∥ lines)

AB = 51.5 sin 61°

= 45.043 m (5 sf)

BC = 78.3 sin 27°

= 35.547 m (5 sf)

AC = 80.59 m (4 sf)

8 DE = 50 tan 31°

= 30.04 mm (4 sf)

$\therefore$ BE = 95.04 mm (4 sf)

$\angle BCE = \tan^{-1}\left(\dfrac{95.04}{50}\right)$

$= 62.3°$ (1 dp)

$\therefore$ ∠BCD = 31.3° (1 dp)

Geometry and ϕ (phi), the golden ratio (pp. 77–81)

The golden ratio, ϕ (pp. 77–81)

$\dfrac{144}{89} = 1.61800$

$\dfrac{233}{144} = 1.61806$

$\dfrac{377}{233} = 1.61802$

$\dfrac{610}{377} = 1.61804$

$\dfrac{987}{610} = 1.61803$

$\dfrac{1597}{987} = 1.61803$

The last two values are the same.

Angles and lengths in a pentagram

1 The external angles of a pentagon add to 360°,

so $\angle BCE = \dfrac{360°}{5} = 72°$

2 $\cos 72° = \dfrac{A}{H}$

$= \dfrac{FC}{1}$

FC = 0.3090

$\therefore$ BC = 0.6180

3 P = 0.6180 Q = 1.6180 R = 2.6180

4 **a** $\dfrac{R}{Q} = \dfrac{2.6180}{1.6180}$

$= 1.6180$

b $\dfrac{Q}{1} = 1.6180$

c $\dfrac{1}{P} = \dfrac{1}{1.6180}$

$= 1.6180$

5 In a pentagram, the length of many line segments are in the **golden ratio** to many other lengths.

Revision 1 (pp. 82–84)

1 **a** *a* = 139°

Ext ∠s in a Δ = into opp ∠s and ∠s in a Δ = 180°.

b *b* = 136°

∠s at a point add to 3600° and vert opp ∠s = 180°.

Δ = 180°.

c *c* = 74° **d** *d* = 99°

e *x* = 115° Reason: corr ∠s =, ∥ lines.

y = 67° Reason: ext ∠s of Δ = sum of int ∠s of Δ.

z = 113° Reason: ∠s on a line = 180°.

f *x* = 12° **g** *x* = 24°

2 **a** 140° **b** Hamilton

c 38.1°S 175.7°E. Accept answers within ± 0.1 degree.

d 145 km. Accept answers within ± 10 km.

80 NM. Accept answers within ± 5 NM.

e

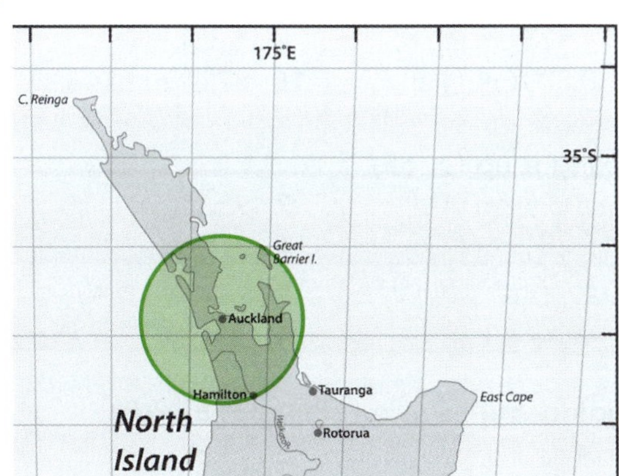

3

 ISBN: 9780170447577

4 Order of rotational symmetry = 3
Order of line symmetry = 3

5

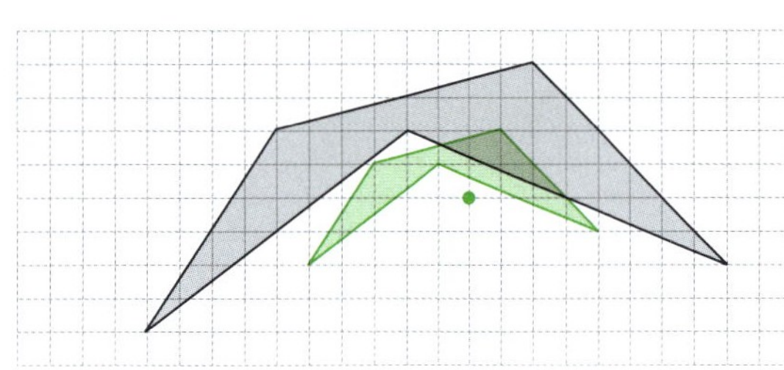

6 a $a = 90$ mm b $b = 57.7$ mm

7 a $c = 41.9$ cm b $d = 68.3$ cm
c $e = 59.8$ cm d $f = 30°$

Revision 2 (pp. 85–87)

1 a $a = 34°$
∠s on a line = 180°.
b $b = 56°$
Ext ∠s in a Δ = into opp ∠s and ∠s in a Δ = 180°.
c $c = 34°$ d $d = 108°$
e $x = 47°$ Reason: alt ∠s =, ∥ lines.
$y = 56°$ Reason: vert opp ∠s =.
$z = 77°$ Reason: ∠s in a Δ = 180°.
f $x = 10°$ g $x = 11°$

2 a 250° b Nelson
c 39.5°S 175.9°E. Accept answers within ± 0.1 degree.
d 400 km. Accept answers within ± 10 km.
200 NM. Accept answers within ± 5 NM.
e 400 km ± 10 km
200 NM ± 5 NM

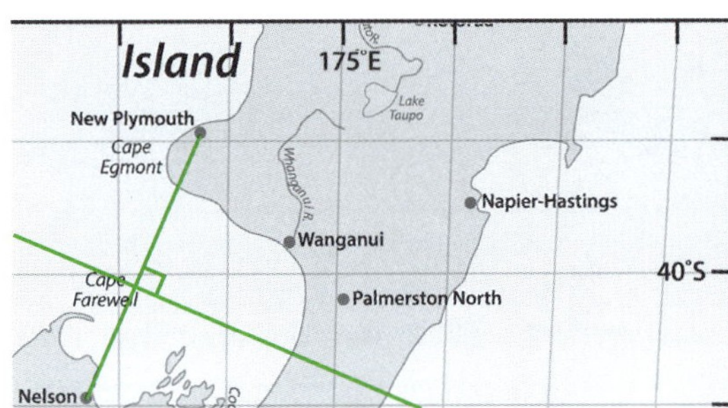

3 $\begin{pmatrix} -6 \\ -3 \end{pmatrix}$

4 Order of rotational symmetry = 10
Order of line symmetry = 10

5

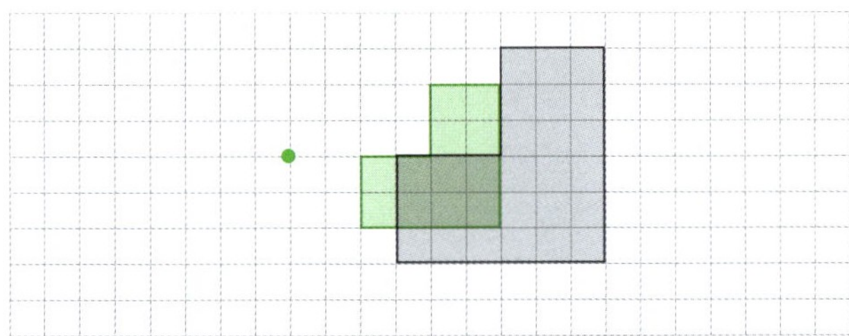

6 a $a = 38.4$ mm b $b = 65.8$ mm

7 a $c = 48.7$ mm b $d = 59.9$ cm
c $e = 61.8°$ d $f = 56.3°$